FRAMING THE CRIMINAL

FRAMING THE CRIMINAL

Crime, Cultural Work and the Loss of Critical Perspective, 1830–1900

David Ray Papke

ARCHON BOOKS

1987

First published 1987 as an Archon Book,
an imprint of The Shoe String Press, Inc.,
Hamden, Connecticut 06514

Printed in the United States of America

The paper in this publication meets the minimum requirements of
American National Standard for Information Sciences–
Permanence of Paper for Printed Library Materials, ANSI Z39.48-1984.

A version of part of the chapter "Legitimate Illegitimacy: The Criminal as Cultural
Worker" appeared originally in *Legal Studies Forum*, 9:2.

Set in Garamond No. 3 by Coghill Composition Co., Richmond, Virginia
Designed by Jill Breitbarth

Library of Congress Cataloging-in-Publication Data

Papke, David Ray, 1947–
Framing the criminal.

Bibliography: p.
Includes index.
1. Crime and criminals—United States—History—19th
century.   2. Crime and the press—United States—History
—19th century.   3. Crime and criminals in literature—
United States—History—19th century.   I. Title.
HV6783.P28   1987   364.1'0973   86-26475
ISBN 0-208-02127-2 (alk. paper)

To my parents,
Raymond and Virginia Papke

Acknowledgments

A cknowledgment pages often thank the tolerant and suffering spouse last, almost as a necessary afterthought. This would be inappropriate for the book at hand since, more so than anyone, Elise Papke contributed to its development and completion. Even while carrying our daughter Tulita, Elise improved my prose, challenged my arguments and added important insights. I thank her for her loving help and for her faith and confidence in the author.

My work on this book in a sense began during my years as a student at the Yale Law School. Many students and faculty members helped me launch an interdisciplinary study of American crime, and Robert Stevens was my most important mentor. He insisted that a student of the law also be a student of history and culture, and he continued in subsequent years to add to my professional development and scholarship.

In Ann Arbor, a dozen friends and advisers at the University of Michigan helped me fight the painful contradictions of graduate school. Personal and intellectual bonds formed with William Loizeaux and Barney Pace proved particularly valuable, and both carefully read and critiqued earlier drafts of this book. Cecil Eby was my most important teacher, increased my fondness for American Studies and chaired my dissertation panel. Thomas Green and Stuart McDougal, respectively, sharpened my appreciation of professionalism and added sophistication to my work in cultural theory.

At the Indiana University School of Law-Indianapolis, I have received generous support from the staff, students and administration. Sue Smallwood, Wendy Hall, Marty Ragsdale, Carol Jansen, Michele Eberwein and Brenda Morrison typed parts of my many drafts. My research assistant Anita Flax not only completed footnote and bibliography work but also shared with me a valuable intellectual dialogue. Most importantly, Dean Gerald Bepko encouraged me to complete this book and to work in areas outside those normally explored by law professors. I thank all of these individuals and my faculty colleagues for their kind assistance.

Contents

I.
Reporting Crime

II.
Imagining Crime

III.
Remembering Crime

List of Illustrations

Preface

Crime is a political subject, but we only partially recognize this. On election day the minority of citizens who vote might opt for an aldermanic or even presidential candidate who promises to "get tough" on crime. In daily conversation pockets of people might complain of threats to property and safety and discuss ways to deal with the "crime problem." Rarely, however, do we critically engage the great volume of crime-related images, statements or messages that cascade into our consciousnesses. Only infrequently do we scrutinize the immanent politics of our crime-related cultural products. Failing to recognize the way crime and the criminal are framed by our cultural experience, we are disabled from developing our own political meanings for crime.

This work attempts to enliven and invigorate our consideration of crime. The work focuses not on the present but rather on the United States of the nineteenth century, in particular, on the urbanizing and industrializing portions of the country from 1830 to 1900. For convenience, I frequently divide these years into subperiods, referring, as is common in much standard scholarship, to the antebellum period, the Civil War decade and the Gilded Age. Yet I also view the years 1830–1900 as a whole period, as a large historical transformation. I am influenced in this regard by historians who have described our nation's nineteenth century as a period of modernization.[1] The United States during these years developed the social structures, economy, values and personality norms of the "modern" society. With the arrival of immigrants and regional variations, the process was hardly simple or one-directional.[2] With class inequalities and active resistance, the process was neither smooth nor merely functionalist.[3] But still, the years 1830 to 1900, rolling, reversing and meandering, were—to use an overworked notion but one that nevertheless seems apt—the beginning of our present.

During these years, an immense variety of crime-related products traveled every avenue into the cultural marketplace. Journalists published thousands of broadsheets, pamphlets, articles and columns concerning crime. Writers of fiction created crime novels, detective stories and serial crime thrillers. Police chiefs, detectives and criminals composed memoirs, confessions and crime-stopping kits. In many instances, artists and photographers elaborately illustrated these works. The large, varied and fascinating body of crime-related work is a significant portion of the period's literary and pictorial production. In addition to rendering and discussing the period's crime, the body of work also illuminates the period in larger, more profound ways. The crime-related products both reflect and actually make visible the crime, social experience and normative restructuring of the modernizing United States.

As I focus on the period and, in particular, its crime-related cultural production, I do not purport to write history per se. This work is instead interdisciplinary; it is a work in American Studies. Frequently controversial and uncertain, American Studies during its thirty years of full flower has proven a scholarly enterprise capable of crossing disciplinary boundaries and providing new insights regarding the American experience. This work, I hope, will in its small way be a part of this exhilarating tradition.

I have indicated the major concerns and argument of the work in its subtitle, "Crime, Cultural Work and the Loss of Critical Perspective, 1830–1900." The terms and phrases of the subtitle designate the major theoretical components that compound into a work titled "Framing the Criminal." Here in the preface, the terms and phrases of the subtitle and of the title itself might profitably be underscored and defined.

Crime

This term, short and seemingly clear, carries a particular meaning in the work at hand. I quarrel with the assumption that crime is a species of phenomenological fact. This assumption of course stalks with bold falseness through many policy studies and scholarly monographs. Surely, much criminology, the eldest bastard child of sociology, embodies the assumption and concomitantly emphasizes "corrections," that is, the control and modification of perpetrators of crime.[4] However, crime is not a discrete and merely controllable social fact but rather those parts of social experience which assorted forces, formations and individuals "label" criminal.[5]

An introductory chapter of this work, relying on popular and scholarly studies of nineteenth-century crime, develops and explores a tripartite typology—personal violence, social disorder and property crime, but this chapter and the eight that follow do not accept the typology as firm and reliable. My argument, both for the nineteenth century and the present, is that crime, broken into categories or as a totality, is not an essential social phenomenon. I assert, as do a small number of other American historians and cultural commentators, that crime is not a dark, static reality but rather is born of a dialectic between occurrence and perspective.[6]

Cultural Work

I employ this phrase, jarring as it may be to some, to avoid the confusion frequently endemic to the more common "culture." Until the eighteenth century "culture" was a noun of process meaning the tending of something, most often crops or animals. But in the eighteenth and nineteenth centuries the term gradually acquired different connotations, in particular, the arts and intellectual activity and subsequently the more anthropological notion of a way of life.[7] Interdisciplinary scholarship of the twentieth century employs the term in both of the latter ways, often simultaneously and often assuming that the former—arts and intellectual life—can indicate or reflect the latter—a way of life.[8] By "cultural work," meanwhile, I hope to suggest a social practice more specific in nature. I take cultural work to be the transformation of ideas, attitudes and impressions as well as writings, drawings, paper and ink into cultural products and experiences. Cultural work is not a whole way of life—one might distinguish it from other types of work; but cultural work is a substantial, diverse and significant part of social activity.[9]

In considering cultural work, I do not restrict myself to either elite or popular varieties, although I do pay more attention to the latter. The very idea of an elite or high culture is a valorizing characterization of certain varieties of cultural work that took hold in Europe and the United States during the nineteenth century,[10] the very period that this work considers. One hundred years later, the differentiation remains powerful both for scholars in the humanities who pride themselves on the study of high culture and for more fledgling groups seeking to bring popular or mass culture into the academy.[11] In reality, the culture industries that emerged in the nineteenth century generated both elite and popular products, and the generation of these products was linked in complex and thorough ways. To segregate the spheres is to obscure the process by which the dominant way of life reorganized cultural work in support of its stabilizing status quo. This process, of course, is ongoing, including as it does both resistance and acceptance and illustrating the complexity of cultural relations and meanings.[12]

The three major sections of this work designate three broad areas of cultural work—"reporting," "imagining" and "remembering." Assorted reporters, journalists and editors report in their work on events that occurred and individuals who lived. Writers and publishers of fiction imagine events and individuals that are not truly social occurrences and actors. Practitioners of crime-related callings remember the events they themselves experienced. My gerunds, I trust, will underscore my concern with the processes of cultural work and be preferable to "newspapers," "novels" or "memoirs," nouns that connote more static entities. To be sure, cultural work does result in products, but those products are not final. Cultural products continue to generate meaning as individuals read and peruse them, and the products also feed back into the production of subsequent products. Cultural work, I am suggesting, is a complex process, one constitutive and dynamic.

As this work acknowledges at many points, developments traced in one of the three major sections of the work are not completely separate and distinct from those traced in the other two sections. Reporting influences imagining and remembering, and imagining and remembering influence both one another and reporting. However, these three broad categories can be thought of as prototypical varieties of cultural work. The categories, rather than the grand transformation occurring between 1830 and 1900, serve as the organizing structure of the work, and the chapter-length discussions fall under the three categorical rubrics. Each category, in other words, spawns its own concerns, and the three categorical treatments are more parallel than sequential.

The Loss of Critical Perspective

All cultural work carries with it either subsconsciously or consciously a perspective on social life. Indeed, crime-related cultural work from 1830 to 1900 was always aligned. It expressed implicitly or explicitly selected events, fictive stories and favored memories from points of view. Men and women in varied production milieux and historical settings offered normative visions of social life. [13]

However, as I have reviewed and studied the development of nineteenth-century American cultural work regarding crime, I have been struck by the gradual loss of critical perspective. For a brief period during the antebellum years, during the first onslaught of modernization, crime-related cultural work was rich in critical perspective; it actively linked crime and politics and drew conclusions from the linkages. Later in the century, as the modern society settled more securely into place, journalism, genres of fiction and memoirs also stabilized and in the process lost a conscious, energetic concern with crime's political meanings and consequences. Politics continued to dwell within the cultural work; cultural work was not, strictly speaking, "depoliticized." But by the end of the century, cultural workers reported, imagined and remembered crime more rigidly and without a critical perspective. As a critical perspective gradually drained from crime-related cultural work, support for a new status quo came increasingly to be cultural work's most significant characteristic.

Framing the Criminal

Overall, crime-related cultural work and its gradual loss of critical perspective between 1830 and 1900 constitute, in my language, a framing of crime and the criminal. I am, of course, not the first to conceive of criminal or cultural "frame." We know well the statement, "I was framed," a refrain from gangster movies and elsewhere, and we use varieties of the statement if not frequently then comfortably in daily discourse. Scholars, meanwhile, have employed "framing" and "frame" to denote not manipulations of the legal process but rather cultural combinations and constructions that put selected phenomena into comprehensive and consumable focus.[14] Frames for these scholars are systems of selection, presentation and accentuation; they are patterned mechanisms of cognition and interpretation that package social experience for producers and purchasers of the frames. Building on both of these usages, I add a political dimension, an assertion that the historical and dialectical process of framing the criminal has political significance.

Between 1830 and 1900, the framing process, the frames, and the foundations, implications and ramifications of the frames changed. These changes did not merely reflect social life but rather functioned politically as part of social life. They contributed to modernization and, more specifically, to a new societal hegemony that not only exercised social control but also gave certain social groups dominance over others. If this process speaks more of restriction and limitation than of freedom and liberation, it nevertheless has major importance for Americans one hundred years later in time. Cultural work of the late nineteenth century denied the contemplators of crime and even the criminals themselves political meanings and alternatives. The framing continues today and, for the most part, remains restricting.

In exploring the framing of the criminal in crime-related cultural work of the nineteenth century, I hope to prove useful to contemporary

Americans. Like many newsmen, novelists, law enforcement officials and criminals of the nineteenth century, we are bewildered and staggered by crime. Like many producers and consumers of crime-related works during the years 1830 to 1900, we are uneasy with our definitions and explanations of crime. By exploring the manner in which Americans of the preceding century framed the criminal, we might better understand the nature and meaning of crime in the final years of our own century. We might even gather to reconsider and alter the criminality in our own lives.

Criminal Conduct in a Modernizing Society:
A Social History of Nineteenth-Century
American Crime

Visitors to the New York Tombs, nineteenth-century America's most notorious urban jail, might at first have found comfort in the confident arrangement of the city's criminals. On the first floor distraught murderers and other "desperate criminals" waited while police, courts and families decided to send them to prisons, mental institutions or the gallows. On the second floor the drunk and disorderly slept off their inebriation and vowed to right their ways or at least to avoid the next police dragnet. On the third floor arrested thieves, pickpockets and burglars played cards and recognized friends in other cells and even among the jailers. The floors were separate, and the criminal designations and divisions seemed certain. But even in the Tombs, the Halls of Justice as it was formally known, visitors would eventually have found a fourth floor, a floor where another group of men and women uneasily passed their time, waiting for the criminal justice system to decipher and label their criminality.[1]

For twentieth-century historians attempting to discuss crime of a century ago, the fourth floor of the Tombs proffers a valuable reminder. One group of these historians, flashy and flamboyant, has provided popular histories of individual criminals and crimes, books designed more for the nightstand than for the research library.[2] Another group of historians, more academic and affiliated with the new social history, has provided more elaborate studies and monographs, often packed with data.[3] The two bodies of historical work have different goals, but the historians in both groups attempt to portray "real life," to isolate individuals and social phenomena. At best, the more sophisticated among them might acknowledge that details elude the historian or that real crime data are "dark" or "black" figures, that is, impossible truly to find. But these acknowledgments are in many cases rhetorical, even stylized, and the historians, both popular and scholarly, go on to speak confidently of crime. Available historical studies of crime are insufficiently fluid and dialectical in their assumptions and methodologies.

For now, the historical studies of nineteenth-century American crime might be used gingerly. Despite their limitations and overstatements, these studies afford insight regarding the general contours of nineteenth-century crime. The literature suggests general American development and also the types of conduct that might be "framed" as criminal. Missing is the agitation and horror of a night at the Tombs, the sense that crime is not easily defined and categorized. But the literature does set the stage for the work at hand.

American modernization began in full force a few decades after the start of the nineteenth century. The nation in earlier years had experienced significant social friction, but in general the American social order before 1830 was relatively stable, with citizens concentrated in cozy towns and farming communities on the Atlantic seaboard, urban centers able to absorb new arrivals, and politics mostly in the hands of traditional elites.[4] In the immediately succeeding decades, meanwhile, parts of the nation were transformed into a modern society. Cities in the East and, to a lesser extent, the old Midwest burst at the seams as their populations swelled with immigrants from Europe and from within America. Factory smokestacks began to vie with church steeples on the urban horizon, and at the foot of the smokestacks the nation's first generation of industrial laborers confronted larger work spaces and more rigid discipline. Traditional elites and the ministry lost sway, and although a degree of social mobility existed, class divisions grew sharper. With good reason, nights before the fire or in the grog shop were increasingly filled with nostalgic memories of a simpler time.[5]

In the context of the rapid modernization of the antebellum decades, urban dwellers quite understandably had difficulty finding their social bearings. They experienced a breakdown of the tighter social networks that had stabilized earlier periods,[6] and their sensations were frequently those of normlessness or anomie.[7] Often they were unsure what was legal or illegal, and sometimes they did not care. Unable or unwilling to internalize the fragmented values of the period, many urban Americans behaved in a destructive or aggressively self-interested manner. Confused or set free by the seeming senselessness of their environment, many acted in ways that could be deemed criminal. With a perceived urban crime wave surging in many directions at once, an 1842 special committee of New York City aldermen was justifiably alarmed:

Notwithstanding the large sums yearly devoted to the administration of justice, crime is still increasing in the city, in all the gradations of guilt, from slight misdemeanors to felonies of the greatest atrocity. The Ordinances of the City, and the Laws of the State, are habitually violated with impunity. The property of the citizen is pilfered, almost before his eyes. Dwellings and ware-houses are entered with an ease and apparent coolness and carelessness of detection, which shows that none are safe.[8]

Data supporting these impressions are difficult to locate and even more difficult to trust, and given the variations in local crime recording, a general statistical study of crime in antebellum America may be impossible. However, social historians have drawn a statistical picture of crime in antebellum Boston. While admitting the arrest records of the Boston police might conceal changes in police procedures, Theodore Ferdinand has observed that the number of arrests per 100,000 residents jumped from less than 700 in 1849 to more than 1900 in 1859. The increase was particularly pronounced for assaults, robberies, burglaries and murders—standard common law crimes that had not been redefined.[9] Roger Lane, meanwhile, has studied Boston court records from the same period. In the misdemeanor courts he finds that criminal cases per 100,000 residents tripled between 1840 and 1860; in the same courts during the same years jail commitments per 100,000 residents jumped from 419 to 548. When Lane turns to grand jury records concerning major crimes, he finds the number of cases per 100,000 residents increased from 89 in 1834 to 117 in 1860.[10] Both Ferdinand and Lane acknowledge that their data measure only those crimes which come to the attention, respectively, of the police and courts rather than crime per se, but the Ferdinand and Lane studies nevertheless constitute evidence of increased criminal activity.[11]

Since the overall social phenomenon of crime consists of complex varieties of social conduct, any categorizing of crime requires caution. The legal categories of criminal conduct, for example, may be useful to a court seeking to determine individual criminal responsibility, but the rigidity of the same categories impedes analysis of crime as a larger phenomenon. Perhaps the best approach is to use only the most general categories, categories with enough conceptual fiber to support analysis but categories that in their very generality serve as reminders of the interlocking character of criminal activity. Three general categories of crime for the antebellum period are personal violence, social disorder, and property.

Personal violence crimes occur in a myriad of individual variations, but the major types include infanticide, child abuse, wife beating, rape and homicide within the perpetrator's immediate circle. With the exception of infanticide, the great majority of perpetrators are males in the early adult years. Most commonly but not exclusively, they are frustrated in their work lives and unable to build strong interpersonal relationships. Barriers to the perpetrator's social and economic aspirations are insurmountable, and against a backdrop of anger, insult, argument and fear, the perpetrator seriously harms a vulnerable victim.[12]

The most striking of these crimes, the one that attracts the most attention, is homicide. In the antebellum period, for example, the 1849 murder of George Parkman by Professor John Webster, a member of the Massachusetts Medical College faculty, convulsed the public. Parkman, a doctor turned money lender, loaned Webster large sums of money, accepting as collateral a mortgage on Webster's home and medical equipment. When Webster proved unable to repay the loans, Parkman threatened to sue, to interrupt Webster's lectures, and to drive the latter from his professorship. Confused and distraught, Webster during a private conference with Parkman in a medical school laboratory slipped into an uncontrollable frenzy:

> At first I kept interposing, trying to pacify him, so that I might obtain the object for which I had sought the interview. But I could not stop him, and soon my own temper was up. I forgot everything. I felt nothing but the sting of his words. I was excited to the highest degree of passion; and while he was speaking and gesticulating in the most violent and menacing manner. . . . I seized whatever thing was handiest,—it was a stick of wood,—and dealt him an instantaneous blow with all the force that passion could give it.[13]

To conceal his crime, Webster then drained the blood from the body, incinerated the head, and placed several limbs in storage vaults. As is the case with most perpetrators of homicide, Webster had not premeditated his act but rather acted in what modern psychoanalysts have characterized as a trance, fugue state, or acute dissociative disorder.[14]

Most other antebellum homicides included similar psychosocial characteristics but less gruesome violence. According to Roger Lane, "The model homicide in nineteenth-century Philadelphia resulted from a brawl or quarrel originating in a saloon but reaching a climax in the street."[15] If not in the street, homicides most commonly occurred in the family kitchen or bedroom, sites of supposed warmth and intimacy.[16] With the exception of the Parkman murder and a few others involving prominent individuals, antebellum homicides usually involved members of the working and marginal classes. The most fragile members of these classes were the ideal candidates to harm members of their immediate circle. For them, the rapidly modernizing society, weak in defining roles and providing reciprocal relationships, was particularly conducive to personal violence crime.

Young males were also the most frequent perpetrators of antebellum social disorder crime, and this variety of crime also resulted in physical harm to individuals known to perpetrators. However, its standard forms and dominant psychosocial underpinnings were different from those of personal violence crime. Most commonly, social disorder crime took the form of disorderly and drunken conduct. Some of the social disorder criminals, to use terms from the era, were "rowdies" or "corner loungers" who clung tenaciously to shreds of material and existential space. Others belonged to volunteer fire companies more interested in squaring off against one another than in extinguishing fires. Still others, usually teenagers, were members of street gangs that toppled apple carts, rang door bells, taunted drunks, and disturbed the peace with the period's shrill whistles.

Developing police departments launched roundups of the disorderly, and in some cases rambunctious mayors themselves physically led the roundup operations.[17] Such dragnets, still a part of police procedures in working class neighborhoods and ghettos, were intimidating but hardly sufficient to stem social disorder crime. In fact, police procedures even created one particularly disruptive antebellum scene: large assemblies outside station houses. The noise and bravado of those gathering to protest the arrest of friends and family members led some to insist their neighborhoods would be more secure if the police based themselves elsewhere.[18]

The frequent riots that plagued antebellum American cities were the largest instances of social disorder crime. Between 1830 and 1860 at least 35 major riots took place in the eastern cities of Baltimore, Philadelphia, New York, and Boston. During the same period Cincinnati, the largest midwestern city, experienced four equally destructive episodes of mob violence.[19] The riots were ignited by social sparks including parades, lectures, elections and even theatrical performances, as in the 1849 Astor Place Riot in New York, which pitted followers of two rival Shakespearean actors and led to 31 deaths when police fired on rioters.[20] However, if specific events set off social disorder, the riots themselves were amorphous affairs. In most instances unorganized mobs vented their frustrations on blacks, Irish Catholics and members of other minority groups. In the words of one historian, the riots were "brutal street plays in which gangs had acted out the fear and enmities of ordinary citizens by attacking their scapegoats."[21]

Riots of this sort reached a midcentury peak in the frightening 1863 draft riots, which ravaged a half dozen cities from Boston to Detroit. The National Conscription Act, the federal government's first major attempt to raise and maintain an army without the aid of state authorities, prompted the riots. The act required all men between the ages of 20 and 45 to register for a draft lottery; particularly irksome to working-class registrants was a stipulation that anyone whose name was drawn could avoid service by paying $300 or by finding a substitute. The rioting began in most cases with attacks on lottery workers and offices, but shortly thereafter rioters forgot the draft and turned to other targets. In New York, where rioting extended over four days and nights and involved an estimated 70,000 participants, rioters first destroyed a Third Avenue lottery office. Fueled by excitement, mobs then raced through the city, burning orphanages, lynching blacks and looting establishments of the well-to-do, most notably the Brooks Brothers clothing store. Before troops ended the rioting, an estimated 500 people had died in "the longest, most widespread, and most destructive riots in American history, with by far the largest numbers of rioters."[22]

Midcentury riots dramatically illustrate a major aspect of nineteenth-century American crime. Like more commonplace social disorder crime, the riots were products of a rapidly changing and disorganized society. Confused instigators and participants longed for excitement and exhilaration. Frustrated and aided by only inchoate political views and vague goals, these criminals, as most perceived them, thrashed desperately about in what seemed an anomic society. What were the social meanings of the world in which they found themselves?

Antebellum property crime involved more planning and a greater degree of criminal consciousness. While personal violence and social disorder crimes were concentrated in ethnic, working class neighborhoods, David R. Johnson's study of the spatial patterns of crime in antebellum Philadelphia suggests that property crime took place primarily in commercial districts and wealthier neighborhoods.[23] Many property criminals were petty thieves who stole goods from the front of stores or poultry from backyards. Others were pickpockets operating in railroad cars or holiday crowds. Still others, the most entrepreneurial of the property criminals, provided illicit liquor, gambling and sex to gentlemen and, more commonly, to the large number of working-class "floaters" moving between eastern coastal cities and new industrial sites in the Midwest.[24] To view antebellum property criminals with awe is to romanticize. Most were low-skilled men and women struggling to make their way in a society they had difficulty understanding.

Some antebellum property criminals found support and direction in the criminal gangs to which they belonged. Bands of criminals had of course also been a part of the traditional social order, as suggested by the emergence of the Mafia in seventeenth-century Italy or by the familiar image of Robin Hood and his Merry Men.[25] However, images of Robin's stable forest outpost notwithstanding, premodern criminal gangs were loosely organized and in general maintained strong ties with their communities. Operating in a largely homogeneous social order marked by sturdy personal relations, traditional gang members rarely projected a criminal self-image.[26] In the modern urban setting, by way of contrast, criminal gangs manifest a greater degree of differentiation from their larger communities. In the heterogeneous society marked by a division of labor, members of urban gangs affiliate with the gang at a younger age and come eventually to look upon crime as an alternative to standard social activity. Indeed, associating primarily and sometimes exclusively with one another, urban gang members develop a recognizable criminal subculture. More so than rural gang members, members of urban gangs perceive themselves as criminals.[27]

Antebellum American criminal gangs stood somewhere between the traditional and the modern. In New York, representative gangs operated in Gotham Court, the Five Points and the Bowery, teeming working-class areas in southern Manhattan.[28] Calling themselves the Daybreak Boys, Plug Uglies and Dead Rabbits, these gangs developed a special argot and structures of command. Mose, the fabled leader of the Bowery Boys gang, had a small entourage, which included a flunky to mind his cigars.[29] But while these gangs manifested some degree of differential association, they remained integrated with their working class communities and had only begun to develop a full criminal subculture. Most likely, they considered themselves roustabouts rather than professional criminals.

The Civil War disrupted criminal activity of all types, and as a result, the nature and level of crime during the war years is difficult to gauge. On the one hand, war itself was an arena for criminal and near-criminal conduct. In camps and combat zones, members of the warring armies committed numerous criminal acts, only some of which were punished by military tribunals. In battle, soldiers engaged in severely antisocial conduct, which in peacetime would most certainly have been considered criminal. On the other hand, the war transported young men, the sector of the general population most likely to commit crimes, away from their home communities. A significant number of these men had committed minor local offenses and then, with the urging of local authorities mindful of available bounties, enlisted in order to avoid criminal penalties. The absence of potential criminals hardly spared cities of the East and Old Midwest from large-scale social disturbances or protected President Lincoln from the murderous plotting of John Wilkes Booth, but it did result in a substantial reduction in everyday crime. The North's prison populations shrank, and in several instances states abandoned plans for newer and larger prisons.[30]

While American men took their criminal ways to the battle fields, American women remained in home communities, where they perpetrated more crime than previously. The number of male criminals before and during the Civil War dwarfed the number of female criminals, but records show clearly that during the war the number of female inmates in New York and Massachusetts jails and prisons and in the Detroit House of Correction grew steadily.[31] Part of the increase was simply a matter of self-interested institutions filling available spaces, but the impact of war on wives and female family members should not be underestimated. Grief, anxiety and confusion created a condition more conducive to forms of irrational conduct that could be deemed criminal. More importantly, deprived of male support, women took rational, albeit criminal, steps to deal with painfully difficult situations. In particular, they turned to prostitution, petty theft, and other forms of criminal activity to support themselves and their families. With their men absent, women during the Civil War were more likely to act as men did during peacetime.

In the years immediately following the Civil War, criminal activity in the East and old Midwest quickly regained its antebellum levels and then rose to even higher levels. The daily papers reported a general crime wave, and court and prison authorities confirmed the development. A large number of post-Civil War lawbreakers were men who had served in the Army or Navy. During 1866, for example, almost seventy percent of those committed to the Massachusetts State Prison and the Eastern Penitentiary at Philadelphia were veterans.[32] Sympathy for men who had exchanged "the blue" for prison colors in fact led to the formation of prisoners' aid societies. Such societies had existed in eastern cities prior to the war, but after the war they sprung up as well in Columbus, Cincinnati, Cleveland, Detroit and Indianapolis.[33]

For some, the increase in crime during the late 1860s has seemed proof that the Civil War destroyed the law-abiding habits of veterans and the general population.[34] Surely this interpretation has some validity. As the sad saga of American World War I and II veterans indicates, returning soldiers often face an excruciating readjustment to society. Fatigued, accustomed to violence, and contemptuous of pain and death, veterans are more prone to criminal conduct than they had been before serving in a wartime military. Nonveterans, jarred first by the war and then by the reentry of men into job markets and personal lives, also experience a postwar readjustment potentially conducive to crime. Yet consideration of increased American crime following the Civil War must also take into account the general state of nineteenth-century American social development. After the Civil War crime increased not only because of returning veterans and a difficult readjustment to peace but also because American society resumed the radical modernization of the antebellum years. From a historical perspective, the decrease in crime during the Civil War was an aberration. In 1865 criminal activity picked up where it had left off in 1861.

It was only in the 1870s that crime began to abate more permanently, a development related to the cessation of chaotic modernization during the last third of the American nineteenth century. The urbanization and industrialization that had begun in the antebellum years continued and in some areas accelerated, but in the Gilded Age the new modern society began in many ways to stabilize. Urban police forces matured and more effectively provided a deterrent or at least a systematic response to crime.[35] Professions such as law, medicine, and architecture organized to control their markets and in the process generated leaders who could take community reins from the debilitated gentry and ministry.[36] Expanded educational systems, buoyed by new compulsory attendance laws, kept large numbers of young males off the streets at least during the daylight hours.[37] As electricity supplemented steam as the chief source of energy, a class of industrial workers learned not only to obey its foremen but also to tolerate the clock and growing production demands.[38] Urban zones became more fully differentiated, dividing the rich from the poor and the commercial from the residential.[39] Considered separately or collectively, these changes brought a new system of order and control to Gilded Age America.

In conjunction with these diverse yet related social and economic developments, a new middle-class ethic and attitude also emerged and stabilized. Surely this ethic had its grounding in certain of the most fundamental institutions of the time: in the period's churches, business enterprises, schools and colleges, even in its middle class in toto.[40] At the same time, however, the ethic factored back into social and economic life. Emanating from changing social life, the ethic was itself a social force. Stressing work, decorum, cleanliness and class awareness, this ethic, in the eyes of recent historians, was also an important aspect of the new social order or hegemony.[41] When urban dwellers, workers and others had internalized the values of this ethic and, indeed, made them part of the lived social process, they were less likely to commit acts perceived as criminal by the middle class. The middle class itself, of course, not only fostered the idealistic system but also for the most part lived by it, that is, made it a subconscious and conscious credo. The ethic was itself one of the gears of modernization, and working with the more distinctly social and economic aspects of modernization, the ethic contributed to the apparent decline in crime.

Statistical studies of crime in Gilded Age America are illustrative. In the case of Boston, Ferdinand's data on arrests for major crimes per 100,000 residents show a precipitous decline from over 2000 in 1875 to less than 1200 by the end of the century. This downward trend is visible both for assault, a routine variety of social disorder crime, and for burglary, a common property crime.[42] In the case of newer cities to the west, the same downward trend occurred. In his study of Buffalo arrest reports, Elwin H. Powell shows that the overall per capita arrest rate for the last third of the century was stationary and that the rate for serious crimes plummeted. In absolute numbers, arrests in Buffalo for assault dropped from 1808 in 1874 to only 988 in 1893; arrests for crimes against property dropped between 1874 and 1883 and then remained stationary for the next ten years.[43] Eric H. Monkkonen, in the only book-length statistical study of nineteenth-century crime, uses more numerous and sophisticated quantifying mechanisms than do other historians, but his conclusions are similar. From the early 1870s through 1885 the crime rate in Columbus, Ohio tended to decrease.[44] Contrary to the still standard assumption that urbanization and industrialization lead to increased crime, studies show crime in the American East and Old Midwest leveled off and in some important cases declined.

While the studies of Gilded Age crime are more numerous and varied than those of antebellum crime, it will once again be useful to supplement the studies by considering certain broad categories of crime. The nation was titillated by Edward Stokes' murder of robber baron "Jubilee Jim" Fisk in 1872, but in general personal violence crime remained sad and familiar affairs. In Baltimore between 1870 and 1872, for example, a half dozen homicides were committed. An iron mill worker bludgeoned a fellow worker to death with a wrench after the latter had accidentally burned him with hot metal tongs. A husband murdered his wife with a rock after finding her in bed with another man. An abandoned mother cut the throats of her four children. Another cooked her infant to death in a kitchen stove.[45] In each instance a frustrating social or economic situation served as a backdrop for panic, violence and death.

Most intriguingly, however, the period's more coherent social structure and increasingly precise definition of social roles led to a per capita decline in personal violence crime. In Philadelphia the annual rate of homicides per 100,000 population significantly declined from 3.3 in the antebellum years to 2.8 between 1860 and 1880, and then to 2.1 between 1880 and 1900.[46] In Buffalo, the number of murders had climbed from 2 in 1854 to 13 in 1874, but then, during a period of rapid local population growth, it dropped to only 6 in 1893.[47] Personal violence crime did not disappear from the metropolis, and it remained particularly prevalent in poor ethnic and minority communities.[48] Yet the declining numbers are even more telling since during the Gilded Age inexpensive handguns were more available. Had antebellum Americans possessed Colt revolvers, a larger number of antebellum homicides would no doubt have occurred, and the contrast between early and late nineteenth-century homicide rates would be more pronounced.

Reactions to the most discussed personal violence crime of the late nineteenth century, the 1892 murders of Andrew and Abby Borden, relate in part to the struggle for and partial achievement of a new social coherence. The murders themselves and the subsequent trial of Lizzie Borden, Andrew Borden's daughter from a previous marriage, took place in Fall River, Massachusetts, a city that illustrated the growing social stratification of the period. While its industry and population grew rapidly in the post–Civil War years, Fall River achieved some overarching stability and order through a rigid division between older Anglo-Saxon families and immigrant working-class families. The two groups had different patterns of consumption, domestic furnishings, speech and clothing styles, and degrees of power. In residential terms, the older New England families, along with members of the new professional and business classes, lived largely on "the Hill," a distinct area in Fall River, while workers lived in the old center city.[49]

Andrew Borden, something of a miser, chose not to live on "the Hill," but all of his friends and relatives were members of Fall River's elite. Borden himself had made a fortune as an undertaker and landlord, and at the time of his murder, he owned a bank, a mill, and many parcels of both city and farm land. When he and his wife Abby were found brutally murdered, much local and national interest in the murder derived from the Bordens' social position. Even members of the elite, models for social life and holders of power, were, it seemed, vulnerable to horrid personal violence crimes.

The allegation that Lizzie Borden, Andrew Borden's unmarried daughter, had committed the crime caused observers and commentators to wonder about the late nineteenth-century family as a guarantor of social balance. In keeping with a development that had begun earlier in the century, middle- and upper-class men and women had increasingly acquired different responsibilities and values. Men worked largely in the public sphere and ostensibly committed themselves to hard work, discipline and success. Their wives and daughters, meanwhile, were increasingly charged with maintaining an orderly home and Christian environment in the private sphere. As "proprietors" of family life, women were to be tender, pious and devoted to their husbands and fathers.[50] Against this backdrop, Lizzie Borden's alleged axing of her father and stepmother was especially shocking. A Fall River jury found her innocent, but the gender-based family, ballast in the hustling society, seemed, at least briefly, less reliable than before.

The gradual stabilization of social life during the Gilded Age also had an impact on the period's social disorder crime. Arrests for drunk and disorderly conduct, commonly over fifty percent of all arrests in a given city, leveled out and dropped during the century's final decades.[51] Part of this trend, of course, relates to the period's per capita expansion of police departments and to improvements in police communication and transportation systems. Additionally, the urban, industrial society generated other institutions conducive to social order, and what Eric H. Monkkonen calls the "Victorian synthesis" provided values and attitudes supportive of the emergent status quo.[52] These general developments, as much as changes in the size and nature of police operations, led to a decline in street rowdyism and public drunkenness.

Even the urban riot, the grander form of social disorder crime, assumed a more comprehensible character during the Gilded Age. In keeping with the patterns historian Charles Tilly has found in late nineteenth-century European rioting, American riots of the Gilded Age most commonly began as rallies, demonstrations, lockouts or strikes and then teetered out of control when police or soldiers entered the scene. This change from the more spontaneous and unpredictable antebellum rioting did not occur at any particular historical moment, and the Election Riot in Philadelphia and the Orange Riot in New York, both during 1871, were reminiscent of the street battles involving ethnic groups in the 1840s and 1850s. But gradually, large-scale disorder in urban America evolved into what Tilly calls "modern collective violence."[53]

In most cases Gilded Age rioting involved formal organizations and shaped political perspectives. In 1873, for example, New York labor and radical organizations drew 7000 supporters to a rally in Tompkins Square to demand that the city create jobs through an expanded public works program. After the city revoked the rally permit on the morning of the gathering, police surrounded and charged the square, provoking a riot of major proportions.[54] In 1877 riots convulsed a dozen cities after railroad unions had struck to protest ten percent wage cuts.[55] In Pittsburgh, where disorder was the most sustained and extensive, strikers, laborers and other supporters maintained a degree of focus even in the midst of the rioting, burning down the railroad depot and destroying 100 locomotives and 2000 railroad cars.[56] In 1886 in Chicago the McCormick Harvester Company locked out its workers. Anarchists from the Black International organized subsequent rallies and militant actions in support of the workers, leading eventually to riots and the Haymarket tragedy.[57] In these examples and others the rioting was as horrifying as that of the antebellum years, but as ironic as it may seem, these riots indicated the growing coherence and stability of urban, industrial life. Many rioters were affiliated with formal organizations and had concrete political goals; often their thoughts and actions reflected a clearheaded class consciousness.

The most striking development in property crime of the same period was the full emergence of professional crime. To some extent, professional crime was an extension of antebellum urban gang activities.[58] The perpetrators of the 1874 kidnapping of four-year-old Charley Ross in Germantown, Pennsylvania, for example, were thought to be members of urban gangs,[59] and one gang, the New York Whyos, was organized enough to publish a price list for its services:

Punching	$ 2.
Both eyes blacked	4.
Nose and jaw broke	10.
Jacked out	15.
Ear chawed off	15.
Leg or arm broke	19.
Shot in leg	25.
Stab	25.
Doing the big job	100. and up[60]

Given the larger picture of modernization, it is clear that professional crime was not a truly distinct social development. It was instead a striking, illegitimate variety of the specialization and consolidation that marked the nineteenth century. Much like their criminal brethren,

businessmen and professionals refined their services, products and identities. Indeed, the lines separating professional criminals and the new
society's businessmen and professionals frequently blurred. The latter
sometimes engaged in the shadiest of practices while building their
private empires.[61] Dishonest businessmen even manipulated the pathetic
Grant administration to their advantage, and a few lent their names to the
lists of the period's convicted criminals.[62]

Fully recognizable professional crime came into its own after the
large-scale issuance of greenbacks and state and federal bonds during the
1860s. With a sizeable volume of negotiable paper in circulation,
property criminals began investing time and money in sophisticated
counterfeiting operations and in the robbery of banks and express
companies. With a larger number of impersonal commercial transactions,
criminal entrepreneurs found more opportunities for fraud and forgery.
According to George Bidwell, a forger about whom more will be said, the
first crime that property criminals recognized as truly "professional" was
the Lord Bond Robbery of 1867. Perpetrated on Wall Street itself, the
heist netted a three-man team of criminals paper worth $1,200,000.[63]

As professional crime developed, it called forth a range of support
structures. The pawnbrokers and junk dealers who had purchased stolen
goods from petty thieves were now joined and in some cases replaced by
sophisticated fences.[64] Affiliates of professional criminals maintained a
network of safehouses stretching at least from Boston to Baltimore, and,
as the example of Howe & Hummel indicates, some attorneys put aside
their general practices to specialize in criminal law. With a half dozen
lawyers and an equal number of clerks, the firm represented New York's
major brothel owners and fences as well as Chester McLaughlin's Valentine Gang of forgers and General Abe Greenthal's Sheeney Mob, a
nationwide syndicate of pickpockets. In 1878 Howe & Hummel collected
a one-time fee of $90,000 from George Leslie, alias "Western George,"
for defending him against charges of robbing the Manhattan Savings
Institution, but more typically the law firm's stable and semipermanent
relationships with its criminal clients included an annual retainer.[65]

An evening with Fredericka "Marm" Mandelbaum illustrates the
state to which late nineteenth-century professional crime had evolved.
Mandelbaum, a New York City matron of the immediate post-Civil War
years, trained young pickpockets, supplied money and pull for colleagues
under arrest, and between 1864 and 1884 fenced an estimated $10
million in stolen goods.[66] In the second-floor living quarters above her dry
goods store at 79 Clinton Street, Mrs. Mandelbaum uncorked the finest of
wines from her wine cellar and served sumptuous repasts from an antique

sideboard. The guests included prominent members of America's light-fingered fraternity—Red Leary, Big Frank McCoy, Langdon Moore and Michael "Sheeney Mike" Kurtz—as well as visiting lawbreakers from Canada, Mexico, and Europe. According to New York Chief of Police Walling, "The receptions were conducted with as much attention to the proprieties of society as though Mrs. Mandelbaum's establishment was in Fifth Avenue instead of in a suspicious corner of the East Side."[67]

With professional criminals enjoying postprandials at Marm Mandelbaum's, America had become a modern society. The chaotic social change that had jarred America during the first half of the century had been supplanted by modern social routines and stable institutions. The urban, industrial society—a new hegemony—had come into its own. An integral part of that society, crime tended to decline on a per capita basis while simultaneously taking new forms representative of the new society.

As the nineteenth century's reporters, imaginers and rememberers tried to capture these developments, they too functioned in a modernizing society. However, their cultural work was not merely a reflection of changing social life and criminal conduct but rather a cultural practice that complexly derived from and contributed to modern social life. As the bases, form, content and thrust of this crime-related cultural work changed between 1830 and 1900, the criminal frames of the modern society emerged. The work and its frames are the subjects of the chapters that follow.

I.

REPORTING CRIME

2.

Rogues and Fiends:
Criminal Frames in the Traditional Street Literature

The work of the social historians, both popular and scholarly, supplies a sense of the nature and quantities of crime in nineteenth-century America, but as the preface of this work suggested, crime in a given historical juncture cannot be grasped merely with specific reports and data. The phenomenon of crime is not simple and essential but rather complexly dialectical. In our time as well as in the past, crime's identity, magnitude and character depend on available cultural conceptualizations. An exploration of the foundations and contours of the dominant criminal frames must be added to the specific reports and data in order to appreciate fully the way in which crime was conceived.

Subsequent parts of this work will consider the way writers of fiction and memoirists, respectively, imagined and remembered crime, but this part of the work concerns crime reporters. Crime reporters are writers, editors and publishers who produce verbal and, to a lesser extent, pictorial accounts of crime from a third-person perspective. Crime reports or accounts need not appear in periodical media, and they do not necessarily have the daily timeliness which, in our hurried, "the clock is ticking" context, sometimes seems a prerequisite.

Of course, to speak of crime reporting is to kindle thoughts of newspapers, and most certainly newspapers were familiar to American colonists as early as the seventeenth century. The London *Gazette,* founded in 1665, crossed the Atlantic in numbers surpassing the colonists themselves, and in Boston in 1685 and New York in 1696, colonial printers contracted to republish the newspaper on North American soil.[1] Subsequently, during the first decades of the eighteenth century, truly indigenous weekly newspapers attracted what was in the time substantial circulations of 600 to 1000 and were regularly purchased by tavern and innkeepers for the enlightenment and amusement of their customers.[2] However, up and down the Atlantic seaboard, eighteenth-century newspapers devoted the great preponderance of their space to government proclamations, European politics and wars, and ship departures and arrivals. Newspaper editors, assuming they even acknowledged a newspaper specialty that might be called crime reporting, limited it to an occasional paragraph concerning a counterfeit, a murder, or a runaway slave or bond servant.[3] The dominance of newspapers as crime reporting institutions was to come only in the nineteenth century.

The notion of a society without substantial newspaper crime reporting provides a pleasant pause. Did the absence of newspaper crime reports help preserve the social connectedness of the traditional society? Were social stability and integration more possible when the press did not label criminals? Perhaps, but in the case of western society such an hypothesis would have to be tested much earlier than the seventeenth and eighteenth centuries. For if newspapers did not print extensive or numerous reports, the citizens of western Europe and North America nevertheless knew no shortage of printed crime reporting. An ephemeral yet abundant street literature reported on crime in great detail.

This largely forgotten street literature began appearing in western Europe and the British Isles shortly after the invention of the printing press.[4] Widely distributed as early as the sixteenth century, this crime-related reportage included jest and chapbooks tracing the lives of criminals, accounts by Robert Greene and Thomas Harman among others, sketches of prison life, gallows pronouncements, lexicons of criminal cant and a staggering array of broadsheets.[5] Indeed, the production of crime-related street literature became so large in the eighteenth century as to provoke a written reaction. Daniel Defoe and Henry Fielding in England and P. L. de Lacretelle in France published pamphlets designed as much to condemn the crime-related publications as to report on crime.[6]

In the North American colonies of the Atlantic seaboard, certain of the crime-related publications had unique religious underpinnings, while others were secular. In a religious vein, Puritan ministers not only earnestly delivered execution sermons but also promptly published them for sale.[7] Additionally, some ministers published crime-related accounts that were less sermons than they were narratives.[8] In a more secular vein, eighteenth-century North American publishers printed and sold crime-related materials comparable to the varieties also available in England and France. Boston in the early 1700s had at least seven printers and nineteen sellers of printed materials,[9] and at least one of them, J. Allen, who was affiliated with an English printer in Cornhill, printed several crime pamphlets which survive. Similar to pamphlets that were available in other reaches of the colonies, Allen's pamphlets reported on recent local crimes, in one case a man who murdered his wife and sister and in another the murder of a cook on a ship in Boston Harbor by a displeased diner.[10] Not all of the colonial street literature concerned sensational crimes; indeed, some dealt not at all with crimes but with funerals, civil proclamations, fires or blazing stars.[11] But surely, the *Pennsylvania Gazette,* a Philadelphia newspaper, had crime-related street literature partially in mind when in 1764 it reviewed the year's events and rhymed:

> Pamphlets have madden'd round the Town,
> And drove poor Moderation down. . . .[12]

After the Revolution, a wide range of crime-related street literature continued to appear. One publication, *The Memoirs of the Notorious Stephen Burroughs,* first published in 1798, was so popular that printers in fourteen towns and cities published no fewer than thirty varieties of the work.[13] Beyond publications concerning individual crimes, criminals, trials and executions, a short-lived crime magazine, *The American Bloody Register,* appeared in 1784. Its publication included illustrations and also promised, via advertisements, that many subsequent issues would be forthcoming.[14]

Slipping a tattered, cracking piece of eighteenth-century street literature from an envelope under the watchful eye of a twentieth-century research librarian is a charming experience. The exhumed cultural artifact, after all, has its winning aura. However, in a society less print-saturated than our own, crime-related street literature was less quaint. Indeed, while the content of the literature attracted the colonial reader's attention, the literature's very form also won respect. When the rapidly expanding American legal profession of the later eighteenth century sought a medium for the first published case reports, it drew upon street pamphlets as a model.[15]

The two most common types of crime-related street literature from the late eighteenth century were the broadsheet and the pamphlet. The broadsheet was customarily folio-sized. Printed on one side with runny lampblack and oil, it had a headline in large type across the top and several columns of reporting or, on occasion, verse. Similar to the older chapbooks, the octavo-sized pamphlets were more elaborate. They ran two to twenty-five pages and had long, descriptive titles and irregular combinations of typefaces. In both types of street literature the most common illustration was a crude woodcut of the presumed criminal hanging by a rope. This ubiquitous illustration was virtually a folk label for the literature.

Publication of the crime-related street literature continued to thrive during the first decades of the nineteenth century. Surviving from this period are not only numerous individual publications but also a bound 1812 collection, *The Criminal Recorder or, An Awful Beacon to the Rising Generation of Both Sexes*.[16] Individual items in the collection are standard, but its preface intriguingly conveys a doubleness of tone and apparent purpose. This doubleness, coming as it does just before the period that is the true launching point for the study at hand, deserves special note. According to the *Criminal Recorder's* unnamed compiler, the collection's American and English crime reports are "authentic monitory stories of guilt and misery." Adult citizens could use the collection as a "convenient auxiliary" to steer their children away from crime.[17] However, after this statement of moral purpose, the compiler adds, "Let it not be hastily supposed by the gay and youthful, that this volume is a dull or canting lecture upon religion and morals."[18] As the nineteenth century began to unfold, American crime-related street literature was already one dash of morality and many more of entertainment.

According to one scholar, street literature, crime reporting included, began to disappear in the United States around 1825,[19] but this traditional cultural form need not be rushed so hastily from the scene. During the antebellum decades and even after the Civil War, the traditional literature continued to enliven the nation's streets and homes. Crime-related street literature production underwent a rudimentary industrialization in the context of a rapidly expanding cultural commodity market, but industrialization notwithstanding, printers continued to draw on the cultural norms that had dominated crime reporting during the preceding centuries. The processes were modern, but, at least temporarily, the frames were predominantly traditional.

If the broadsheets and pamphlets first appeared in Europe, so too did the industrialization of their production. The change was most striking in England during the 1820s when, aided by a stable of regular writers and a store of reusable ballads and woodcuts, broadsheet and pamphlet printer James Catnach and his chief rival John Pitts began systematically manufacturing half-penny and penny pieces of crime-related reporting.[20] Certain of the production and marketing procedures of Catnach and Pitts suggest the aggressiveness of the industry. Both printers regularly produced broadsheets purportedly featuring condemned criminals' scaffold speeches, but some of these broadsheets appeared before the criminals actually rode to the scaffold.[21] Both publishers also systematically plagiarized market proven items from one another and from other smaller producers.[22] In 1823, relying on a battery of presses capable of only 200–

300 copies per hour, Catnach produced no fewer than 250,000 broadsheets and short pamphlets concerning John Thurtell's murder of gambler William Weare.[23] So commercially successful were reports on the murder that the always resourceful Catnach even produced a final broadsheet headed "WE ARE alive again." Much like twentieth-century supermarket patrons misled by the headlines surrounding the checkout counter, many of Catnach's eighteenth-century customers might have assumed "WEARE" was not dead after all.[24]

In the United States the development of an efficient specialized industry began only a few years later. With improved presses, the American crime-reporting concerns had an industrial capacity larger than that of the London concerns of the 1820s. No one concern rivaled Catnach in size, but employing dozens of clerks, editors and writers, American printers such as Samuel N. Dickinson of Boston and Robert Desilver of Philadelphia supplied their street hawkers and itinerant agents with a steady flow of marketable crime reports. The greatest number of surviving antebellum reports come, predictably, from the cities of the Eastern seaboard and from Cincinnati. In addition, dozens of smaller concerns stretching from Portland and Augusta, Maine, in the North through Ithaca and Troy in upstate New York to Indianapolis, Louisville and St. Joseph's in the Old Midwest also produced crime-related literature.[25]

When produced by the larger concerns, the street literature was likely to be more elaborate and shaped. The broadsheet, for example, long a specialty of the small independent artisan printer, seems, if surviving pieces of antebellum literature are an indication, to have disappeared by the 1830s. Octavo-sized pamphlets, meanwhile, survive in abundance. Their typefaces were more uniform than earlier, and printers sometimes covered them with cool green or warm pink wrappers. Most commonly but by no means exclusively, these pamphlets were twenty-four or forty-eight pages in length. Aware that the potential consumer might want length for his purchase, the craftiest of the publishers sometimes made their publications seem longer by numbering the first page somewhere in the teens or by slyly skipping page numbers in the middle.[26]

One sign of the increased sophistication of the crime pamphlets was their illustrations. The familiar folk woodcut of a criminal hanging dead and doomed from a rope did not disappear completely, but in the products of the larger concerns it was gradually replaced by more elaborate illustrations geared specifically to the crime or criminal being reported. One illustration from the 1824 pamphlet concerning the robbery and murder of a Mr. Bonsall of Upper Darby, Pennsylvania, nicely straddles the pictorial divide.[27] On the right is the traditional

24

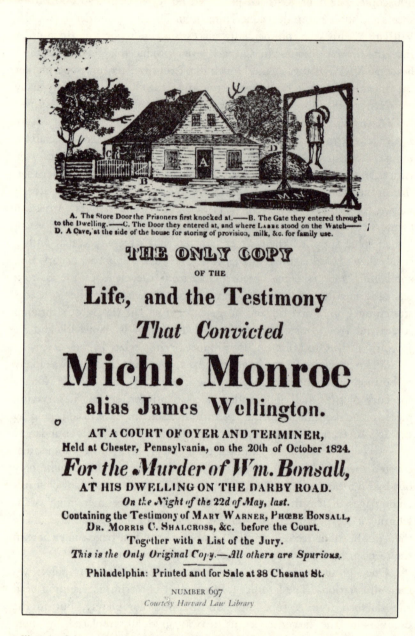

Illus. 1. Crime pamphlet title page and drawing including the traditional symbolic hanging on the right and the four stages of a crime on the left (1828).

woodcut, but on the left is a complicated four-stage scenario, indicated by letters, showing the steps of the crime.

The written texts of the pamphlets included, as they long had, bits and pieces of indictments, courtroom testimony, medical reports, formal verdicts and confessions, but editors also supplied a fixed narrative voice integrating the materials. The stylized narrative could, for the perceptive reader, call attention to itself. In the 1846 *Life and Confessions of Henry Wyatt, Who Was Executed at Auburn, For the Murder of James Gordon, A Fellow Convict,* the narrative voice is supposedly that of the robber, counterfeiter and murderer, Wyatt himself. However, while he proves articulate, particularly for a former mill worker, "Wyatt's" inclusion of a facsimile of his prison suicide note shatters the facade of authorship:

> Eye bid this hellish world A dew for I
> believe I shall go to heaven
>> Nothing moore at Present
>>> Henry Wyatt
> [Endorsement.] Mr. Pettibone sheriff of
> cauga county, NY eye take this plan to
> save you the painful Jobb[28]

In the Wyatt pamphlet and others, physical touches and text were the work of skillful, increasingly sophisticated production workers.

Indeed, the increasingly skillful writers and editors apparently felt little of the modern journalist's compulsion for accuracy. Liberties were regularly taken with the facts of a crime or a trial, prompting one modern scholar to insist on separating fact from fiction in the nineteenth-century street literature.[29] Admittedly, certain of the firms—Barclay's of Philadelphia or A. R. Orton of Baltimore—specialized in completely fictitious reports.[30] They disguised their fiction by giving specific execution dates and places and by placing narration in what was supposedly the hands of a respected clergyman. Even aside from these "cocks," the term Catnach and Pitts had applied to completely fictitious reports,[31] fact and fiction blended blithely throughout the reporting. Attempts to divide the two require not only caution but also a healthy amount of scholarly trepidation.

Perhaps some readers of the crime pamphlets would have welcomed a consumer advocate who might have alerted them to the bogus reports or stretched facts, but most antebellum readers worried little about the lines dividing fact and fiction. More important and more rewarding in terms of reading experience was the presence in the pamphlets of recognizable criminal frames, that is, constellations of words, images, conceptualizations and judgments that made the reported crime or criminal easily accessible. On this score, despite the rudimentary industrialization, the printers and publishers rarely disappointed. In essence, the street literature concerns relied on two frames, the rogue and the fiend, both of which had existed for centuries. The only major addition was the roguish fiend or, if you will, the fiendish rogue, a criminal characterization that combined the two standard frames.

The rogue was a picaro or trickster, almost always a man with a long history of tawdry adventures and crimes against property. The term itself, according to Dr. Johnson, Noah Webster, and others, derived from the Latin *rogator,* meaning beggar or asker, but C. J. Ribton-Turner, a late nineteenth-century scholar of English crime-related ephemera, noted that in the sixteenth century Gaelic, Scottish and Icelandic forms of the term were in usage. Most directly influential in the derivation of the English term "rogue," at least according to Ribton-Turner, was the Manx *rueg,* meaning enemy or plunderer.[32] As early as 1572, the term "rogue" appeared unambiguously not only in English usage but also in English statutes.[33]

Publishers and readers, of course, concerned themselves not with roguish etymology but with specific incarnations. Charles Moore and William Stuart epitomized the rogue type. The 1854 pamphlet regarding the swindler Moore promised in its subtitle a "Revealing History of the Most Remarkable Robberies, Forgeries, Kidnapping, Counterfeiting and Gambling Operations."[34] Born in Boston where his father ran an importing business, Moore launched dozens of frauds and criminal schemes. Later, he moved to New York and then to Marseille, where he continued his wily ways. Stuart, dubbed "The First and Most Celebrated Counterfeiter of Connecticut" in a pamphlet subtitle, mastered other sorts of crime as well.[35] In his own words, Stuart was,

> the chief of the gang—planner of operations, and more thoroughly versed in the tactics of roguery than any of them. . . . I was never disconcerted, but calm and deliberate or wild and turbulent, as occasion seemed to require.[36]

While serving a short term in a Danbury, Connecticut jail, Stuart was offered a gill of rum by the jailer for every rat he trapped. The classic rogue, Stuart trapped one rat, hid it, and then collected on it every day for a month.[37]

Rogue pamphlets regarding Moore, Stuart and countless others continued a criminal framing common in the eighteenth-century street literature about Johnathan Wild, Dick Turpin and Jack Shepard and suggested by even the sixteenth-century conny-catching pamphlets. On the one hand, the pamphlets disavowed criminal purpose. Predictable statements extracted from a rogue moldering behind bars or awaiting the hangman told readers of the sadness and disgrace immanent in a life of crime. According to Charles Moore, his story might perhaps "be the means of inducing others, who have started on the road to the gallows—dissipation—and who are not entirely hardened, to pause in their career and be warned by my terrible fate."[38] The counterfeiter William Stuart echoed these sentiments:

> My experience has been sad and severe. Comforts never arise from dissipation, wickedness and crime. Pure and rational enjoyments never spring from vicious propensities. Indulgences in errors never gladden the heart permanently, nor light up the smiles of happiness on the circumstances of men.[39]

On the other hand, the pamphlets were full of smartly executed schemes, crafty prison escapes, and vaguely hinted liaisons, all presented with an eagerness bordering on enthusiasm.

Were the disavowals louder than the enthusiasm? If modern literary criticism has accomplished nothing else, it has demonstrated that a text is "plural," that it is read in different ways by different readers or, in fact, by the same reader at different times.[40] Hence, some antebellum publishers and readers undoubtedly took the disavowals of criminal purpose seriously. However, American publishers were surely aware of the fortune James Catnach and John Pitts had amassed,[41] and like them were anxious to manufacture crime reports that would captivate consumers. Ultimately, the publishers wanted hungry purchasers more than forewarned citizens. Readers seeking moral tracts could find on the market no shortage of more genuinely religious and moral works and presumably turned to the rogue literature with other thoughts in mind. Enmeshed in tinier struggles against the same laws, constabulary, and well-to-do citizens that the rogues topped, readers looked for and found in the pamphlets soothing victories over the same foes who made difficult their own daily lives. More generally, readers of the rogue pamphlets found in them valorizations of self-reliant individualism. In an era in which an ethos of individualism was emerging and even stabilizing, reading about an individualistic rogue was an especially pleasant experience.[42]

Fiend pamphlets, meanwhile, traced their lineage as far back as fifteenth-century Paris when Parisians read of a barber from the Île de la Cité who had murdered a score of customers and neighbors. With the barber relocated from the Île de la Cité to Fleet Street, similar reports were sold in seventeenth and eighteenth-century England.[43] As pamphlets about the barber, recently used as a basis for the successful Broadway production "Sweeney Todd," suggest, the criminals on whom these pamphlets reported were not property but rather personal violence criminals, most often murderers. The criminal acts of these individuals were prompted by any number of circumstances—foiled robberies, insurmountable gambling debts, love affairs, or disputes over land, liquor, or slavery. Regardless of the circumstances, however, the literature casts the criminal as a fiend, that is, a diabolical, frenzied person. Imagine the following criminals called forward by a cultural bailiff in deathly detail: Thomas Barrett of Massachusetts, who savagely raped the seventy-year-old Mrs. Houghton and then murdered her;[44] Robert McConaghy of Pennsylvania, who demonically choked, shot and beat to death his mother-in-law, wife and five children;[45] Andrew Hellman of Maryland, who chopped up his wife with an axe, attempted to bury the body parts, but in the midst of his monstrous carnage left several limbs lying about his home.[46] In each case the relevant pamphlet stressed the manner in which the criminal was overwhelmed by rage; the pamphlet cast him as berserk, violent, evil—in a word, as a fiend.

Reading these fiend pamphlets over 100 years after their initial publication, a reader might find his or her own criminal frames intruding on the nineteenth-century one. Each of these criminals manifests severe psychosocial disorder and cries out, at least implicitly, for counseling, but for antebellum readers the fiend pamphlets were not clinical studies but pulsating titillations. Pushing beyond the basic fiendishness in the pamphlets' portrayals to certain secondary elements that repeat in good numbers of pamphlets facilitates speculation regarding the specific reading experiences the publishers produced and the readers presumably relished.

One standard subtype is the report on a prominent citizen's perpetration of a violent crime. There is no shortage of pamphlets concerning the lives and deeds of lawyers, doctors and dentists, the new professionals of the modernizing society. How titillating it was to read of Dr. John Hardenbrook, who in 1849 poisoned his wife with strychnine and then cleaned her stomach in a purported autopsy.[47] Just as fascinating were the horrible acts of ministers. When the body of Sarah Cornell, a Fall River working girl who was five months pregnant, was found hanging from a haystack pole, mobs surrounded the home of the Reverend Ephraim

Avery, and the New England conference of the Methodist Church raised $6000 to defend one of the leaders of its flock.[48] Afterwards, no fewer than twenty-one pamphlets reported on the murder and Avery's subsequent trial.[49] These pamphlets both drew on and fueled the public's fascination with the misconduct of a prominent man and in part caused Cornell's humble grave to become a veritable shrine of populist titillation.[50] Turning the pages of pamphlets regarding Hardenbrook, Avery and others, the average citizen found special delight in the misdeeds and the punishment of members of social elites.

Another subtype of fiend pamphlet, easily the most common, prefaced the criminal act and punishment with accounts of illicit, often adulterous heterosexual activity. John Erpenstein, for example, had left his wife and three children in Germany and engaged in an affair with Dora Muller. When his wife trailed him to New Jersey, he served her a bread-and-butter sandwich laced with arsenic.[51] Maurice Antonio shared both the home and the wife of Ignacio Pinto, but finally, unable to tolerate a triangular relationship, he murdered Pinto and buried his body under the barn.[52] Contemplating the social and personal foreplay in these and countless other murderous pamphlets, readers vicariously escaped the sexual and moral codes that strapped them. They held hotly in their hands a type of pornography that, by twentieth-century standards, is so tame as almost to elude recognition. At the end, of course, when illicit intimacy gave way to rage and violence, the fiend pamphlets launched into predictable moralizing, but for many readers this moralizing was only a palate-cleansing sorbet at the end of a delightfully spicy reading experience.

While almost all of the rogues in the pamphlet literature were men, a good number of the fiends were women. In a period in which, according to recent scholarship, American middle-class women were increasingly confined to a private sphere and this gender restriction was held out even to working-class women as a normative model,[53] the presence of female fiends is intriguing. For some, the amorous activities of a woman, against the backdrop of gender ideology, were all the more pornographic. Women in particular, when their resident patriarchs were at the office or busy in the fields, could slip a pamphlet out of their knitting or plates and vicariously experience the sexual adventures missing in their own lives. Reading of Isabella Narvaez, the "Female Fiend and Triple Murderess," who murdered one husband with prussic acid, a second with a hatchet, and still a third with a dagger,[54] female readers might even have found a cultural vent for a man-hating urge literally engendered by grinding, draining private captivity.

A combination of the two basic criminal frames was the roguish fiend. Pamphlets utilizing this combined frame reported the life of a property criminal who, after a career of wit and dexterity, committed a personal violence crime in a fit of rage or passion. In their earlier pages, roguish fiend pamphlets employed the images of the trickster; later, the same pamphlets switched to monstrous, savage imagery. The 1846 pamphlet concerning Henry Wyatt, cited earlier, is a good example. Its early stages chronicle in exuberant detail Wyatt's long life of pickpocketing, counterfeiting and burglary and, with an eye to an anticipated linkage of heterosexual activity with enraged crime, dwell as well on his intimate liaisons. In the end, Wyatt commits a brutal murder in upstate New York, and the pamphlet converts the rogue into a fiend, moving smoothly from one frame to another.[55] Not only the rogue and the fiend but even the hybridized roguish fiend had been a mainstay in the street literature for three hundred years.[56]

During the second half of the nineteenth century, crime pamphlets passed from the scene. Ted Peterson, the scholar who has most seriously studied the British pamphlets, rings the death knell for the British industry in 1871, when collectors began gathering street literature for nostalgic purposes.[57] In the United States, where the industrialization of pamphlet production began a few years after it did in England, production of the pamphlets continued almost until the end of the nineteenth century. The Barclay concern in Philadelphia, which in the years preceding the Civil War had primarily published "cocks," began after the War to report on actual crimes and criminals.[58] Edward Stokes's shooting of Jim Fisk or Charles Guiteau's assassination of President Garfield led to dozens of pamphlets,[59] and even as late as 1892 the murder of Andrew and Abby Borden resulted in pamphlets suggesting Lizzie Borden had wielded the bloody axe.[60]

Perhaps selected late nineteenth-century crime pamphlets are culturally significant. Pamphlets, such as those concerning the 1878 murder of Mary Stannard of Madison, Connecticut, or the robberies and murders perpetrated by the linguist Edward Ruloff in upstate New York,[61] reflect the period's interest in popular science. The pamphlet about Jesse Pomeroy, the "Boy Fiend of Boston," and the murders he committed suggests the age's new concern with childhood.[62] Additionally, there were groups of pamphlets showing a new sensitivity to social disorder crime as allegedly perpetrated by the Mollie Maguires and Haymarket rioters.[63] Overall, however, the vestigial production of original crime pamphlets during the last third of the nineteenth century is difficult to interpret in toto.

As for the traditional rogue and fiend frames, it was the latter that manifested the greater staying power. Virtually all of the late nineteenth-century pamphlets focus on personal violence crimes, and the great majority of them employ the language, images, conceptualizations and judgments that marked the fiend pamphlets from the 1830s and 1840s. Fiendishness as a criminal frame remained responsive to the personal violence crime which was part of the social life of the growing cities and also of the more traditional towns and villages. Roguery, meanwhile, certainly had potential correlations to the shady scheming of the era, but the dominant ideology of the era deplored such conduct and in subtle ways undermined the viability of the rogue frame.[64] To cite only one example, the period's enthusiastically produced and widely read rags-to-riches stories and novels cast the ingenious property criminal in undeniably negative ways.[65] All of this having been said, however, traditional forms of crime reporting—the fiend and rogue frames—appeared in nothing approaching their early nineteenth-century magnitude.

How might developments within nineteenth-century street literature be succinctly characterized? Riding as they were on the first waves of nineteenth-century modernization, the crime pamphlets represented both the old and the new in crime reporting. Their novelty resided primarily in their rationalized, industrial production in the context of an expanding cultural commodity market. Once something of a folk product, produced by independent artisan printers, the crime-related street literature of the antebellum years adopted the social and economic moorings so typical of a modern commercial nation. Yet as this change took place and as the literature became a more elaborate, standardized cultural product, street literature producers continued to use traditional criminal frames. New modes of production did not, at least immediately, carry with them new notions of crime and the criminal.

This is not to argue, of course, that the rogue and fiend frames did not acquire new accents and subtleties in the antebellum context. In a society full of robust entrepreneurs and champions of private property, pamphlet reports on rogues seemed more pointed. In the growing cities where factories belched smoke into the air and residents fretted over apparently anomic conditions, reports on murderous fiends served as the reference points in the search for new social norms.

However, these accents, derived from the midcentury juncture, were less potent than those which might have been available had the rogue and fiend frames given way to something new. As had long been the case, the apparent disavowal of crime in the rogue and fiend frames was matched by the reports' excitement about crime. The rogue frame, pitting the careerist property criminal against the well-to-do, the police, and the law, delighted readers who struggled less successfully against similar foes in their own lives. The fiend frame, culminating in a monstrous personal violence crime, offered amorous, illicit sexual activity as well, and readers found in it a variety of pornography. These most fundamental elements of the crime reports had attracted readers for centuries.

In rough terms and with a nod to at least one hybrid, the rogue and fiend corresponded, respectively, to property and personal violence criminals. However, as will be true with other culturally conveyed criminals considered in this work, the assorted rogues and fiends were not merely "gathered up" from social life. There were, to be sure, careerist property criminals and enraged murderers, but these men and women were not rogues or fiends per se. They became rogues and fiends in the context of reigning social relationships, cultural alternatives and ideologies; in particular, they were encased in well-established structures of meaning. Consumers, who shared many of the social rhythms and attitudes of the producers, recognized and enjoyed the criminal portraiture with reference to the same structures of meaning. The frames encased the criminals as much as the criminals prompted the frames.

Crime reporting of this sort was, of course, living on borrowed time. Daily newspapers were shortly to overwhelm the crime pamphlets. New reportorial frames would replace the rogue and fiend frames. Yet the broadsides and pamphlets should be held firmly in mind. They provide the dominant criminal frames of a society more traditional than the one that would emerge. The broadsides and pamphlets illustrate the mutual involvement of crime and cultural work.

3.

Politicized Crime Journalism:
The Midcentury Cheap Press

In his 1967 study of deviance in Puritan society, the scholar Kai Erikson suggested that sustained social turmoil brings with it institutions and "deployment processes," which both respond to and clarify new modes of criminal conduct.[1] If Erikson's basic insight is applied to early nineteenth-century American society, a new understanding of the period's surge in prison construction, establishment of citywide police forces, and expansion of metropolitan police courts emerges. These new institutions helped Americans comprehend the crime and, more generally, the new social rhythms that rocked the urban East and the young cities of the old Midwest. These institutions and their processes socially delineated and placed the criminal and, in so doing, gave the modernizing nation useful and meaningful ways to chart its course of development.

Erikson's observations are also useful in a study of crime-related cultural work. For not only social institutions and deployment processes but also cultural institutions and the products they generated delineated criminals differently during the 1830s and 1840s. The traditional pamphlet literature, as the previous chapter suggested, had limited potential for this. Despite rudimentary industrialization, the producers of pamphlets continued to generate pamphlets in which the portrayals of criminals were frozen. However, new producers and products of the 1830s and 1840s—penny dailies and the *National Police Gazette*—experimented with new crime-related portrayals and images. During a brief period of social restructuring, crime and the criminal were innovatively framed.

Standard works have for many years given the penny press and, to a lesser extent, the *National Police Gazette* a special place in journalism history.[2] Challenged in recent years but as yet untoppled, this scholarship promotes a generally positive and melioristic interpretation.[3] "Journalism history," according to a leading spokesman for the interpretation, "is the story of man's long struggle to communicate freely with his fellow men."[4]

The heroic leaders of the forces desiring better communication have been the enlightened editors who make publications available to more and more readers. The journalistic publications, meanwhile, have become more objective, reliable, and socially responsible. The struggle continues, but over time journalistic publications have become increasingly valuable and indispensable for the reading public.

On a certain level, this paradigmatic interpretation helps illuminate journalistic developments of the 1830s and 1840s. Prior to 1830, newspapers in the United States were expensive; in the second and third decades of the nineteenth century they usually cost 6 cents per issue. Their circulations, by modern standards, were quite small, ranging from a few hundred to a maximum of 4000, and two types of newspapers dominated. One type, almost always sporting the word "advertiser," "commercial" or "mercantile,"[5] was in essence a business page as newspaper. It devoted almost all of its space to commercial information, advertisements and schedules of ship arrivals and departures. The second type was the party organ, ranging from *The Washington Globe,* which President Jackson made into the semiofficial newspaper of the Democracy, to smaller sheets affiliated with local parties and factions.[6] More ephemeral than the mercantile newspaper, the party-affiliated newspaper offered primarily political commentary and opinion. Together, the two types of newspapers had a lock on American newspaper journalism.

In subsequent decades, the mercantile and party-affiliated newspapers continued to appear, but the penny dailies and, eventually, the *National Police Gazette* joined them on the market. Beginning with Boston's *The Evening Bulletin* and Philadelphia's *The Cent,* both founded in 1830, the new newspapers initiated significant changes in American newspapers. Calling themselves "heralds" and "tribunes," "stars" and "suns," they achieved circulations five and even ten times larger than the older newspapers. They abandoned an emphasis on commercial notices and political commentary and began reporting what might seem to the twentieth-century reader factual news. According to the established historical paradigm, the cheap press began expanding newspaper readerships and producing objective news, highly valorized goals that later newspapers would even more fully achieve.

Yet is the paradigmatic interpretation of the cheap press of the 1830s and 1840s in itself satisfactory? Generated primarily by academics in journalism schools, the paradigm suffers from a type of tunnel vision, tracing the line of newspaper development without paying enough attention to changing social situations and without critically exploring the political significance of the new newspapers.[7] The circulations of the penny dailies and, a decade later, the *National Police Gazette* were both greater *and* different. Readers came largely from the ranks of mechanics, artisans, office workers and small merchants—urban social groups whose members' work experiences and social status were changing.[8] The journalism of the new newspapers was not simply more objective but was of a decidedly different cast. It still included mercantile and political events but stressed romances and scandals, sports and amusements, crime and arrests. While the readers reached for the new newspapers, the newspapers reached for the new readers, providing types of news that were marketable. The newspapers engineered a significant expansion of the cultural commodity market. More significantly for the study at hand, the newspapers manifested a critical perspective. They introduced readers to a new society, and in the process they spoke for what they took to be the readers' interests in the world taking shape around them.

The present chapter is concerned with these developments and, particularly, with the crime journalism that was a part of them. Such penny dailies as *The Sun* and *The Herald* gave crime journalism much more space and prominence than had previously been the case. Pacesetters for the new newspapers of the 1830s, *The Sun* and *The Herald* placed crime in frames responsive to the emergence of new social groups and to the changing social hierarchies and configurations. So critically charged was their cultural work that in 1840 traditional elites reacted sharply to the new newspapers' journalism and criminal frames. Reaction apparently triumphant, the *National Police Gazette* then appeared in 1845 and, more vigorously than even its predecessors, resumed the critical crime journalism that *The Sun* and *The Herald* had initiated.

A comprehensive description or analysis of crime reporting in the 1830s and 1840s is a project too large for the chapter at hand, but an exploration of New York City developments is manageable and particularly suggestive. In 1830, New York City had almost 203,000 residents,[9] nearly twenty percent of the nation's urban population, and its mechanic and artisan classes were growing at an especially rapid pace. Due to its busy harbor and connection via the Hudson River to the Erie Canal, New York already had more business and shipping activity than Boston and Philadelphia. Most importantly for immediate purposes, New York during these decades was beginning to surge ahead as the nation's publishing and cultural center. Two New York City newspapers, *The Sun* and *The Herald,* staked claims to being the nation's two largest daily newspapers. Their crime reporting was innovative and, for some, troubling indeed.

The first issue of *The Sun* appeared on the streets of New York on September 3, 1833.[10] Benjamin H. Day, the newspaper's founder, was the son of a Massachusetts hatter and a printer, who had failed nine months earlier in an attempt to publish another penny daily, *The Morning Post*. According to limited biographical information, Day had ties to the radical artisans' movement of the period.[11] Additionally, Day's job-printing trade had suffered as a result of the 1833 depression, and he hoped *The Sun* might repair his losses. For the first issue, Day wrote all the news copy, lifted advertisements from other papers, and even set the type. One historian with a taste for metaphoric euthanasia overstates the case when he asserts Day's efforts drove "a knife into the sclerotic heart of ancient journalism,"[12] but surely Day was ambitious. "The object of this paper," Day announced in the top left corner of his first front page, "is to lay before the public at a price within the reach of every one, ALL THE NEWS OF THE DAY, and at the same time afford an advantageous medium for advertising."[13]

Given the size of the space with which Day worked, his capitalized claims seem more hopeful than realistic. The earliest issues of *The Sun* had four small pages measuring 8 × 11¼ inches with only three columns to the page. The first, third, and fourth pages, recalling the mercantile dailies, had columns of shipping notices, commercial advertisements, and a listing of available New York bank notes. The remainder of those pages were devoted not to what a modern reader might consider news but rather sketches, poems, and announcements of record-breaking apples, lemons, and, in one case, a sheep yielding 19 lb of fleece. News coverage gradually infiltrated these pages, but at first it appeared almost exclusively on the second page. This page contained in the first and subsequent issues a large number of one- and two-paragraph news items from both the city and around the country concerning fires, accidents, building projects, marriages, and deaths. Strikingly absent was reporting on national politics. Underscoring the fact that the absence of national political news was a matter of choice rather than an oversight was a report in *The Sun*'s May 9, 1834 issue. The report highlights a series of United States Senate debating points, resolutions, amendments, and votes, never once mentioning the substance of these matters. The report wryly concludes, "Nothing of importance was done in the lower house."[14]

By the standards of the time, an unusually large portion of *The Sun*'s contents was crime-related. In the first issue alone there were one-paragraph reports on a murder in Columbus, the robbery of the Boston to Lynn stage, a double execution in Connecticut, a prison insurrection, and a burglary at 50 Exchange Place in Manhattan. Each of these reports was straightforward and without opinionated commentary. In subsequent issues similar items continued to appear, bearing succinct titles such as "Thief Taken," "Robbing a House" and "Double Murder." In addition, early issues of *The Sun* had a daily column titled "Police Office," concerning cases in New York's lower criminal courts, and short editorials suggesting that the local watch was as ineffective as the watch in New Orleans or Havana or deploring the leniency of local judges. In fact, even *The Sun's* advertisements hinted of crime. Interspersed among the commercial notices were personal notices offering rewards for the return of lost or stolen property, most notably watches. According to one commentator who later condemned such notices, pawnbrokers and fences followed them closely and then launched negotiations with criminal victims for the return of their property.[15]

In the context of nineteenth-century crime reporting as a whole, *The Sun's* short reports on crime, the trials of criminals, and criminal punishment are perhaps the most significant. They are the start of a generic crime reporting that later became a journalistic mainstay. In the context of the antebellum years, though, *The Sun's* daily "Police Office" column was the most intriguing. Most commonly appearing on page two, the column reported on developments in New York's Police Court. New York officials had established the court in City Hall in 1798. It grew steadily during the first decades of the nineteenth century and by the 1830s had a branch where the Bowery and Third Avenue split.[16] Similar in procedures and size to lower criminal courts in Boston, Philadelphia, Baltimore and other larger cities, New York's Police Court epitomized the expanding lower tier of the criminal justice system in the 1830s.

While a half-dozen magistrates presided over New York's Police Court, the reporter George W. Wisner presided over *The Sun's* daily column concerning it.[17] Wisner joined *The Sun* only a week after its initial appearance. Day originally paid him $4 per week to cover the New York Police Court, but Wisner lent a hand with other aspects of *The Sun* as well. He and Day eventually had a falling out regarding the newspaper's position on slavery,[18] and Wisner moved west to become a prominent Michigan legislator and journalist.[19] However, in the early days of *The Sun,* Wisner's daily column and other work led to his listing on the newspaper's masthead as a co-owner.[20]

Wisner and, one assumes, assorted assistants recounted in the "Police Office" the stories of thousands of men and women "brought up" for petty crime. Some were personal violence criminals who had beaten spouses, friends or neighbors. Others were social disorder criminals, most commonly men who drank until they were "blue" and stirred up a ruckus.

Still others were property criminals charged with picking pockets, pilfering merchants' goods, or swiping household items. Other than the word "prisoner," which *The Sun* regularly used to designate those appearing before the court, the newspaper did not use a standard label for these men and women. It disdained labels such as "rogue" and "fiend," which were common in the pamphlet literature. It also differed from the prosaic twentieth-century legalist who, in the process of dumping these men and women into the gray anonymity of criminal records, might have labeled them "misdemeanants." The prisoners were individuals, and even though libel suits could and did result,[21] *The Sun* called each and every one by name.

In formal terms, *The Sun*'s "Police Office" was rich in special touches and unique compositional devices. Wisner's reports of crimes and subsequent courtroom developments are often punctuated by numerous dashes between prose fragments. Born perhaps of a hurried court reporter's note taking, the dashes nicely suggest—the fragmentation—and the confusion—of antebellum social life—and courtrooms. The column's characterization is surprisingly strong, given the limited space. In the midst of the column's six to twelve short daily reports, tight, dramatic scenes in which actors speak for themselves frequently appeared. Designated as "Mag.," "Watch.," "Wit.," and "Pris.," the actors playfully and forcefully reveal their characters through dialogue, often in distinctive dialects. Wisner's own voice often surfaces at the end of these scenes, noting that the magistrate sent an inebriate to a place "where the people drink cold water"[22] or that a lock thief "was placed under the security of locks which he will find more stubborn things to walk off with, or through, than those he pilfered."[23]

To be sure, few relished an appearance in the "Police Office," but overall the column is surprisingly gentle, almost pleasant. The court itself seems a friendly enclave on the frayed edges of the city's social coherence where simple men and women show composure and confusion, dignity and weakness. Individually identified and able to turn a smart phrase, the criminals as well as the watchmen, victims and others seem people of fiber and verve. Many may have beaten, become disruptively intoxicated, or stolen, but the "Police Office" invites readers to delight and suffer along with them. *The Sun*'s column is empathic. It tells the reader that the criminals are us, the workers of the city, and that all is well and good when, as is often the case, disputes are solved and reconciliations are achieved in the courtroom.

The Sun's "Police Office" column and crime reporting in general were central to the make-up and success of the newspaper. Some sense of how earnestly *The Sun* took its crime reporting can be gained from the newspaper's vigilance in monitoring crime reporting elsewhere. In the February 11, 1834 issue, to cite only one example, *The Sun* under the heading "Plagiarism" noted that *The Evening Star* had stolen a crime report from *Mornings at Bow Street,* a book of London tales and anecdotes. *The Evening Star,* it seems, had made only those changes in the original text "as were necessary to adopt it to the American market."[24] In 1835, when *The Sun* gradually began to cover national political news, its crime reporting actually influenced and shaped this coverage. Rather than allowing the more conventional variety of opinionated political reporting to creep into its pages, *The Sun* instead presented news from the United States Senate and House of Representatives in columns of capsule reports that closely resembled those of the "Police Office."[25] The citizens of New York, it seems, appreciated the amount, forms and tone of crime reporting in *The Sun.* The newspaper's circulation jumped to 8000 after only six months and 15,000 after fifteen months.[26] In 1835, according to its own claims, *The Sun's* circulation surpassed "that of any other daily newspaper in the Union."[27] Although not as pathologically as the boy in *The Sun's* sixth issue who was so fascinated by crime and punishment that he accidentally killed himself while simulating a hanging,[28] *The Sun's* readers delighted in the subject of crime.

The Herald, meanwhile, appeared on the streets of New York less than two years after *The Sun.*[29] Its founder was James Gordon Bennett, a Scotsman who had immigrated to North America at the age of 24 and worked in Halifax, Boston and Charleston before earning a reputation as a New York journalist specializing in Wall Street reports. In May, 1835, having already failed in two previous attempts to launch penny dailies, Bennett assembed a mere $500 in capital and, working in a Wall Street basement on a desk made of a plank and two flour barrels, put out the first issue of *The Herald.* Shortly thereafter, a fire destroyed *The Herald's* headquarters, but Bennett was not deterred.[30] He moved to new offices, stationed reporters in Europe and American regional centers, and during his second year of operation raised his newspaper's price to two cents. The latter move, although a bit staggering for the laboring mechanic, seems not to have impeded *The Herald's* circulation growth. The more prosperous members of New York's working and middle classes adopted the newspaper as their own. By 1840, *The Herald* had 20,000 daily readers, second only to *The Sun* among American dailies.[31]

During its earliest years *The Herald* resembled *The Sun,* consisting of four pages only slightly larger than pieces of twentieth-century business stationery. Playful sketches and advertisements dominated, respectively,

The Herald's first and fourth pages, while editorials and short, briefly titled news items clustered on the second and third pages. The news items included reports of accidents, fires, and storms as well as a daily "money article," theater notices, and spicy reports on the upper crust. Overall, the newspaper attempted to capture and convey the events and texture of the new urban society that was beginning to supplant the traditional agrarian order. Indeed, even such light-hearted sketches as "Rural Life" by "A. Jaunt," which appeared on the front page of the first issue after the fire, revealed *The Herald*'s urban, modernizing perspective. After a sweet "ramble in the woods" and several moments of introspection perched on "some ambitious root," "Jaunt" returns to the city "more serene and calm than before,"[32] but return he does. Like *The Herald* for which he wrote, the author looked at and experienced the world from a bustling urban locus.

Not surprisingly, crime-related editorials, columns and reports were also staples in *The Herald*'s daily fare. However, for the time being at least, these journalistic forms remained fluid, and *The Herald* shaped them differently than did *The Sun*. *The Herald*'s editorials about crime and the criminal justice system, for example, were longer, more frequent, and more aggressive than those in *The Sun*. They grumbled about the police, the courts and the prisons, and one special ongoing concern was the perceived similarity between sophisticated property crime and the activities of Wall Street speculators. Perhaps this analogizing derives from Bennett's early experiences as a Wall Street reporter and his determination to provide intensive business news coverage in *The Herald*. However, as subsequent discussions will indicate, this challenging analogy was also posed in other works of the period. Cultural workers commenting on the modernizing society, not merely James Gordon Bennett, perceived similarities between bank robbers and confidence men on the one hand and financiers and stock manipulators on the other. The work of the latter, *The Herald* insisted, was "generated in the dark—and consummated in the dark. . . ."[33]

With regard to a Police Court column, *The Herald* announced plans at the end of August, 1835 to begin a new and different type of column, one veritably Shakespearean in inspiration:

> The mere barren record of person and crime amounts to nothing—to something less than nothing. There is a moral—a principle—a little salt in every event of life—why not extract it and present it to the public in a new and elegant dress? . . . if a Shakespeare could have taken a stroll in the morning or

afternoon through the Police, does any one imagine he could not have picked up half a dozen dramas and some original character? The bee extracts from the lowliest flower—so shall we in the Police Office.[34]

The columns that followed treated one case at length rather than reporting on six or twelve. They also included some delightful imagery, for example, a description of sailor Jack Gooney leaving the courtroom after drunk and disorderly charges against him had been dropped: "Jack, after rapping his knuckles on the desk by way of applause to the magistrate, hoisted the top sail, let go the anchor, and made sail in a style out of the office, firing salutes of indignation with his gleaming black eye, on the watchman and all in attendance."[35] However, despite *The Herald's* ambitiousness and flair in its Police Court column, the column in fact shared many of the features of similar columns in *The Sun* and other newspapers. More significantly, for reasons never explained, *The Herald* abandoned the column in the process of regearing itself following the fire.[36]

While *The Herald* posed particularly pointed questions in its crime-related editorials and abandoned experiments in its Police Court column, it was actually in the area of crime news reporting that the newspaper made the biggest change. During its first year of publication, *The Herald* ran daily a few short crime reports. Occasionally the reports were humorous, as in the case of a Grand Street urchin who left a gentleman with a crate of oranges worth fifty cents when he purportedly went down the street to change the gentleman's five dollar bill.[37] More often, however, the crime reports, as in *The Sun,* were short, simple and straightforward. Then, in the spring of 1836, Dorcas Dorrance, a prostitute from Augusta, Maine, who had moved to New York and taken the name Helen Jewett, was found in a brothel, dead from three-inch-deep hatchet wounds to her head. The chief suspect in the murder was the nineteen-year-old clerk Richard P. Robinson, who had visited Jewett on the night of the murder and whose cloak was found near the scene of the crime. The Jewett-Robinson affair fueled a crime-reporting extravaganza unrivaled in the prior history of newspaper journalism in the United States.

In terms of cultural work, the case prompted changes in placement, magnitude and style in *The Herald's* crime reporting. Starting with *The Herald's* initial report on the crime in its April 12, 1836, issue, reports concerning the case appeared not on the newspaper's center pages but rather at the top of its front page. In addition, the reports were hardly a paragraph or two of unadorned prose. Instead, they routinely ran several columns and, filled with details and opinions, constituted an expansive new form of crime reporting. The reports described for the readers scenes at the morgue, at the graveyard, at the Tombs, and at Rowina Townsend's City Hotel, the brothel where Jewett worked. They noted Jewett's preferences for green dresses, the works of Byron, and customers who were lawyers and brokers,[38] and they detailed as well Robinson's home life, work habits, and relationships with other clerks. When the scene finally shifted to the courtroom, the reporting included descriptions of those in attendance, reactions to judicial rulings, and column after column of verbatim testimony. Through it all, the tone was mysterious and moralistic.

To say that *The Herald* had found both a criminal case and a mode of crime reporting that fascinated readers is an understatement indeed. According to one historian, *The Herald*'s circulation tripled during the two months it gave front page coverage to the murder and the trial.[39] In addition, other New York newspapers quickly recognized the lucrative resource that *The Herald* had not only located but also manufactured. They scurried to match *The Herald*'s coverage in both volume and form, and a particularly animated rivalry developed between *The Herald* and *The Sun*. The former, although it had originally called Robinson "a villain too black a die for mortal,"[40] said he was innocent. The latter, on the basis of its own investigations, declared that he was guilty. When in early June, 1836, the jury acquitted Robinson, *The Herald* rejoiced at the courtroom scene:

> The cheerings and huzzas were tremendous—in vain the court
> assayed to stop them . . . they might as well have tried to
> choke the current of a river with sand, as to put a stop to the
> hearty outbursts of honest acclamation that rang again and
> again through the hall.[41]

Less pleased, *The Sun* stressed not the courtroom reaction but rather that of the community. Throughout New York, *The Sun* asserted, people were saying "that any good looking young man, possessing or being able to raise among his friends, the sum of fifteen hundred dollars to retain Messrs. Maxwell, Price and Hoffman for his counsel, might murder any person he chose, with perfect impunity."[42]

How genuine was the disagreement between *The Herald* and *The Sun?* Undoubtedly it was based on differing convictions, but at the same time it included certain mitigating elements. The different stances, to begin with, were good for both newspapers' circulations. The disagreement was cultivated with an eye to boosting newspaper sales. More importantly in the context of present concerns, both newspapers cast the murder and subsequent trial in similar political terms. Questions of Robinson's guilt aside, *The Herald* and *The Sun* saw an established elite lurking behind the scenes, engaging in immoral behavior and then seeking special treatment in the criminal justice system. For *The Herald,* the whole affair was a "mysterious juggle," and the newspaper told readers, "Look to it—look to it."[43] Men of wealth, "some of them worth $150,000,"[44] sought to obscure their brothel-visiting proclivities and to incriminate a humble clerk for a heinous crime in *their* sinful pleasure palace. For *The Sun,* Robinson himself, endowed with money and powerful friends, was the representative of the immoral, manipulating elite. To set him free, as the courts had done, was to perpetuate that elite's special privileges and dispensations. The characterizations that the newspapers employed and the specific reactions to the verdicts that they proffered were different, but both *The Herald* and *The Sun* similarly cast the Jewett murder and Robinson trial as episodes in the period's struggle between classes.

Police Court columns, crime-related editorials and reporting on crimes and trials illustrate how critical alignment was pointedly a part of the early penny press' criminal frame. Political parties and factions were not the keys to this alignment—*The Herald* spoke for *The Sun* as well when it vowed to avoid "the dirt of party politics."[45] The keys were instead the newspapers' reactions to and support for emerging social groups. *The Sun,* perhaps, spoke more forcefully for mechanics and artisans, in Day's words, "the operative classes of society."[46] *The Herald,* as its two-cent price suggests, tended to peg itself one notch higher on the antebellum social ladder, to the city's clerks, office workers, and small merchants. However, neither of the newspapers strove for precisely segregated consumer groups. Generally, *The Sun* and *The Herald* stood with the emerging working and middle classes *in toto.* Day and Bennett, a printer and an immigrant, respectively, were men who had risen from humble origins. Their newspapers concomitantly were rising voices of the new social classes; and the crime journalism in *The Sun* and *The Herald* championed mechanics, artisans, clerks, and small merchants over the traditional landed and mercantile elites, which well into midcentury held power in the modernizing nation.[47]

Were the messages of *The Sun* and *The Herald* heard? Could readers decode the newspapers' politics? The mushrooming circulations of *The*

Sun and *The Herald* suggest that the metropolitan working and middle classes recognized their journalistic tribunes. Even more strikingly, spokesmen for traditional elites and values shouted back. As the social restructuring of the 1830s carried forward into the next decade, these spokesmen vigorously attacked the newspapers and their crime journalism.

The attack on the cheap press and particularly on *The Herald* was known in the period as the "moral war."[48] As the very name of this 1840 undertaking as well as the role played in it by Protestant ministers suggest, the "moral war" could be seen as an overlooked part of the revivalism of the antebellum decades. Convincing and provocative recent scholarship has shown how pervasively this revivalism affected labor movements, family life, and political parties during this period,[49] and presumably it played a role in journalism as well. However, at the same time, an interpretation of this sort may be incorrect. While the war makers may have found comfort in their moral self-impressions, the war's actual discourse revolved around "sensationalism" rather than articulated moral principles. While ministers played a major role, newspaper editors and writers were actually the chief combatants. Fundamentally, the war involved journalistic standards, institutions, and cultural workers.

Surely the cheap press had done its best to get under the skin of traditionalists. During the late 1830s the eccentric Bennett in particular had delighted in his journalism's ability to shock. Language, Bennett assumed, was an instrument that he as a prominent editor could sharpen and improve, and he flaunted his disdain for linguistic prudery, substituting "legs" for the prescribed "limbs," "skirts" for "linens," and "pantaloons" for "unmentionables." "Petticoats—petticoats—petticoats—petticoats," he had blustered, "there—you fastidious fools—vent your mawkishness on that."[50] Moving from individual words to larger forms, he also covered in irreverent detail the expensive parties of the city's oldest and wealthiest families, the wrongdoings of prominent bankers, the romantic affairs of the upper crust, and the duplicity of Protestant ministers. Most extensively, as demonstrated, he made politicized reports on New York's crime a daily newspaper staple.

For several years the six-cent dailies, most of which still clustered in the Wall Street area, let Bennett's journalism pass, but when Bennett ridiculed another editor's physical handicap,[51] the war was on. Editors of *The Evening Signal, The Evening Star,* and *The Courier and Enquirer,* New York's most successful newspapers prior to the advent of the penny press, called on New Yorkers to close down *The Herald.* Without acknowledging the struggle between social groups that was so much a part of the recent journalistic developments, the editors deplored *The Herald's* brand of journalism as "sensationalist." Rarely contemplated but often employed, the term was a sweeping pejorative designating, more than anything else, normative disapproval. More specific and certainly more graphic were the terms applied to Bennett. *The Evening Star* called him a "common bandit" and "turkey buzzard," and not to be outdone, *The Evening Signal* labeled him a "venomous reptile."[52]

For his part, Bennett at first retaliated with more of the "sensationalism" the attackers deplored, but the attackers did not desist. They attracted support from newspapers in Boston, Albany, Philadelphia and Baltimore, and several English newspapers even joined the fray. With the newspapers' urging and approval, members of the New York establishment boycotted the businesses that advertised in *The Herald,* pressured hotels to remove *The Herald* from their reading rooms, and refused to buy from street vendors who sold *The Herald* along with other cultural commodities. When, by Bennett's own admission, *The Herald's* advertising income and circulation dropped precipitously,[53] he agreed to modify the crime coverage and other forms of reporting that had so offended his enemies. The more moderate approach, Bennett said in one last burst of effrontery, was a gift to others at the time of his wedding.[54]

With *The Herald* licking its wounds, the traditional journalists and their allies had reason to be confident regarding the future. In Massachusetts, Peleg Chandler, a respected member of the American Antiquarian Society and Massachusetts Historical Society, comfortably launched a series of crime reports, educational and proper, which were to innoculate against future outbreaks of sensationalism.[55] However, in 1845, barely a year after Chandler's second volume appeared, the first issues of the *National Police Gazette* rolled off the press. In newspaper editors' offices on Wall Street, in the studies of respected ministers, and in stately homes in the exclusive residential areas of Washington Square, Astor Place and Gramercy Park, genteel eyebrows must have raised. While the penny press had served up a daily ration of crime reporting, the *Gazette* offered a weekly feast. In fact, it actually outstripped *The Sun* and *The Herald* in championing the interests of emergent social groups and criticizing traditional elites. Surveying New York and the nation, the *Gazette* was certain the working and middle classes most needed and deserved protection from criminals and that the established and wealthy were often the most dangerous malefactors. For one brief period in American history, at least, politicized cultural workers were determined to frame the criminal in aggressively political ways.

The founders of the *Gazette* were Enoch Camp and George Wilkes, two prototypical figures of the period.[56] Camp stood on the hustling, accumulating beachhead of the new society. The leader of a New York City law firm that had briefly employed Wilkes as a clerk, Camp also invested in a range of business ventures. He was an entrepreneur and a good one at that. The son of a New York cabinet maker, Wilkes also had an eye for the smart business deal, but more so than Camp, he brought critical consciousness to his social practices. He believed mechanics, artisans, and small merchants, even saloon keepers, should have the same political rights as the landed or mercantile elite. Wilkes briefly edited the *Subterranean,* a journal concerning New York politics with a particularly vigilant eye for the wrongdoings of the elite, and his early journalism proved so pungent that he was sued several times and served a four-week sentence in the Tombs for criminal libel. While imprisoned, Wilkes continued to sharpen his alignment, and he composed a short volume on the horrors of the Tombs, which contributed to the defeat of Mayor Robert Morris in New York's municipal election.[57] The same volume endorsed in passing the penny press which was altering the nature of New York newspaper journalism. "*The Herald,*" Wilkes wrote, "is the only diurnal I care about reading, and is, according to my notions, the best specimen of a *newspaper* I ever saw."[58]

Even before Wilkes left the Tombs, Camp approached him with an idea for a new crime periodical.[59] The two men surveyed the trans-Atlantic field of publications and found no shortage of models for their venture. In England, the *Quarterly Pursuit* and the *London Police Gazette,* government-sponsored sheets for local magistrates, described fugitives.[60] Of a slightly different nature was the *Newgate Calendar,* an authorized publication of the Ordinary of Newgate Prison, which attempted to educate the public with histories, sentences, confessions and, in some cases, last words of Newgate prisoners.[61] In addition, both types of English publications had their more commercial derivatives. The *London Police Gazette,* for example, had led quickly to *Cleave's Weekly Police Gazette* and the *Sporting and Police Gazette,* popular newspapers of the 1830s.[62] The *Newgate Calendar* had spawned such mass publications as *The Malefactor's Register* and *The New Newgate and Tyburn Calendar,* among others.[63] If the state had an interest in reporting crime, so too did enterprising entrepreneurs.

In formal terms, the periodical that Camp and Wilkes founded resembled both these English publications and the penny dailies of New York. Early issues of the *Gazette* were octavo-sized with eight pages to an issue and only four columns to the page. The front page had subscription and advertising rates at the top of the left-hand column and longer features. The back pages were filled with advertisements for early consumer goods—"sarsaparilla," bedsteads, eyeglasses, and pistols called "Home Protectors"—and for professional services. In keeping with the *Gazette*'s original partnership agreement,[64] Enoch Camp's advertisements for legal services customarily headed the latter, and rental agents, debt collectors and private detectives, an intriguing assembly of operatives, were also regular advertisers. On the second, third, and fourth pages were editorials, short news reports, and assorted columns. Overall, the small weekly was chock-full of print.

Apparently, the *Gazette* found an immediate place in the marketplace and in the hearts of advertisers. The *Gazette* sold on the newsstand for five cents or on an annual subscription basis for two dollars, and its circulation jumped from an initial 8600 in 1845 to 40,000 in 1850.[65] Advertisements consistently filled a quarter to a third of the *Gazette,* but they too increased in number as the weekly expanded to a larger size with eight columns to the page. Initially, advertising rates were one dollar and fifty cents for the first insertion, respectively, of twenty or ten-line "squares."[66] By 1850, rates had risen to ten cents per line.[67] The penny dailies should perhaps have been concerned with the *Gazette*'s success, but endorsements of the *Gazette* from the dailies suggest that they welcomed the new weekly to the ranks of inexpensive newspapers.[68] Bennett himself called the *Gazette* "a very interesting new weekly" and praised the well-written features and useful statistics in the *Gazette*'s first issue.[69]

One reason for both the *Gazette*'s success and its endorsements from the penny dailies may have been its crusading, public-spirited tone. The *Gazette* perceived itself as more than a profit-seeking periodical capitalizing on popular fascination with crime. At least during its earliest years, the *Gazette* had a mission: the suppression of the nation's growing criminal menace. The publication's bold prospectus, adorned with a woodcut of a classical goddess holding the scales of justice, bemoaned the "hordes of English and other thieves, burglars, pickpockets and swindlers" whose "daily and mighty exploits" so troubled the nation. The prospectus described the *Gazette* as "an untiring and ubiquitous minister of public justice" prepared to expose criminals "to the public gaze until they become powerless from the notoriety of their debasement."[70] Subsequently, the *Gazette*'s weekly editorials, running in length from a few lines to a few columns, picked up where the prospectus left off. In early issues of the *Gazette,* the editors called for information on specific crimes, ran the names of United States Army deserters, exposed fraudulent copper mines, and produced a list of "rich thieves."[71] "Being already in possession of a most comprehensive correspondence to all parts of the country, and having made arrangements with some of the ablest and most experienced officers ever attached to the police," Camp and Wilkes announced in their tenth issue, we are ready "to receive communications of all kinds of police matters, and to attend to all kinds of police business."[72]

In conjunction with its avowed crime-stopping, the *Gazette* had special groups it championed and others it attacked. The *Gazette*'s favorites were the same as those of *The Sun* and *The Herald:* mechanics, artisans and small merchants, members of the emerging classes, which the *Gazette* took to embody the industry and integrity of the Republic. Imbued with democratizing instincts and classical liberal values, the *Gazette* was determined to protect these classes' property. The names, descriptions, and addresses of criminals that the *Gazette* published would presumably help these deserving groups protect themselves from thieves. In addition, the *Gazette* told artisans and merchants how to spot bologna made of horse flesh, how to regain stolen goods, and how to mark what was perhaps their most important personal machine, the timepiece.

Those whom the *Gazette*'s editorials designated arch foes were not so much criminals in general but rather those citizens with old or large wealth who could manipulate the criminal justice system. The *Gazette* continually railed against the police force's susceptibility to bribes, the grand jury's subservience to bankers and brokers, the courts' granting of bail to gentlemen, and the executive's pardons of the well-to-do. Speaking specifically of the bail system but echoing its standard class-oriented criticism, the *Gazette* asserted, "Under the same rule the Devil himself would be discharged from custody if Mammon would 'go his bail,' while the angel Gabriel would be sent to the Tombs for want of wealthy friends."[73]

Overall the *Gazette* appeared to be an immense Chinese menu of crime reporting. Missing is any coverage of minor crimes such as those reported by *The Sun*'s "Police Office," but energetic *Gazette* writers reported on a wide range of felonies in both New York and other cities. Long feature articles described illegal lotteries and detailed the criminal offenses of temperance advocate John Gough, whom *Gazette* reporters caught, literally, with his pants down.[74] Hundreds, indeed thousands of short paragraphs provided reports on crimes, the apprehension of criminals, and criminal trials. Columns headed by the names of a dozen cities offered summaries of crime-related developments in those cities. Like a Chinese menu, however, the *Gazette* in reality featured a central core of dishes, each laced with variable trimmings. Subtly yet effectively, these dishes had a critical perspective comparable to that of the *Gazette*'s editorials.

Predictably, the most frequent reporting concerned crime against property. Heralded by a listing of thirty-four *bona fide* property criminals in the initial issue,[75] the property crime reports included a multitude of shorter articles as well as longer, detailed accounts of lives devoted to property crime. When readers grumbled that the latter were always "to be continued," Camp and Wilkes defended their cultural work. "Some of our readers complain at having the story lengthened out," an editorial in the fifth issue stated, "but if they will devote a moment's reflection to the subject, they will see that a story so crowded with interest and complicated mystery could not be unravelled in a smaller space."[76]

In both the short reports and the longer, serialized "Lives," *Gazette* writers routinely used the word "rogue" to designate their criminal subjects and, given norms in the pamphlet literature of the period, the word undoubtedly created traditional expectations for some readers. These expectations notwithstanding, the harsher, more prosaic "felon" more accurately indicates the cultural frame that the *Gazette* used for property criminals. Indeed, the *Gazette*'s detailed accounts of criminal careers were called the "Lives of the Felons" series. Missing in these "Lives" and in shorter property crime reports as well was any delight in the resourceful lawbreaker. From the *Gazette*'s perspective, pickpockets, burglars and confidence men were not picaresque tricksters but rather mean, willful predators who harmed and exploited industrious workers and merchants. Dan Schiller, a twentieth-century scholar who has carefully studied and even quantified aspects of the thirteen "Lives" in the *Gazette*'s first 101 issues, argues that they collectively suggest a nineteenth-century social nightmare. In Schiller's opinion, the "Lives" suggested that self-interested usurpers of property were thriving while the feeble criminal justice system did little to deter or punish them. A lockean world in which private property was secure threatened to become hobbesian.[77]

While the traditional rogue frame might privately have pleased the property criminals placed in it, the felon frame led to decidedly different reactions. The very first issue of the *Gazette,* which detailed the activities of the swindler Robert Sutton, alias Bob the Wheeler, so offended one of Sutton's sons that he went on a tear against the *Gazette*'s defenders in the Gin and Calamus Hall on Delancey Street. In the barroom melee, Jonas Burks, the Hall's proprietor, lost several fingers and part of an ear, and one Croucher Collins died.[78] Only a few months later, Sutton himself, recently released from a prison, outdistanced his son. With a gang of toughs including Dingdong Kelly and Resurrectionist Downer, a grave robber, Sutton attacked the *Gazette*'s offices at 27 Centre Street. After the dust had settled, three men were carried out dead.[79] Members of the New York underworld launched still another attack in 1850, and during the attack criminal figures Country McCloskey and Nobby McChester not only destroyed the periodical's presses but also killed Andrew Frost, the *Gazette*'s star reporter.[80] Clearly, New York's more sophisticated property criminals considered the *Gazette* both noxious and effective. The perpetration of property crime was difficult enough without a periodical using a felon frame to highlight it.

Although, as a champion of petit bourgeois property rights, the *Gazette* was less interested in personal violence crime than it was in property crime, reports on the former nevertheless constituted the periodical's second major crime reporting staple. The earliest issues of the *Gazette* included on their center pages columns starkly titled "Seductions," "Rapes" and "Murders," which contained one to twelve capsule crime reports. In addition, longer accounts of single personal violence crimes occasionally stretched for several columns. As early as the fourteenth issue, in fact, the *Gazette*'s front page illustration, until then used to depict an event, location, or individual from the "Lives of the Felons" series, portrayed "The Boston Tragedy," the murder of adulteress Mary Ann Bickford by her lover Albert Tirrell.[81] Showing Bickford in bed with her erect breasts pointing upward and Tirrell, muscles taught, wielding a mean razor from his crotch, the illustrations promised the type of pornographic titillation that a reader might also have found in *The Herald*'s descriptions of Madame Townsend's brothel or in the period's fiend pamphlets. Indeed, in both its coverage of "The Boston Tragedy" and in other personal violence crime reports, the *Gazette* frequently employed the word "fiend" to designate the criminal perpetrator.

Yet as in the case of its property crime reports, the *Gazette*'s use of a criminal keyword familiar from the street literature did not necessarily mean the *Gazette* also used a traditional criminal frame. Consistent with its politics, the *Gazette* specialized in personal violence reports that illustrated either the wrongdoings of a property elite or that elite's ability to manipulate the criminal justice system. Not all of the personal violence reporting had this angle, but in its fortieth issue the *Gazette* emphasized the class origins of a dastardly seducer in a capsule report:

> Seduction and Suicide.—One of the fiends in human form that haunt our cities recently seduced the only daughter of a poor widow, in Philadelphia, and then induced her to enter a brothel to hide her shame. The blow crushed the parent, reason tottered on its throne, and on Tuesday last, during a

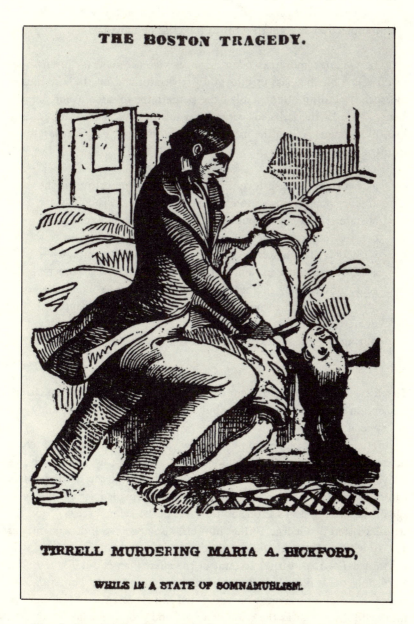

Illus. 2. Drawing of a violent murder from the *National Police Gazette* (1845).

paroxysm of despair, she jumped from her lonely attic room to
the pavement, death ending her sufferings. The conscience of
the wretch that produced this act may twinge, but yet he will
be tolerated as a gentleman, in the class he moves.[82]

The *Gazette*'s more extended personal violence reports, meanwhile,
also dwelled on the class origins of a perpetrator and on the way money
and social standing often enabled the perpetrator to circumvent punishment. Tirrell, the alleged perpetrator of Bickford's murder, had a
$30,000 fortune. When the jury found him innocent, the *Gazette* felt the
acquittal was:

> a result that can scarcely be believed, and conjecture in the
> absence of apparent reason for such a perverse decision has not
> abstained from the imputation of some indirection among the
> constituted authorities. . . . The man's character is entirely
> without relief, his case entirely undeserving of sympathy—
> scarcely of commiseration. Indeed, we do not know a character
> more unsoftened, in the whole dark catalogue of homicide.
> . . . The natural termination of such a career from degree to
> degree is to the extreme of guilt, and if justice had been done
> during the late trial, the gallows would have been its punish-
> ment.[83]

Tirrell's wealth, his employment of sophisticated lawyers, and the latter's
concoction of a defense of somnambulism, the *Gazette* was sure, allowed a
guilty man to go free.

Perhaps the best example of how a vigorous democratic credo
influenced the *Gazette*'s personal violence reporting was the weekly's
revival of the Jewett-Robinson affair, which had so decorated the penny
dailies' pages several years earlier. The *Gazette* provided serialized coverage of the affair in 1848 as one of its "Lives of the Felons" series,[84] and the
serial, written by George Wilkes himself, also appeared independently as
a small volume.[85] Highly fictionalized, the serial and volume more closely
resembled *The Sun*'s earlier account of the affair than it did *The Herald*'s.
According to Wilkes, Jewett had been the intelligent and honest daughter of a humble artisan who sadly fell into prostitution. Robinson,
meanwhile, was cast as the scion of an old and prominent family and the
colleague of decadent, justice-evading gentlemen. As in its editorials,
short articles and "Lives," the *Gazette* was prepared to locate in crime a
story of class inequality and manipulation.

The contrast between the crime journalism of the pamphlets and broadsides and that of *The Sun, The Herald* and the *Gazette* is striking. While the pamphlet and broadside crime reporting, stretching from Elizabethan times into the rudimentary American industrialization of the early nineteenth century, consistently employed the "rogue" and "fiend" frames for the criminal, *The Sun, The Herald,* and the *Gazette* in diverse ways opted for and experimented with new frames. Crime, as the preface to this work argued, is not essential social fact but rather is born of a dialectic of social development and cultural comprehension. Furthermore, while certain criminal frames such as the "rogue" and the "fiend" can be relatively bereft of political meanings, newer frames found in the "Police Office," front-page feature articles, and the "Lives of the Felons" series can abound in them. Journalistic children of a tumultuous historical juncture, *The Sun, The Herald,* the *Gazette* and their crime journalism illustrate the political potential that the criminal frame possesses. However, as the next chapter will indicate, the innovative and the critical themselves can evolve into the standard and the static. The budding of a consciously critical framing of the criminal does not guarantee its full flower.

4.

Information and Entertainment: Journalistic Frames for the Modern Society

Riding the Staten Island Ferry to Manhattan, a sharp-eyed passenger might glimpse, if the angle is just right, the spire of the Trinity Church peeking from among large office buildings. The nineteenth-century skyline of Christian steeples, the passenger might reflect, has given way to a twentieth-century skyline of business columns. However, in the final decades of the nineteenth century, a third type of building dominated the view. In 1875 the Florentine campanile of the Tribune Tower rose from mansard shoulders to 260 feet, only 26 feet shorter than Trinity Church, New York's tallest structure. In 1890 the Venetian World Building rose even higher to 309 feet and became New York's tallest building.[1] During these years New York City and the more developed parts of the nation abandoned an earlier form of social life in which family, community and deference reigned and committed themselves to the rhythms and structures of modern society. The daily newspaper cast its shadow over this transformation.

The newspapers that raised these confident buildings were themselves very different from the dailies of the antebellum period. In only a few decades the daily press had evolved from small, loosely structured operations to large, highly organized corporations. During the Gilded Age, certain of these corporations produced and sold an increasingly generic, often staid crime journalism, which purported to be informational. In the 1890s *The New York Times* became a paragon in this regard. Simultaneously, Joseph Pulitzer and William Randolph Hearst introduced a "new journalism." More entertaining than informational, the "new journalism" included animated and accentuated coverage of crime. With the informational journalism selling largely to urban elites and entertainment journalism to workers, the two varieties of crime journalism became American newspapers' dominant frames for crime and the criminal.

Almost one hundred years later, the two varieties of crime journalism, both parts of larger journalistic enterprises, remain powerful. The two varieties of crime journalism, as cultural processes and products, are even more hulking than the buildings in which they were developed. Unlike the crime journalism of the cheap press of the mid-nineteenth century, bourgeois and mass crime journalism fail to provide critical interpretations of crime. They provide information and entertain, but they also invite readers to accept the modern society in which they live.

Large and important daily newspapers flourished on the Eastern seaboard and throughout the old Midwest during the Gilded Age,[2] but as had been the case thirty years earlier, New York was the center of American daily journalism. The home of over one million people and soon to add outlying towns to the metropolis,[3] New York in 1870 housed a dozen daily newspapers, the largest of which led the nation in both circulation and sophistication. As an examination of these dailies during the 1870s suggests, they presented a surprisingly coordinated and similar front. Solid and steady, the dailies reported on crime and other subjects in ways not designed to fire political passion.

The two largest dailies in New York during the 1870s were *The Sun* and *The Herald,* both of which claimed circulations of 100,000 in 1872.[4] *The Sun,* which had passed earlier from Benjamin Day to a brother-in-law Moses Beach and his sons, had changed hands again in 1868, when Charles A. Dana purchased it.[5] A former Brooks Farm socialist, Chicago journalist, and assistant secretary of war, Dana led a revival of the city's first penny daily, which, during the final years of the Beaches' control, had languished slightly. Although Dana raised *The Sun*'s price to two cents, the newspaper remained the favorite among New York workers.[6] Its rival *The Herald,* meanwhile, boasted of correspondents throughout the world and was known as the nation's preeminent news gatherer.[7] The resourceful James Gordon Bennett had held the reins of the newspaper and, presumably, whipped its horses until his health failed in the late 1860s. When he died in 1872, his son James Gordon Bennett, Jr., assumed control. Unpopular with newspaper historians,[8] Bennett, Jr., spent as much time in Paris as he did in New York, but under his quirky, autocratic leadership, *The Herald* remained the nation's most prominent daily and in the course of the 1870s surpassed *The Sun* in circulation.

Vying with *The Sun* and *The Herald* for both New York readers and national prominence were *The New-York Times* and *The Tribune,* each of which had more specialized social identities. The circulations of *The New-York Times* and *The Tribune* during the 1870s were roughly half those of their two larger competitors, but these totals were large enough to rank both newspapers among the nation's ten largest.[9] Henry Raymond, a graduate of the University of Vermont, leader of New York's Republican Party and one-time United States congressman, had tailored *The New-York Times* to the tastes of New York's more prosperous citizens.[10] During eighteen years as editor he had largely kept an early promise "to get into a passion as rarely as possible."[11] After Raymond's death in 1869, his financier George Jones acquired the newspaper and with the assistance of assorted editors remained faithful to Raymond's promise. In the offices of *The Tribune* the crotchety Horace Greeley had long occupied the boss' chair.[12] His newspaper was a pacesetter in the coverage of national politics and the arts. To some, *The Tribune* seemed a "radical" organ,[13] but this radicalism appealed more to readers in New York's upstate "burned-over" district than those in New York City. When, politically and physically crushed by an unsuccessful run for president, Greeley died in 1872, his associate editor Whitelaw Reid acquired the majority interest in *The Tribune,* in part through the support of the capitalist Jay Gould.[14]

From the perspective of standard journalism histories, the deaths between 1869 and 1872 of Bennett, Sr., Raymond and Greeley make the three-year period an important watershed in American journalism history,[15] but lionizing necrologies of "great men" notwithstanding, the passing of a generation of owner-editors appears to have had little impact on the corporate identity and commercial success of New York's leading dailies. While during the antebellum years Benjamin Day and Bennett, Sr., had been able to launch their dailies with limited capital, New York's dailies by 1870 had become heavily capitalized. Despite the changes in ownership prompted by the deaths of owner-editors, all four newspapers were tightly held corporations whose stock was rarely available on the market.[16] One observer estimated in 1868 that the annual cost of publishing either *The Herald* or *The Tribune* was between $800,000 and $1,000,000,[17] and the cost of successful corporate ventures of course falls below the ventures' revenues—sometimes by staggering margins. One reason for the newspapers' commercial success was their ability to tap a growing pool of consumers. The average daily circulation of the four newspapers had doubled during the 1860s,[18] and while *The Sun* had raised its daily price to two cents, the other three newspapers sold during the 1870s for even a penny or two higher.

In addition to greater income from sales, increased income from advertising also swelled the New York dailies' accounts during the 1870s. Contributing to and profiting from this increase were advertising agencies. Several agencies that specialized in the sale of print media space established themselves in New York in the 1860s and 1870s,[19] and they proved more efficient and resourceful than the individual agents who had represented newspapers prior to the Civil War.[20] The production of consumer goods, after all, had greatly diversified and expanded, and, prepared to offer much more than soda and guns to national markets, producers of consumer goods looked to the newspapers, another consumer good, as a place to advertise their wares. At the end of the decade currently under consideration, the compilers of the national Census in 1880 did not mince their words: in their opinion, the growth of the American newspaper was "hardly paralleled by that of any other phase of industrial development in the United States."[21]

While newspapers' sales and advertising income grew, so too did their staffs.[22] In the 1830s Day and Bennett, Sr., had served, at least briefly, as their own chief editors, reporters, compositors and even printers, but by the 1870s New York's leading newspapers all had large, highly differentiated staffs arranged into hierarchies. At the top of the hierarchy was the publisher-owner, but he was now assisted by managing, night, foreign, financial, city and literary editors.[23] On the very bottom were the battalions of newsboys who not only sold the dailies citywide on a piece rate but also captured the imagination of the period's commentators on the urban scene.[24] A notch higher and actually working in-house were a range of clerks, secretaries, compositors and printers. Some of the latter had for decades been members of unions, an affiliation that apparently had not been enough to impede the declining social prestige of the printing trade over the preceding thirty years.[25]

Most intriguing among the different types of Gilded Age newspaper workers were the reviewers and reporters. Emily Bettey, who was a full-time reporter for *The Sun* during the period,[26] perhaps looked upon reporting as a wonderful new career opportunity for a woman, but Bettey's male colleagues at *The Sun* and elsewhere were less delighted with a position precariously posed between careerism and occupationalism.[27] Harry Marks, like many of the reporters of the period who jumped frequently from one newspaper to another hoping to catch a break, sensed the contradictions of the reporter's position. Reporters, Marks was certain, were "no longer mere machines for reporting speeches or chronicling the dry details of daily occurrences." Still, earning only twenty-five or thirty dollars per week, most reporters in Marks' opinion were "poor men."[28]

The actual newspapers that the New York daily press of the 1870s produced were larger and more frequently issued than those of the antebellum years. While earlier *The Sun* and *The Herald* had consisted of four small pages with only three or four columns to the page, the dailies during the early Gilded Age consisted of eight or even ten larger sheets with six or seven columns to the page. Increasingly, there were morning and evening editions, the latter being one of the most striking newspaper developments of the period,[29] and *The Herald* even issued a foreign edition in Paris. Following the lead of *The Tribune,* the dailies also issued Sunday editions during the 1870s, appealing to readers outside the city and invading what had previously been a newspaper-free Sabbath.

With large morning, evening and Sunday editions rolling off the presses in Printing House Square just across the street from New York's City Hall, Gilded Age readers clearly had more journalism to read than ever before. Indeed, the average reader likely found it impossible to read the newspaper fully, and as the newspapers grew, they developed formats which facilitated selective reading. The format of the newspaper became homologous to the differentiation of its editorial categories, and although segregation of standard types of news was not complete, readers knew in general where in the newspaper to turn for international, national, local, financial, arts and sports news.[30] *The New-York Times* routinely headed a section "City and Suburban News" and then marked off subsections devoted to "New-York City," "Brooklyn," "New Jersey," and eventually "Staten Island." In addition, single-column headlines sometimes arranged in multiple decks further facilitated a selective reading or even a quick review of the newspaper's contents. *The Herald* included a daily listing of its major reports and their locations, and the harried city dweller, in a rush between commitments, could get by with a glance at this useful table of contents.

In terms of general appearance and organization the four newspapers did not differ significantly from one another,[31] and as the 1870s went forward, even political differences between the dailies became increasingly difficult to decipher. To be sure, editorials continued to appear, but now frozen into a few columns of a page in the center of the newspaper, they had been supplanted in importance by the news reports. As in the case of *The New-York Times'* attack on the Tweed Ring during the early 1870s,[32] the newspapers sometimes aggressively blended opinion and news, but in general none of the newspapers were consistent crusaders with distinct journalisms to match.[33] Occasionally, readers found opinions and judgments popping fleetingly from between the lines, but more customarily, the short news reports and most of the longer ones as well lacked overt political alignment. Indeed, since well before the Civil War, the major dailies had been affiliated with one another and with the Western Union Telegraph Company in the country's first "wire service."[34] Starting even, with the same international and national news, the newspapers did relatively little to develop contrasting political presentations of the news.

Crime news itself, a journalistic initiative that had been pursued with so much vigor in the antebellum years, showed many of the tendencies toward segregation and depoliticization that marked Gilded Age dailies as a whole. During the 1870s crime news was a regular and stable part of the New York daily newspaper, but at the same time it hardly dominated or invigorated the newspaper as it had earlier. Filling roughly five percent of the space, crime news was less significant in the newspaper's daily make-up than international news, national political news, financial news, and even theater and book reviews. With the exception of occasional reports on major crime developments, crime news was written tersely and without flair.

As part of this development, the criminal court columns, which *The Sun* in particular had pioneered, largely disappeared. Such columns with their sympathetic attention to the working men and women "brought up" in the misdemeanor courts had continued into the 1850s, usually bearing the title of "Police Intelligence" or "Legal Reporter." But even at that point one might have predicted their demise. The columns of the 1850s focused as much on criminal cases in the higher Court of General Sessions or Court of Oyer and Terminer as they did on the Police Court; and as the anonymous lumping together of petty criminals in the following item from a column indicates, reporters no longer used the columns to suggest individuality or sympathy:

Heavy Haul of Disorderlies.—About seventy persons were arrested yesterday for drunkenness, disorderly conduct, petit larceny, &c, in six of the upper Wards, and all were disposed of at the Jefferson Market Police Court. This is an unusually large number.[35]

After the Civil War when the major New York dailies interred this form of crime news, no one seemed to care.

Short, straightforward crime reports of the sort that had dotted the antebellum newspapers, meanwhile, continued to appear during the 1870s in a largely unchanged form. If these reports concerned crime outside New York, they tended to appear on the center pages of the newspaper, mixed among the less significant national and international news. They most commonly concerned murder and took the form of single, tightly packed paragraphs. If the reports concerned crime-related developments in New York, they routinely appeared on the page or pages of the newspaper most devoted to city news. *The New-York Times,* for example, placed local crime news in its "City and Suburban News" section, while *The Sun* encased it in a "Life in the Metropolis" section. In the other dailies as well, the placement and form of local crime news suggested that dailies no longer took local crime to be a particularly significant part of social life. Equaled or even exceeded in prominence by comparable reports on accidents, speeches, parades and suicides, the local crime reports of the 1870s rarely suggested character, explored class relations, or developed the political aspects of a crime-related situation.

Concomitant with these developments, the New York dailies of the 1870s began to abandon the courts and shift to the police department as a source of crime reports. The shift is understandable in light of growing pressures on reporters to produce news regularly. In the courts, after all, days could go by full of absences, continuances and mundane developments. The police department, meanwhile, was a steadier source of information regarding arrests and investigations, and more so than the courts, it could be counted upon by crime reporters for daily materials, which were convertible into "news." Production convenience, however, carried with it a change in perspective.[36]

Since the change is lasting, it deserves careful consideration. In the courts, particularly the lower courts, a guilty verdict was more likely than not, but a guilty verdict was not predetermined. The courtroom remained a public forum, and although a virtual adjunct, the reporter was still on the layman's side of the bar, watching from a friend's or an average citizen's perspective. An attitude sympathetic to the accused or at least neutral was more likely. As the reporter came to rely on the police department, his perspective came to change. The department, although supposedly sharing the courts' commitment to truth and justice, was in fact even more committed to the preservation of social order and to convincing the public of the department's forcefulness. The police, as later chapters of this work will indicate, were often secretive and viewed journalists suspiciously, but those officers who dealt regularly with the press developed working relationships and friendships with newsmen. The latter, for their part, welcomed the development, in part because of the way it facilitated their daily news production. In the process reporters came to share the police department's perspective. "A Good Catch," a typical short crime report from *The Herald,* sported not only a heading likely to please policemen but also the deceptively routine assertion that the prisoners, arrested for selling bogus steamship tickets, "were identified by detectives sent by Superintendent Walling of New York, as notorious thieves."[37] Rather than exploring and critiquing the uncertain and sometimes biased fissures between legitimacy and illegitimacy, reporters working regularly with the police used arrests as certain indications of illegality and wrongdoing.

Occasionally, crimes, arrests and court developments spawned more extended coverage, series of articles that would follow a crime story over several days or even a front page report that filled a half-column or more. An example of a crime that received significant newspaper coverage was the previously mentioned 1874 kidnapping of Charley Ross, the four-year-old son of a wholesale dry goods dealer in Philadelphia. *The Herald* preceded the other dailies in reporting on the Ross case,[38] but eventually coverage in *The Sun*, *The New-York Times* and other New York dailies followed. The Ross case became the first nineteenth-century kidnapping to attract major newspaper coverage. Exploiting their police department connections to the fullest, the newspapers suggested that the crime had been perpetrated by New York criminals. Sustained coverage of the kidnapping of the symbolic Gilded Age child no doubt helped circulation, but the kidnappers and poor Ross, for that matter, were never found.

While coverage of the Ross case was more extended than most, it nevertheless exemplified the development of major crime reports of the Gilded Age. The core genres, only sprouting in the 1870s but recognizable for the twentieth-century reader who encounters daily their ongoing weediness, included the crime perpetration piece, the arrest report, the investigation account, the trial summary, and the punishment report. These genres most certainly did not dominate the staid New York dailies of the 1870s, but they nevertheless appeared frequently enough to become standard by the end of the decade. Furthermore, within each genre more specialized types emerged. Hence, the report of the Ross kidnapping and its apparent appeal to readers prompted dozens of other kidnapping or child-stealing accounts, all within the basic crime perpetration and investigation genres.

Particularly noteworthy as a crime-related genre and subtype were, respectively, the punishment report and account of an execution. Earlier in the century a hanging had been a convulsive public affair. Thousands gathered and, boisterous and often drunken, lent a degree of spontaneity and unpredictability to the affair. The traditional pamphlet and broadside literature had vigorously reported this scene, drawing out its drama and inviting readers to reflect on the troubling phenomenon of murder by the state. In the 1870s, New York hangings were more likely to be semiprivate affairs conducted almost clinically in the bowels of a prison. *The Sun*, *The Herald*, *The New-York Times* and *The Tribune* usually reported executions on their front pages. To the extent that the general public learned of and reflected upon these hangings, it did so primarily through the generic frame provided by a daily newspaper report. For his part, the newspaper reporter covering an execution, echoing in a limited way the pamphlets, invoked the drama of the event, but at the same time he conveyed it with increasingly prosaic generic elements: the grieving relatives, the last hours of the condemned, his or her behavior en route to the gallows, and, of course, the condemned's last words, if any. Predictably employed, the generic elements made executions seem almost routine. Often, as in *The Herald's* 1877 report on the execution of Poindexter Edmonson, an execution article barely mentioned the social context of the crime and the punishment. Edmonson, desperate about ends that did not meet, had feuded with the man who owned the house in which he lived and finally killed him. For *The Herald,* the affair was hardly complex or rich in social meanings: "Yesterday, the condemned felon who had always been a most wicked and blasphemous man, professed religion, and received the ordinance of baptism by sprinkling at the Reverend John Haynsworth. . . ." It was simply a "Hangman's Day."[39]

The New York dailies' coverage of major social disorder crimes of the 1870s is a telling example of the growing importance of genres in Gilded Age crime reporting. As noted in the first chapter of this work, major social disorder crime of the period differed significantly from the more spontaneous, less directed rioting of the 1840s and 1850s. By the 1870s, its major outbursts ironically evidenced the increased stabilization of social life by involving unions and other organized groups with concrete goals and political programs. In 1877, for example, the owners of the Baltimore and Ohio Railroad, the nation's largest line, announced ten percent wage cuts for all of its employees, and in response workers in Martinsburg, West Virginia, the Baltimore and Ohio's main terminus, struck. The strike spread first to Baltimore and then west to Pittsburgh, Ohio, Indiana and Illinois. In the course of the strike, workers derailed trains, burned down depots, and, buoyed by the support of family members and other workers, managed at least briefly to bring United States rail service to a halt.

How did the New York dailies cover these developments? Their editorial position was not surprising. Themselves major business institutions, the newspapers deplored the actions of the strikers. In an editorial titled "Taking the Railroad Riots by the Throat," *The Herald* declared, "The law must be enforced and the rights and property of the railroad protected at all hazards. . . ."[40] *The New-York Times,* in an editorial of the same day, found it "difficult to conceive of a more unjustifiable and unreasonable strike"; in its opinion, the strike was "nothing more than a rash and spiteful demonstration of resentment by men too ignorant or too reckless to understand their own interests."[41]

The newspapers' news coverage, meanwhile, was more intriguing. First surfacing as short articles in the national news sections on the newspapers' middle pages, the coverage then burst prominently onto front pages as state militias proved unable to control the outraged workers and as President Hayes sent federal troops to West Virginia. The form of the news articles resembled closely that of Civil War dispatches. As during the Civil War, daily coverage consisted of two, three, even a half dozen dispatches from different locations, printed one after another without being coordinated into one report. At the end of a string of dispatches, unadorned lists of the dead and the wounded appeared, much as they had after dispatches concerning Civil War battles.

Surely this reporting suggested class bias. The strikers and their fellow workers donned the figurative clothes of a well-remembered enemy, the Confederate Army; according to the dailies, the strikers had generals and morning musters. State militias and federal troops protecting railroad interests, by contrast, were the heroic, transmogrified Union Army. Additionally, the reportage illustrated in a specialized way the powerful influence of genres in daily crime reporting. Editors and reporters, faced by a different, particularly threatening social development, did not experiment with new forms of reportage. They did not even rely on the crime-related genres that had emerged and begun to stabilize during the 1870s. They turned instead to the generic larder, and seasoned and reheated the well-preserved war news genre that had so dominated their pages and boosted their circulations during the early 1860s. The newspapers framed social disorder criminals in a warlike manner.

From the perspective of the standard journalism historians, the 1870s represent another step forward.[42] Picking up where the penny press had left off, newspapers of the period supplied more and more citizens with news. The news itself was increasingly "independent" and "objective." Yet if scrutinized more carefully, the changes seem less appealing. The social turmoil and cozy newspaper operations of the antebellum years had spawned a fluid, opinionated newspaper journalism. The large, rigid and hierarchical newspaper institutions of subsequent decades manufactured a more static, less critical product. Crime reporting in particular illustrated the change and strongly suggested a bourgeois informational frame for crime and the criminal, which, by the end of the century, would be one of only two available on American newsstands.

Any complacency the leading New York dailies felt during the 1870s did not survive the 1880s and 1890s. During the final decades of the nineteenth century Joseph Pulitzer's *The World* and then William Randolph Hearst's *New York Journal* took over first place in newspaper sales in the metropolitan area. However, while these journalistic newcomers shook the New York and national newspaper establishments, their so-called new journalism did not facilitate recognition of the axes and tensions of modern society. It was instead a brand of entertainment journalism. It thrilled and titillated, but steeped in melodrama, it relied largely on depoliticized frames.

Like the most successful New York daily newspaper editors before them, Pulitzer and Hearst came to Gotham from elsewhere, but unlike their predecessors, both came to New York with substantial editorial experience and large bankrolls. Pulitzer was born in Hungary,[43] the son of a Magyar-Jewish father and an Austro-German mother, and he first made his mark in the United States among the German associations and political clubs of St. Louis. He worked for Carl Schurz as an editor on *Die Westliche Post,* served in the Missouri legislature, and during the late 1870s and early 1880s made *The Post-Dispatch* St. Louis' leading evening newspaper. One key to the success of *The Post-Dispatch* was the paper's crime-related crusading, which exposed, among other things, the corrupt awarding of public utilities and police protection of illegal gambling rings. Happy with his achievements, Pulitzer set out for a European vacation, but when he stopped in New York on the way, he learned that *The World,* a lagging morning daily, was for sale. Postponing his plans to visit the Old World, Pulitzer purchased *The World* from Jay Gould for $346,000 and published his first issue on May 11, 1883. In subsequent years *The World,* even more than Pulitzer's St. Louis operations, became the base of his newspaper empire.

In the same year that Pulitzer purchased *The World,* Hearst enrolled as a Harvard College undergraduate.[44] The only son of a California pioneer who had made a fortune mining the silver of the Comstock Lode, Hearst was not destined to become a distinguished alumnus of fair Harvard. He gave his pet alligator liquor to drink, liked to stage ostentatious fireworks displays, and found his only undergraduate success as business editor of *The Lampoon,* a campus humor magazine. At the end of his junior year, he was expelled for decorating chamber pots with the visages of William James, Josiah Royce and other faculty members. Enthusiasm and bravado intact, Hearst returned to California and convinced his father to name him editor of *The Examiner,* a San Francisco daily. Having worked for a summer as a cub reporter for *The World,* Hearst was determined to duplicate its brand of journalism on the West Coast. In large part, he succeeded, converting a newspaper that had been primarily a support organ for the Hearst family interests into a popular daily. In 1895, seeking bigger challenges, Hearst purchased *The Morning Journal,* a New York daily that Pulitzer's brother Albert had founded, and renamed it the *New York Journal.* With $7.5 million from the sale of mining stock, "Willie," as his mother called him, moved east to tussle with the nation's newspaper giants. His reputation among fellow editors would never approach Pulitzer's,[45] but changes Hearst and the *New York Journal* made in daily newspapers were as substantial as those made by Pulitzer and *The World.*

The large, one might even say stupendous success of *The World* and *New York Journal* during the final decades of the nineteenth century dwarfed any prior successes in daily journalism. Having inherited a daily circulation of 15,000, Pulitzer built it to 100,000 in sixteen months.[46] Initially, *The Herald, The New-York Times* and *The Tribune* attempted to keep pace by lowering their daily prices,[47] but *The World* surged ahead. In September, 1886, its circulation reached 250,000, a national record, and Pulitzer marked the achievement by giving his editors silver medals.[48] Starting a dozen years later, the *New York Journal* achieved a daily circulation of 150,000 after a few months under Hearst and then jumped to 1.5 million a year later.[49] Simultaneously, the two newspapers' staffs grew appreciably, reaching 1300 in one case,[50] and the very size of *The World* and the *New York Journal* expanded from sixteen to twenty-four pages. With more pages, advertising inches stretched miles.[51] The then crime reporter Lincoln Steffens said in 1897, "The magnitude of financial operations of the newspaper is turning journalism upside down."[52]

The journalism that Hearst, Pulitzer, and the two newspapers championed was called "new journalism." Pulitzer had become fond of the phrase during his St. Louis years, and when he moved to New York, he was known as a "new journalist." Hearst had studied the production of the "new journalism" in *The World's* offices and also in Boston offices of other practitioners before bringing it to San Francisco.[53] Later, when he began publishing the *New York Journal,* he proclaimed his newspaper the great exemplar of the "new journalism." To guarantee that he duplicated Pulitzer's initiative carefully, Hearst even hired away many of Pulitzer's top editors and reporters.[54]

What was "new journalism?" Traditional treatments cite its independence from party affiliations, emphasis on news gathering, and crusades in the community interest,[55] but these features do not distinguish it from what came before. All of these features were mainstays in the daily journalism of the 1870s and, in certain cases, even the cheap press of the 1830s and 1840s. Instead, "new journalism," as a variety of cultural work, was distinct because of its new format techniques and popularized content. *The World* during the 1880s and then both *The World* and *New York Journal* during the 1890s devoted important space and increased attention to disasters, scandals, gossip and crime.

Crime coverage of the 1880s and later ideally illustrates the contours and trust of "new journalism" as a whole. Local news, especially crime news, was perhaps the chief staple of *The World*. It appeared in the newspaper's "Metropolis by Day" section, which resembled the local news sections of *The Sun*, *The Herald*, *The New-York Times* and *The Tribune*. More significantly, it also appeared in positions of importance and prominence in the newspaper. While other newspapers routinely devoted their front pages to international and national political news, Pulitzer devoted large portions of *The World*'s front page to crime news. He considered the right-hand column of the front page the most important column in the newspaper,[56] and this was often devoted to crime reports. *The World* of January 1, 1884, for example, was a typical issue from midway through Pulitzer's first year of publishing the newspaper. It had six major reports beginning at the top of the six front-page columns. Two concerned national politics and one a fire, but the other three concerned crime. One story, with a Maine dateline, reported a murder, and the other two, without datelines and therefore local, reported the theft of $2000 from a New Yorker in a Second Avenue elevated station and the disappearance of both a jewelry salesman and his $30,000 in stock.[57] Hearst in the 1890s also gave crime reports front-page prominence and, if anything, flaunted such stories even more than Pulitzer. Often, like creeping vines, they inched left from the right-hand columns across the whole front page of the *New York Journal*.

The more prominently placed crime reporting of both newspapers was accompanied by eye-catching headlines and illustrations. Both devices, while eschewed by the mainstream dailies, were common in the weekly press, particularly in the *National Police Gazette*. In the years preceding the Civil War, the original founders of the *Gazette* lost enthusiasm for their endeavor, and it had passed eventually to George Matsell, the son of an early nineteenth-century New York bookseller, who subsequently became New York's Chief of Police. After the Civil War the *Gazette* had changed hands again, coming under control of the buoyant Irish immigrant and entrepreneur Richard K. Fox.[58] Under Matsell and particularly under Fox, the *Gazette* greatly expanded its use of large headlines and illustrative materials. The format techniques were picked up by such look-alikes as the *California Police Gazette* and the *Illustrated Police News,* and, conceivably, the *Gazette*'s techniques and concomitant commercial successes influenced New York's "new journalists" as well.

Whatever the direct lines of influence, *The World* and then the *New York Journal* employed in their enlarged, more prominently placed crime stories a different style of headlines and illustrative materials than that found in the established post-Civil War dailies. *The World*'s headline writers, although in the 1880s still restrained by print size and single-column width, coined for early issues the likes of "A Mother's Awful Crime" and "Love and Cold Poison." The writers also showed a knack for alliteration: "Baptized in Blood," "Terrible Times in Troy," and "Jim-Jams of the Jury."[59] A decade later the *New York Journal,* adopting techniques first used in Chicago,[60] began publishing headlines in larger typefaces and spanning several columns. On November 10, 1896, one routine issue of the *New York Journal* included the following half dozen headlines: "One Gun Killed Two Men," "Lovers Were Thieves," "Axe Didn't Kill Her," "He Robbed Small Boys," "His Murder Clueless," and "Closing in On Robbers."[61] Abstract yet pungent, these headlines captured the reader's attention with their crime-related declarations. Presumably, they also invited readers to buy newsstand issues in order to read further accounts of personal violence and property crimes and of criminal investigations. In *The World* of the 1880s, front-page diagrams and maps of crime scenes stood beside the headlines,[62] and the newspaper also published drawings of criminals. In the 1890s the *New York Journal* expanded use of such illustrative materials, and after 1897 photographic halftones increasingly replaced hand drawings.

The headlines and illustrations matched the style and content of the actual crime reports no less than the style and content of the reports matched the headlines and illustrations. In particular, *The World* and the *New York Journal* produced and sold headlines, illustrations and accounts of personal violence crime. To be sure, journalistic renderings of social disorder crime (brawls in working-class neighborhoods and strike-related riots) and of property crime (robberies, burglaries and business frauds) did not disappear, but the producers of new journalism were particularly animated and skilled in their coverage of beatings and murders within intimate social groupings, particularly within families. The headlines, illustrations and accounts were shocking. Most commonly, they stressed the "human interest" elements of a story, the personalized individual touches which awakened readers' disgust or sympathy.[63]

This reporting was journalistic melodrama. In a rough way it paralleled certain of the crime news genres that had become standard in the older dailies, but more importantly it embodied the features of melodrama itself. In the summer of 1885 *The World* gave great prominence to personal violence crimes both in New York itself and in surrounding areas. "Fate of a Gambler's Wife," for example, told the sad story of Adele O'Thayne, a Vassar graduate and daughter of the owner of several laundries, who fell in love with and married August Erwin, a womanizer and gambler. With her father pressuring her to leave her husband, Adele quarreled with August, and the latter shot her.[64] In Middle Haddam, Connecticut, meanwhile, Herman Hurd, a man who drove good horses, lived well, and squandered family monies, pummeled his sister Mrs. John Dart after a quarrel over a family inheritance thought to total several hundred thousand dollars.[65] In both cases, the backdrop was the family. The victim was pure, honest, or at most led astray, and the criminal perpetrator was careless, deceitful, mean, and ultimately violent. Surely the actual crimes took place, but in these cases as well as in hundreds of others, the headlines, illustrations and accounts framed the criminal melodramatically.

Riding into this melodramatic frame is the hero, and given the dualistic, Manichean nature of the frame, the hero is customarily as noble as the criminal is villainous. Often, a policeman, a judge, or an outraged community assumed the heroic role, but in certain cases *The World* and *New York Journal* cast themselves as heroes. In 1892, *The World* and particularly reporter Isaac D. White used a button and two inches of cloth found at the scene of the attempted murder of Russell Sage to trace the would-be killer to Boston and eventually to identify him.[66] All of White's deductions and exploits were reported faithfully in the newspaper. In June of 1897, when police found the dismembered limbs of a man in the East River and in different locations on the East Side, the *New York Journal* began coverage of what would become known as the Guldensuppe murder case. The newspaper offered a $1000 reward for "information or clues, theories and suggestions" that would solve the murder, and it published not only color prints of the oilcloth in which the body parts were found but also sketches of the body parts themselves.[67] The newspaper boasted of throwing the "entire force of its news-gathering machinery into the work, under the personal direction of the best editorial brains in the world."[68] Due at least in part to the newspaper's efforts, police eventually identified the limbs as those of William Guldensuppe, a Turkish bath rubber. A loyal *New York Journal* reader from Astoria, Queens, recognized the oilcloth facsimile and remembered who had purchased it, and the purchaser, Mrs. Nack, and her lover, Martin Thorn, were indicted for their murderous termination of a romantic triangle. Only then did the

Illus. 3. Headlines and drawings regarding the Guldensuppe case from the front page of *The World* (1897).

New York Journal, the self-styled journalistic detective hero, rest. The criminals' "conviction and punishment," a Hearst editorial announced, "are now left in the hands of justice."[69]

Melodrama, some have argued, need not necessarily be opprobrious.[70] However, in the case of *The World*'s and *New York Journal*'s crime journalism, cultural work that did not purport to be fiction but rather reports on actual crime-related developments, melodrama is troubling. By selecting out for emphasis personal violence crimes, this journalism gave misleading impressions regarding the variety of crime in the urban environment; by accentuating a crime's most shocking elements, it reduced the social complexity of crime-related situations; and by melodramatically casting victims, criminals, and criminal pursuers in white and black, it ignored the more profound social and political aspects of crime.

Pulitzer, Hearst and their editors no doubt appreciated the nature of this crime journalism. Pulitzer, in fact, attempted to justify it. Crime thrives if allowed to remain secret, he said, and prominent newspaper coverage brings it into the open, thereby enabling law-abiding citizens to combat it.[71] Furthermore, he argued, sensational news in general was a way to bring readers to the editorial page, in his opinion the most important part of the newspaper.[72] Pulitzer, at best, might be credited with a type of functional hypocrisy. Fond of asserting "I want to talk to a nation, not a select committee,"[73] he nevertheless did so with criminal frames that left him with an $18 million fortune at the time of his death.[74] Hearst, always the more admittedly commercial of the two editors, offered no rationalizations for the journalistic melodrama.

In essence, the crime journalism of *The World* and *New York Journal* was a designed commercial product. Placed prominently on the front page and highlighted with bold headlines and flashy illustrations, it framed the criminal in a melodramatic fashion. Men and women from all walks of life read it, but in general it appealed not to elites but rather to the masses, most notably workers and recent immigrants. Tired or bored, they found in this journalism relief from the strain and the ennui of their lives, but laying down an issue of *The World* or *New York Journal,* they rarely had any greater sense of what caused their strain and ennui in the first place.

At the very turn of the twentieth century, certain community leaders took a stand against the journalism of Pulitzer and Hearst. The attackers dubbed their journalistic foe not "new" but "yellow" journalism. Inspired by cartoons featuring a child in a yellow dress—the so-called "yellow kid"—which ran in the late 1890s in both *The World* and *New York*

Journal,[75] the phrase "yellow journalism" connoted journalistic titillation and scare tactics. For journalism historians, who have adopted the phrase as a descriptive category without carefully exploring its normative thrust, this variety of journalism is most distasteful when considered in conjunction with the Spanish-American War. Undoubtedly, Pulitzer and Hearst beat their journalistic drums loudly regarding Spanish conduct in Cuba and thereby contributed to the United States' enthusiasm for war. But "yellow journalism" as a critical phrase in its own period connoted more than jingoism. It applied as well to other types of reporting in *The World* and *New York Journal;* among these types, crime reporting was perhaps the most notorious.

The most agitated critics of yellow journalism were in fact newspapers. Yellow journalism was an immensely successful commercial product, and it not only attracted large readerships but also cut into and impeded the growth of the circulations of the more traditional newspapers. The same had been true of Bennett, Sr.,'s journalism in 1840, but by 1900 the combatants and mode of combat had changed. In 1900 the newspapers that deplored Pulitzer and Hearst's brand of journalism were not traditional commercial weeklies but rather, like their enemy, large urban dailies. While in the antebellum period a rival newspaper editor such as James Webb of *The Courier and Enquirer* might register his displeasure by caning Bennett, Sr.,[76] the large newspaper institutions of 1900 attacked in other ways. When traditional Chicago newspapers tried to drive Hearst's *American* off the streets of the Windy City, for example, the newspapers turned to an increasingly sturdy underworld and criminal thugs to menace Hearst's drivers, hawkers and customers.[77]

Beyond the onslaught from traditional newspapers themselves, the 1900 campaign against yellow journalism also differed from the moral war of 1840 in the support groups it attracted. In the earlier fray, established Protestant ministers had been the commercial weeklies' strongest ally in battling Bennett, Sr., and these ministers did in fact understand the fight to be "moral." In 1900 the dailies deploring yellow journalism attracted support less from the ministry and more from professional and business groups. Rather than rising from the pulpit, professionals and businessmen spoke out at white collar lunch meetings or in proper club rooms. The yellow journalism, they asserted, was not so much immoral or sinful as it was improper and irresponsible. Particularly telling was Hearst's rabid commentaries on President McKinley, examples of which were found on the person of Leon Czolgosz, McKinley's assassin.[78] From the perspective of professional and business elites, which had largely supplanted the ministry in social hierarchies by the turn of the century, yellow journalism could actually inspire and fuel the most heinous of crimes.

In the end, the great agitation regarding yellow journalism led to only minor changes. Pulitzer seemed stung by the criticism, and busily constructing and maintaining his reputation as a "great" American newspaper publisher, he slightly moderated aspects of his newspapers.[79] Hearst was less daunted, and under both his leadership and the leadership of others, yellow journalism remained a mainstay in American newspapers. When the smoke from the battle over yellow journalism cleared, fully one-third of the nation's dailies remained yellow.[80] Later, after World War I, these dailies would strongly influence the operations and news reporting in the nation's first mass tabloids.[81]

Perhaps the struggle against yellow journalism would have been more successful if middle- and upper-class urbanites had been left with no choice but yellow newspapers. However, with the exception of those members of the comfortable classes who could not resist peeking at accounts of the most recent criminal atrocities and scandals, the yellow newspapers were read largely by the swelling ranks of laborers and industrial workers.[82] The newspapers' elaborate illustrations and large headlines, Pulitzer and Hearst knew, appealed to readers whose English reading skills were only minimal.[83] Clerks, professionals, businessmen and comfortable housewives read instead newspapers that resembled and were derived from the staid newspapers of the immediate post-Civil War decades. Proper, calm and only passingly concerned with crime coverage, these newspapers gave middle- and upper-class readers reports that were congenial to bourgeois activities and ideologies. In particular, they embodied the belief in objectivity and fact that was central in the self-congratulatory "science" of late nineteenth-century professionalism and business and that will also surface in other types of cultural work to be considered shortly.

The model and the pacesetter in the latter regard was *The New-York Times*. In the early 1890s, the newspaper had fallen on hard times, and its daily circulation had dropped to a paltry 9000. However, in 1896 Adolph S. Ochs, the experienced publisher of *The Chattanooga Times,* arranged an elaborate refinancing of the newspaper, dropped the outdated hyphen from the newspaper's name, and began to build *The New York Times* into a paragon of bourgeois journalism.[84] Shortly after taking control, Ochs announced a contest for a new slogan, ran daily columns full of entries, and chose "All the World News, but not a School for Scandal" as a winner.[85] Designed to boost circulation, the campaign also made clear *The*

New York Times would be different than the yellow newspapers. It would be careful and thorough, restrained and dignified. While the contest winner was quickly put aside in favor of a slogan concocted by Ochs and his editors, this alternative slogan conveyed much the same sentiment. Appearing first on the editorial page in October, 1896, and then in a small box on the top of the front page on February 10, 1897, the slogan read: "All the News That's Fit to Print."[86]

With the nation saying goodbye to its first full century, two types of newspapers, one mass and one bourgeois, provided two varieties of daily newspaper journalism. Both types of daily newspapers, of course, were large corporations selling cultural products, but their differing readerships and journalistic characteristics gave the types distinctly different identities. One attracted immense readerships consisting primarily of workers and published an animated, scandal seeking brand of journalism. With giant headlines and elaborate illustrations, the journalism constituted a form of entertainment. The second type, epitomized by *The New York Times,* attracted a smaller but still large readership consisting primarily of more prosperous and comfortable men and women. It published a more subdued journalism, one designed to inform rather than to entertain. Given the large number of American dailies at the turn of the century, certain dailies of course combined characteristics of the two types, but still the types were sturdy building blocks for the whole edifice of daily journalism. Almost a century later, they remain central in American newspaper publishing, buying and reading experiences.[87]

Both prototypical enterprises included a variety of crime journalism. Mass crime journalism, best illustrated in the 1890s by Pulitzer's *The World* and Hearst's *New York Journal,* often dominated the newspapers' front pages and spun melodramatic crime stories. Bourgeois crime journalism, epitomized at the turn of the century in Ochs' *The New York Times,* was consigned to less than prominent parts of the newspaper and occupied a mere five percent of total space. Restrained and purportedly factual, it was less a series of stories than a run of grinding, unadorned reports. Neither crime journalism was more inherently "news." Both were instead conventional modes of journalistic narrative, developed and sold by either mass or bourgeois newspapers.

Surely the two varieties of crime journalism, as is true of all cultural artifacts, had political alignments, that is, they expressed, "explicitly or implicitly, selected experience from a specific point of view."[88] The mass crime journalism spoke to and for the often sad and abrupt experience of urban workers and immigrants; the bourgeois crime journalism represented the more controlled and confident perspective of the professional or

businessman. However, while both varieties were in this sense compan-
ionable with class structure, neither afforded political meanings derived
from class. Neither articulated class commitment. Mass crime journalism, titillating and relieving with its moralistic stories in black and
white, and bourgeois crime journalism, reporting a grey, uninterpreted
world of fact, failed to capture the radiant colors of crime in turn-of-the-
century America. In tandem, the two varieties of crime journalism had
replaced the critical crime journalism of the cheap press, which had
flourished during the earlier, more jagged burst of nineteenth-century
modernization. The mass and bourgeois varieties of crime journalism
framed crime and the criminal without making an active, open choice of
position. By so doing, they deprived readers of a powerful means of
recognizing and criticizing their world. They were crime journalisms of
and for the modern society.

II.

IMAGINING CRIME

5.

Pointed Political Meanings:
Popular Antebellum Fiction

The history of crime-related fiction is more difficult to trace than the history of crime-related journalism. A great number of stories and novels, perhaps even a majority of all fictional works, portray crime in one way or another. Despite the established institutions of fiction production, authors of fiction have greater freedom in their works than do journalists. Readers of fiction, turning the pages of lengthier and more complex cultural commodities, are more likely to find and create variable meanings. For these reasons and others, a study of crime-related fiction must start with admissions of selectiveness and trepidation.

Yet, this scholarly caution notwithstanding, crime-related fiction did play an important role in the nineteenth-century framing of crime and the criminal. If crime, as the first part of this study argued, is not an essential social fact but rather is recognized through a combination of occurrence and perspective, crime-related fiction contributed to the process. Particularly significant, for purposes of this chapter, as well as for the chapter which follows, are the production and products of popular crime-related fiction. Certain imaginers of crime—cultural workers engaged in the production of popular fiction—attempted quite consciously to plumb the complex subject of crime. Their legions of readers, many first-generation consumers of fiction, found in the reading experience suggested frames for crime and the criminal.

Some of the frames, especially those with which fiction publishers and writers experimented during the antebellum years, invoked pointed political meanings that readers could apply to their social environments and individual lives. In the second half of the century, new frames emerged which lacked the critical thrust of the frames that were used earlier. How complete was the transformation? How do popular crime-related fiction of the antebellum and post-Civil War periods compare to one another? Answers to these questions must be preceded by explorations of the two bodies of work.

The chapter at hand will consider antebellum crime-related popular fiction and its frames. Working in the midst of rapidly expanding popular fiction production, imaginers of crime such as Edgar Allan Poe, Joseph Holt Ingraham, Edward Z. Judson and George Lippard wrote crime-related fiction set in the city. The four did not maintain this focus in all of their works, and all were influenced by British and European fiction. But still, Poe, Ingraham, Judson and Lippard in different ways framed the criminal critically. Lippard's *The Quaker City; or The Monks of Monk Hall* in particular offered countless readers the opportunity to critique and make political sense of the world into which they were racing.

During the antebellum years popular fiction found a home in jaggedly modernizing America. As was the case with the proliferating and expanding newspapers of the period, no single factor explains the increased production and consumption of a given variety of cultural work. The population of the United States, especially in the urban areas, grew rapidly, and the expanded system of public schools, lyceums, libraries and cultural enrichment programs helped create a public that might buy and read fiction. Publishers realized that a market for fiction had emerged, and new developments in printing technology enabled them to generate products rapidly and with less expense to themselves. Introduced in 1825, the Napier steam press produced 2000 copies per hour, and the Hoe rotary press of 1847 multiplied the Napier production rate by a factor of five. Improved binding machines, book plates, and ink and paper production processes also made it increasingly feasible to turn out mass-produced fiction. Expanding systems of roads, canals and railroads facilitated distribution, and the literate public with increased leisure time trooped enthusiastically to the street vendor, book shoppe or railway station bookstall.[1]

Fiction production of the period was less predictably systematic but more lively and buoyantly enterprising than fiction production in the twentieth century. One major wing of the fiction industry engaged in magazine publishing. According to Frank L. Mott, 4000 to 5000 new magazines were launched in America between 1825 and 1850; while the average new periodical survived only two years, the number of extant magazines jumped from roughly 100 to 600 during the twenty-five year span.[2] These magazines sometimes included small notices and professional "cards" on the final pages of an issue, but in general they relied on subscriptions rather than advertising for income. Many of the magazines, most notably women's magazines such as *Godey's Lady's Book,* included both short and serialized fiction between their covers. In addition,

American magazine publishers such as Park Benjamin and Rufus Wilmot Griswold placed "extras" or "supplements" of their periodicals on the market, and these inexpensive volumes, selling for twenty-five cents to fifty cents, contained works of serialized novels reprinted in toto.

More established publishing houses, which had previously printed clothbound volumes of fiction that sold for one dollar or more, took note of the growing market and success of the magazine publishers. The likes of Harper & Brothers and Carey & Hart had themselves long pirated from England and Europe many of the works they sold to elite audiences, but they nevertheless protested the sale of fiction at prices lower than their own. Eventually, Harper & Brothers and others resolved to fight the new fiction entrepreneurs on their own terms, and during the early 1840s they began to publish fiction in paperbacks, which sold for prices comparable to the extras and supplements. In 1820 the annual gross trade in books had been only $2,500,000, but due to the efforts of the new fiction entrepreneurs and changes accepted by the established houses, gross trade increased fivefold by 1850.[3] A large percentage of the mushrooming book production took the form of novels and anthologies of short fiction by Americans, published in both hard and paper covers.[4]

Much of the indigenous popular fiction seemed to discerning commentators of the period unimpressive. Nativist thrillers laced with sinister nuns and priests were popular with male readers,[5] while women apparently preferred moralistic domestic novels by Mrs. E. D. E. N. Southworth and Mrs. Mary Jane Holmes and by such verdant authoresses as Fanny Fern and Grace Greenwood.[6] Nathaniel Hawthorne, supposedly frustrated by the lack of recognition accorded his own works, called these authoresses "a d——d mob of scribbling women." "I should have no chance of success while the public taste is occupied with their trash," he complained in a much quoted letter to his editor, "and should be ashamed of myself if I did succeed."[7]

However, while Hawthorne disdained an affiliation with popular tastes in fiction, Hawthorne himself as well as other venerated authors in American literature did in fact rank among the best-selling writers of fiction. According to lists compiled by twentieth-century scholars, Hawthorne's *Twice-Told Tales* was a best-seller in the late 1830s, while his *The Scarlet Letter* and *The House of the Seven Gables* were best-sellers in the 1850s. Several novels by James Fenimore Cooper, Herman Melville's *Moby Dick,* and Edgar Allan Poe's *Tales* also appear on the best-seller lists for the antebellum years.[8]

Admittedly, the majority of these canonized works have relatively little to yield regarding crime in the modern city. Although crime is portrayed in all these works, the works in general eschew the urban scene and opt instead for a natural setting, one perhaps carrying an implicit critique of modernization but one without attempts at urban canvasing.[9] The major exceptions are stories by Edgar Allan Poe.

A treatment of three of Poe's popular crime-related stories is forthcoming, but Poe's involvement with antebellum fiction production in itself also deserves attention. Although excellent biographers have chronicled Poe's life,[10] these biographers have not sufficiently emphasized Poe's experiences as a cultural worker in a particular historical juncture. Instead, they have stressed notions of the tortured artist, struggling, discovering and writing alone, or, more recently, they have placed Poe in the variegated romantic movement.[11] Neither perspective is wholly satisfactory. Even a writer as poignantly alone as Poe did not work in true isolation. Even a writer as aware of international literary developments as Poe did not function simply within a literary movement.

Poe's youth and earlier efforts as a cultural worker set the stage for the portion of his life that is most relevant to the work at hand. Born in 1809 in Boston of poor itinerant actors, Poe was orphaned at an early age and then raised in Richmond and London by the Scottish-American tobacco merchant John Allan. Disastrous enrollments at the University of Virginia and West Point followed, and after Poe's expulsion from the latter, Allan disowned him. Still in his early twenties, Poe then turned to cultural work for a livelihood. He wrote stories, poems and reviews for prevailing fees; he plagiarized and was plagiarized; and his work appeared in a wide range of antebellum cultural commodities—magazines, papercovered pamphlets and bound anthologies. A different man in this context might have become an efficient and well-compensated hack, but Poe was too eccentric and idiosyncratic for that. Yet Poe's experiences as a cultural worker do constitute the social origins of his imaginative work, and they also illustrate the rhythms and frustrations of antebellum fiction production.

The year 1840 found Poe and his curious family resettled in Philadelphia after previous stays in Baltimore, Richmond and New York. Maria Clemm, Poe's aunt, happily shopped, cooked and sewed for her "Eddie," while Poe lovingly called her "Muddie" or mother. Virginia, Poe's childbride and cousin, had become an adoring if fragile wife.[12] Poe himself sold his stories and essays on a freelance basis to assorted periodicals, customarily earning four to five dollars per page.[13] He also worked as a part-time literary editor for *Burton's Gentleman's Magazine,* a monthly compendium of poems, short stories, theatrical gossip and literary criticism. Like many of his other work relationships, Poe's relationship with William E.

Burton, an English comedian just two years his senior, was stormy.[14] When, in May of 1840, Burton refused to publish Poe's review of John L. Carey's *Domestic Slavery,* Poe resigned in a huff from what he angrily called the "Gent's Mag."

During the final months of 1840, Poe engaged in a variety of projects, ranging from an attempt to launch *Penn Magazine,* a literary periodical that he could call his own, to campaigning for the Whig William Henry Harrison in the Philadelphia area. The tasks were a strain, with capital eluding his proprietary dreams and swirling crowds turning the local election into an extended brawl. Poe retired to his home, disabled by the nervous illness that on more than one occasion had proven his mean nemesis. Then, toward the very end of 1840, Poe began to use his pen to make sense of the world around him and to lift himself from his malaise. One of his new stories was "The Man of the Crowd," a sad ramble through the dark streets of London but at least narrated by a character who, like Poe himself, had been ill but now finds himself "in one of those happy moods which are so precisely the converse of ennui."[15]

The story appeared in the last number of *Burton's,* which had by this point been purchased by cabinet maker turned lawyer George Graham, and early in 1841 Poe called on Graham to see what further stories he might write for the new *Graham's Magazine.* Graham in turned offered him an editorial position. Poe accepted and, while continuing to solicit backing for his own *Penn Magazine,* went to work preparing the April, 1841, issue of *Graham's.* Due in part to Poe's efforts, the magazine quickly emerged as perhaps *the* most successful of the antebellum period's new leisure periodicals. Combining stories, poems and sketches with sheet music for popular songs and full-page illustrations of women's fashions, *Graham's* attracted in the early 1840s as many as 25,000 subscribers and prompted one later commentator to compare it to the twentieth century's *Saturday Evening Post* and *Ladies' Home Journal.*[16] With *Graham's* thriving, Poe was at least temporarily secure. He bought red carpets and a tea set for Mrs. Clemm and a harp and piano for Virginia. After a day in his office and a meal at Mrs. Clemm's table, Poe could seat himself at his writer's desk, temporarily at ease with his life.

But as was always the case during his adult years, Poe had little time to savor a successful interlude. In early 1842 his life went sour. When Virginia ruptured a blood vessel in her throat while singing, doctors discovered her tuberculosis. Poe moved the family to the outskirts of Philadelphia, hoping the more peaceful setting would be good for Virginia's health. At the office Poe encountered and generated friction, and when it appeared that Graham intended to replace Poe, the latter resigned his editorial position. Poe then attempted to leave magazine work, but when Robert Tyler, son of the president, failed to secure a custom house position for Poe, the exit routes seemed blocked.

In 1843 Poe's plans for his own magazine again fell through, and a new leaflet series of his stories failed to sell. Poe experienced a paranoia born of his entrepreneurial and marketing failures. At wit's end, he became convinced that a Philadelphia clique was conspiring against him. In April, 1844, in what must have been a wretched mood, Poe moved his family back to New York. The move did little to restore Virginia's health, and over the next three years she slowly died. Yet somehow Poe continued to write and to work as a magazine editor. In New York during the mid–1840s Poe published his most famous poem, a number of original stories, and even a collection of works. He also worked as many as fifteen hours a day editing the *Broadway Journal,* only to see the periodical fold.[17]

During these years, Poe, despite his successes, was continually frustrated in the workplace and the market, and indeed, his biting and incessant commentaries on other cultural workers led to heated controversies and growing animosities. In 1849, the final year of his life, Poe concluded it was not merely assorted editors and literary figures who were undermining his efforts but rather the entire northern literary establishment. He decided to move south and looked in particular to Richmond as a place where he might find peace of mind.[18] As illusory as his many previous dreams, this planned escape from the entire modernizing North did not succeed. Inebriated and delerious, Poe was found in a Baltimore public house after a local election, and he died shortly thereafter.[19]

Overall, Poe's travails in fiction production during the 1840s do not distinguish the years from other periods of his adult life, and the stories he wrote during these years do not constitute Poe's full fiction production. Poe was not an "everyman"—insanity ran in his natural family, growing up in an adopted family without permanent standing harmed him, and his marriage was unusual and draining. Poe nevertheless fully experienced the uncertain rhythms of antebellum fiction production. This production was expanding but also chaotic. Fiction-publishing periodicals were being founded and folded daily. In keeping with the midcentury norm of jumping from one occupational field to another,[20] many individuals temporarily tried their hand at periodical publishing and editing, and fiction writers had strained and tenuous relationships with transient publishers and editors. Anthologies, cheap paperbacks and cloth-covered volumes competed with periodicals for the fiction-buying public's dollars, and international literary freebootery was common.[21] If Poe's crime-related stories set in the modern city manifest a richly critical vision of crime and society, the stories' material and social origins help explain this vibrance.

Three of Poe's stories from the 1840s—"The Murders in the Rue Morgue," "The Mystery of Marie Rogêt," and "The Purloined Letter"— deserve special attention.[22] Critics have generally grouped these stories as Poe's detective stories, and indeed, there is some validity to this grouping. One might question several of the clues in "The Murders in the Rue Morgue" or the deductions in "The Purloined Letter,"[23] but the tales do invite the reader to join in solving a criminal mystery. The word "detective" does not appear in the tales or, for that matter, in print prior to 1843,[24] but the tales do feature a superb detecting character in C. Auguste Dupin. When measured against the rules for detective fiction, which appeared as long ago as the 1920s,[25] Poe's tales seem veritable literary common law on which later codifications were based.

However, approaching the stories merely as detective stories is unsatisfactory. Ex post facto generic appreciation of the three tales fails to capture the reading experience that these stories provided in the 1840s. Some antebellum readers may have known that Poe himself grouped the three stories as special "ratiocinative" tales. A few may have taken note of Poe's reminder in "The Purloined Letter" that readers intrigued by C. Auguste Dupin could also find his exploits chronicled in two earlier tales. But the majority of readers certainly did not approach the tales as generic exemplars. As subscribers to *Graham's Magazine* or *The Ladies' Companion* or as recipients of a Christmas gift volume, they were most likely middle class urbanites. After a day in an office or in the home, they looked generally for stories that might provide relaxation or insight. They approached Poe's tales not as detective fiction devotees but more generally as fiction consumers and readers.

In hopes of capturing the meanings of the three stories in their original context, generic concerns may be set aside. Consideration of general fiction elements—narration, setting, plot, and characters—holds more promise as a way to grasp the response of antebellum readers. This type of consideration reveals that Poe's tales invited contemplation regarding crime and society. The tales illustrate the potential of imaginative work to eschew comforting frames for crime and the criminal.

Readers of the three stories learn early that their narrator is a gentleman. Although his name and origins never appear, the narrator's comments on the peculiarities of the French suggest that he might be American. Financially secure, he can reside in Paris and amuse himself hunting rare books and attending dramatic productions. Finding the company of Chevalier C. Auguste Dupin "a treasure beyond price,"[26] the narrator rents and furnishes a secluded home where he and Dupin can enjoy "the twofold luxury of meditation and a meerschaum."[27] This residence in the Faubourg St. Germain proves ideal for considering fictive crime and attempts at its detection, both of which the narrator does in a first-person voice.

The effectiveness of the narration in the three stories should not be underestimated. Later, the narrating and observing colleague of the detective figure became a mainstay in detective fiction, most notably in Conan Doyle's Watson. In the early 1840s it worked on its own terms. Quickly recognizable, Dupin's gentleman companion wins the reader's trust. He is precise and articulate; he conveys amazement at what transpires. Perhaps only in "The Mystery of Marie Rogêt," in which Dupin's own lengthy analyses of newspaper accounts overwhelm the narrator, does the voice unsatisfactorily convey a story. In the two other stories, the antebellum magazine reader found the unnamed narrator a congenial storyteller, so congenial as to elude any formal recognition as such. The narrator not only stands apart from crime and its detection but also ponders them with intense introspection. The narrator gives readers a good vantage point while simultaneously providing a truly contemplative mode. Reading the stories through the narrator, the reader is invited, even encouraged, to ponder crime and society. The mind of the narrator is inquiring, critical, often unsettled, and the reader's engagement with the three stories rests on a well executed narrative contract.

The setting for "The Murders in the Rue Morgue," "The Mystery of Marie Rogêt" and "The Purloined Letter" is, as suggested, neither Philadelphia nor New York but rather nineteenth-century Paris. In the French capital the wealthy may live in pleasant hotel suites, but their clandestine ways lead them to house their servants elsewhere. The less well-to-do live not with robust extended families but rather with widowed mothers and sycophantic companions. Their residences are time-eaten, grotesque homes or dark apartments on side streets. Shielded by pulled shades or closed shutters, the residents slumber "tranquilly in the Present, weaving the dull world . . . into dreams."[28] Outside, ambitious men and, most shockingly, young women pursue their fast-paced callings. Even after dark, crowds push up against the pedestrian, incomprehensible foreign languages fill the air, and desperate adventures infest neighborhoods. With newspapers screaming of "Extraordinary Murders," the night walker is aware that crime and violence play all night.

Most antebellum readers were likely to find this setting captivating. In effectively crafted images, Poe supplies a cityscape, forms a social activity and modes of personality. He creates a recognizable world. The images are economical and telegraphic, and they do not deter a short story reader from quickly engaging other elements of the stories. The images are unified in their eeriness and melancholy. The stories fulfill not only a narrative contract but also a mimetic one as well.[29]

Yet at the same time Poe's setting is hardly routine. Poe set his stories in Paris instead of in any number of American cities that his readers might have known well. One biographer has explained Poe's choice by suggesting he spent 1832, the "missing year" of his life, in the French capital.[30] Another has noted his familiarity with "Unpublished Passages in the Life of Vidocq, the French Minister of Police," a popular series of antebellum magazine articles.[31] More generally, the setting resonates with original readers' assumptions regarding life on the continent. The Parisian world epitomizes decadence and connotes a social environment that could both fascinate and sober the reflective antebellum American. Is this our future? Is this the world into which we are entering? Certainly it led the antebellum reader to consider in juxtaposition the urban America in which he or she lived.

With engagement achieved through narration and mimesis, antebellum readers could follow the stories' plots and characters. Always difficult to distinguish from one another, the sequencing of fictive events and the compounding of character can nevertheless be appraised in relative terms. In Poe's stories the former is simple: a horrible and unsolved crime haunts Paris, Prefect G— of the Paris police discusses the crime with Dupin and the narrator, Dupin makes one or two investigative forays, Dupin offers a solution to the crime.[32] Plotting is predictable, and indeed, the reader knows early in each story that Dupin's solution is forthcoming. Characterization, meanwhile, is quite striking. More so than the sequencing of fictive events, Poe's characters shape and give energy to the tales.

As with setting and narrative voice, Poe's choices in characterization are economical—the major characters are only three in number. One is the previously discussed introspective narrator, and the other two are the Prefect G— and Dupin. While the Prefect G— is minor when compared to the latter, the prefect is superbly wrought. This functionary, according to "The Murders in the Rue Morgue," is too cunning to be profound.

> In his wisdom is no *stamen*. It is all head and no body, like the pictures of the Goddess Laverna, —, or at least, all head and shoulders, like a codfish.[33]

When the prefect comes to visit, the "leaden-footed" hours drag by.[34] Easily piqued by his failures, he gushes on about a case and asserts, "with a peculiarly Parisian air,"[35] that his reputation and honor are at stake.

Somehow, the prefect can never comprehend Dupin's ways. "Ha! ha! ha!—ha! ha! ha!—ho! ho! ho!," he roars, "Oh, Dupin, you will be the death of me yet!"[36]

Unlike the prefect, C. Auguste Dupin has a complete name, and Poe's tales delineate this character more fully. Dupin is a gentleman from an excellent, illustrious family whose voice, usually in rich tenor, can on occasion rise to a treble. Unfortunately, this character has largely "ceased to bestir himself in the world, or to care for the retrieval of his fortunes."[37] During the day he prefers to remain indoors, customarily reading, writing and conversing in the armchair in his fourth-floor book closet. Sometimes wearing green spectacles, he enjoys his pipe more than the prefect's complements or his male companion's fawning. At night Dupin, in his most curious *bizarrerie,* sallies forth into the streets, "roaming far and wide until a later hour, seeking, amid the wild lights and shadows of the populous city, that infinity of mental excitement which quiet observation can afford."[38] On one such sally, Dupin astonishingly synchronizes himself with the sequence and speed of the narrator's thoughts. After fifteen minutes of silence, he articulates exactly what his companion is thinking.[39]

Dupin's most notable conduct has to do with his crime solving. His motivation springs primarily from a fascination with difficult puzzles, but Dupin nevertheless accepts payment from Prefect G— for his work. Dupin's approach to detection is, of course, chiefly analytic; he can reassemble clues par excellence. However, Dupin is not simply a reasoner. As the narrator notes, there is in fact "a double Dupin—the creative and the resolvent."[40] In considering clues, leads and motivations, Dupin manifests an aesthetic appreciation for crime. The butchery in "The Murders in the Rue Morgue"—one dead woman rammed up a chimney and another virtually beheaded—strikes Dupin as "excessively outré."[41] The problem in "The Purloined Letter" is perhaps too simple, "a little too plain."[42] If Prefect G— is inept, it is because, unlike Dupin, he is deficient as a sensitive, artistic man.

Later writers of detective fiction also juxtaposed unimaginative professional police with inspired amateur detectives, and indeed, this particular juxtaposition of characters became one of the genre's most admired conventions.[43] Antebellum readers, however, neither had nor needed detective fiction conventions. As noted in the first chapter of this work, antebellum American cities were confused and distressingly anomic. As yet unorganized into metropolitan departments, antebellum police failed to control mushrooming crime. Appropriately abbreviated and partial in name, the Prefect G— was referential. Readers could find in him a version of their own police. Dupin, meanwhile, constituted an alternative. An aristocrat and member of the traditional elite, he could alleviate the malaise of fictive crime and society in ways the Prefect G——, a symbolic representation of the rising urban classes, could not.

Reading experience complete, antebellum readers extinguished their lights with some feeling of peace. However, wrapped tightly in their night covers or trudging along the muddy streets to the next morning of work, some readers no doubt returned to the stories less comfortably. Poe's carefully crafted narrative voice, setting and characters do not offer any lasting assurances. They do not offer meanings that are comforting. Instead, they suggest that crime remains horrible, that it remains a haunting and mysterious part of social life.

In "The Murders in the Rue Morgue" and "The Mystery of Marie Rogêt," the criminal milieu is the working world of Paris, and specification of a crime and a criminal prove difficult. In the former a widow and her daughter are murdered savagely, but Dupin's investigation reveals that the perpetrator is a sailor's escaped "Ourang-Outang." Perhaps the sailor is guilty of removing an animal from its natural environment with an eye to profit or of negligence, but Dupin himself declares the sailor is not legally guilty of a formal crime. Mean and irrational, the beasts of the working class prowl Poe's metropolis, but crime and the criminal cannot even be designated. In "The Mystery of Marie Rogêt," a young woman attempts to make her way in the bustling city, but dark lovers, an unwanted pregnancy, and waterfront gangs make the path treacherous. After passers-by pull her bloated corpse from the river, Dupin tells the police how to find her killer, but Poe and his readers knew that the New York murder of Mary Rogers, on which the fiction was based, remained unsolved.[44] Speaking through Dupin, Poe understandably warns of the "infinite series of mistakes which arrive in the path of Reason through her propensity for seeking truth in detail."[45]

In "The Purloined Letter" the criminal milieu is the public sphere, the realm of state politics. The Minister D—— steals an intimate letter from a member of the royal family and uses it to blackmail the victim and further his designs in the political arena. From the beginning of the tale, the crime and the criminal are known, and the ingenious Dupin finds the letter, hidden in the open, in a letter rack on the minister's mantel. But how troubling are the similarities between the criminal and his pursuer. The minister and Dupin share not only an initial but also a much discussed fondness for both mathematics and poetry. In the end, Dupin does not merely retrieve the letter and terminate the intrigue. Instead, he replaces it with a carefully prepared facsimile with the message:

—Un dessein si funeste
S'il n'est digne d'Atree, est digne de Thyeste.[46]

A mean spirit, is seems, is part of both crime and detection. In Poe's mind, criminal and detective blend powerfully into one.

Influenced by developed detective fiction conventions, many readers of a later day read Poe's stories comfortably. In the antebellum period, readers turned the stories' pages disconcertedly. Guided by an introspective narrator, confronted by an alienated and crime-laden cityscape, and engaged by characters with representative class identities, the reader had good reason to ponder the complexities of crime and society. Poe was hardly an enthusiastic democrat; his alignment in the stories is with Dupin, a lonely aristocrat. However, Poe's three stories provocatively explore the open-ended experience and meaning of crime in a modernizing society. Poe's fiction, read at the time of its writing, does not frame the criminal confidently or comfortably. Ambiguity lurks. Objectivity is suspect. These crime-related stories imaginatively critique the sad and painful confusion of modernizing social existence.

After turning to the *Broadway Journal* and his battle with New York literary figures, Poe did not continue to write of crime in the modern city, but other less venerated fiction writers of the 1840s and 1850s did mine extensively a related imaginative vein. While Poe's stories were destined to catch the eye and approval of university-based scholars,[47] the works of these other writers have not found their way into the twentieth-century academy. Their appreciation is largely restricted to their own period. Yet like Poe, Joseph Holt Ingraham and Edward Z. Judson were forceful imaginers of crime-related fiction. A brief consideration of their relevant works will further underscore antebellum fiction production processes and suggest the critical thrust of certain works generated through those processes.

Although Ingraham and Judson were no doubt aware of Poe's works and reputation, it was not Poe but rather English and French writers who most influenced them. Ingraham and Judson knew the early works of Dickens and Balzac. Due to pirated editions of their works, both of the latter attracted large readerships in the United States during the antebellum period.[48] More so than either Dickens or Balzac, the Frenchman Eugène Sue provided the model for the Americans under consideration. According to *The American Review,* Sue easily surpassed Dickens and Balzac in popularity in the United States during the 1840s. Blue-covered editions of Sue's works, the journal reported, occupied "a conspicuous place on the dressing-table of fair ladies and the work-bench of the artisan."[49]

Sue himself was a master of the French *feuilleton* or cheap, pamphlet literature.[50] His *Les mystères de Paris,* a sprawling ten-volume serial, attracted the interest and francs of nineteenth-century Frenchmen. Featuring Fleur-de-Marie, a prostitute, and abundant in crime, violence and sadism, not to mention pointed social conflict, the novel was quickly translated and sold in the United States during 1843.[51] Sue's subsequently written and translated *Le juif errant,* similar in format, tone and concerns, was a comparable commercial success.[52] Surveying Sue's international popularity, no less a social and cultural critic than Karl Marx was prompted to comment. Sue, in Marx's opinion, was "the most wretched offal of socialist literature."[53] In their rich exchange of letters Marx and his colleague Engels deplored writers like Sue who merely attached political opinions, comments and phrases to their literature without subscribing to or articulating a more profound social and historical critique. A writer like Sue, Marx and Engels agreed, produced "tendency literature."[54] In the decidedly nonmarxist cultural commodity markets of antebellum America, such pointed criticism was hardly a factor. Some fifty novels concerning crime and urban life appeared in the United States between 1844 and 1860.[55] Two of the most prominent domesticators of Sue's work were Ingraham and Judson.

Born in obscurity in Portland, Maine, in 1809, Ingraham as a youth served as a crewman on a South American trading vessel and then attended Bowdoin College, eventually graduating at what was for the period the advanced age of twenty-four.[56] He briefly taught foreign languages at Jefferson College in Natchez, Mississippi, and then, during a five-year span in the late 1830s, published no fewer than eighty adventure novelettes, works that Longfellow called perhaps the worst fiction ever written.[57] In 1844, aware of the great attention Sue's writings had received, Ingraham wrote *The Miseries of New York; or, The Burglar and Counselor,*[58] a work aping Sue's longer and similarly named novel of Parisian life.

Edward Z. Judson, best known in later years by his pen name "Ned Buntline," was, like Ingraham, a man with an eye for the smart cultural enterprise.[59] A product of the small village of Stamford, New York, where he was born in 1824, Judson had also gone to sea as a young man and then converted his seafaring experiences into adventure yarns. In 1844, writing in a short-lived Cincinnati literary journal he had founded, Judson deplored Ingraham's dependence on Sue and called on American writers to develop a more truly indigenous literature.[60] However, never a pillar of consistency, Judson in January, 1848, wrote his own largely derivative *Mysteries and Miseries of New York: A Story of Real Life*. When publishers proved uninterested in the work, he himself financed publication of the first volume and sold it in paper covers for twenty-five cents.[61] Berford & Company then brought out the four subsequent volumes of the work as well as the complete bound work.[62] *Mysteries and Miseries of New York* quickly sold over 100,000 copies,[63] and reversing the trans-Atlantic path of Sue's works, Judson's novel appeared in reprints and translations in England, France and Denmark. Subsequently, the playwright Benjamin Baker wrote and produced several plays based on the work,[64] and Judson himself wrote at least four additional volumes, one set in New Orleans rather than New York, which were sequels to his *Mysteries and Miseries of New York*.[65]

Admittedly, these novelettes and novels by Ingraham and Judson deserve low marks if measured by the formal and thematic standards of the American canon.[66] None appear carefully or tightly designed, offering instead sprawling plots that wind their way convolutedly through crime-laden urban panoramas. None present highly defined characters struggling for their independence and meaning but rather many weakly defined characters whose fictive experiences convey collective meaning. However, the antebellum works of Ingraham and Judson *were* immensely popular in their periods, and the authors did understand them to have political significance.

The literary designs and social purposes of Ingraham and Judson compare not to those of antebellum New England literati but rather to those of antebellum journalists. *The Miseries of New York* and *Mysteries and Miseries of New York* are in many ways "journalistic novels." Like the period's newspapers, both informatively sketch new types of crime and provide tours of actual gambling and prostitution establishments. Judson, who also adds glossaries of criminal slang and crime statistics, insists repeatedly in the prefaces of *Mysteries and Miseries of New York* on the work's accuracy. "Though this work bears the title of a novel," he says, "it is written with the ink of truth and deserves the name of a *history* more than that of a romance."[67] For those "city critics" who might doubt him, Judson offers to provide "an original or counterpart for every scene."[68]

Purported accuracy was of course a good marketing ploy, but like the editors of *The Sun, The Herald* and the *National Police Gazette,* Ingraham and Judson had not only profit but also public service in mind. The novelists claim to be cultural police, determined to expose the activities and the elite origins of many criminal perpetrators. Judson says his aim in *Mysteries and Miseries of New York* "is to do good."[69] With an eye to that goal, as well as to sales, Judson sent copies of his novels to the mayor of New York, to several aldermen, and to police headquarters.[70]

In subsequent years, both Ingraham and Judson lost their interest in the miseries and mysteries of the metropolis, and their social commitments shifted significantly. Ingraham in 1855 took orders in the Episcopal church and during his final years wrote primarily religious works, including among others *The Prince of the House of David,*[71] which still appears occasionally on church sponsored reading lists. Judson, always the more rambunctious of the two, was an instigator in New York's Astor Place Riot of 1849. He then composed a ratty string of western adventure stories and launched his promotion of the obscure scout whom the nation would come to think of as Buffalo Bill. Cultural workers peaked by the first bursts of full-scale modernization, Ingraham and Judson temporarily at least had coordinated their opportunism with critical, imaginative portrayals of crime in the city. But opportunism and critical consciousness are uneasy bedfellows, and writers do not necessarily wield to their dying days the pointed literary instruments of their youth.

While Ingraham and Judson became, respectively, a pietistic minister and a hustling entrepreneur, their contemporary George Lippard wrote powerfully of crime in the urban environment and then continued to develop throughout his life the literary and political instruments of his early days. "LITERATURE merely considered as an ART is a despicable thing," he asserted. "A literature which does not work practically, for the advancement of social reform . . . is just good for nothing at all."[72] Lippard's life and his most important work, *The Quaker City; or, The Monks of Monk Hall,* are appropriate concluding focal points in this chapter concerning antebellum crime-related popular fiction.

Born in 1822 in Chester County, Pennsylvania, Lippard experienced a rocky childhood.[73] His mother died during his ninth year, and his father departed for Philadelphia, leaving young George in the care of his aunts. Like Poe, Ingraham, Judson and many other writers of the period, Lippard experimented with other callings before settling finally into cultural work. The ministry was his first choice, but he was disgusted with "the contradiction between the theory and practice" of Christianity.[74] He then turned to the practice of law but concluded that lawyers and the law in general did not serve justice.[75] In 1840, Lippard attempted to write a novel.[76] Fiction was at first difficult for him and did not provide a livelihood, but Lippard also worked for the *Spirit of the Times,* a lively Philadelphia penny newspaper, writing reviews, news reports and a police court column. The journalistic experience in conjunction with his growing political commitment enabled the would-be novelist to find his literary voice. In 1842, the *Saturday Evening Post* published serially *Herbert Tracy*,[77] Lippard's first full novel, and the still young Pennsylvanian's work as a fiction writer swung into gear.

Lippard's most significant and widely noticed novel of the 1840s was *The Quaker City; or, The Monks of Monk Hall.* Published first in 1844 and 1845 as a ten-installment paper-covered serial, *The Quaker City* appeared shortly thereafter in one hastily bound five-book volume.[78] Selling rapidly at the rate of 60,000 copies per year, the novel then went through twenty-seven domestic and several foreign editions by 1850.[79] Resigned but still wry about the literary piracy of the period, Lippard praised one "beautiful edition in four volumes . . . bearing the imprint of Otto Wigland, Leipsic, as Publisher, and the name of Frederick Gerstaker, as the Author."[80] According to Lippard's chief biographer, *The Quaker City* was the best selling American novel before *Uncle Tom's Cabin* of 1852.[81] *The Quaker City*, Lippard himself said in 1849, "has been more attacked, and more read, than any work of American fiction ever published."[82]

The reaction to the novel, not surprisingly, was strongest in Philadelphia itself. As convulsed by the forces of modernization as any American city of the antebellum period,[83] Philadelphia, as Poe would have confirmed, was on edge. *The Quaker City*, inspired at least in part by an actual Philadelphia murder,[84] provoked many of the residents of the actual Quaker City to denigrate or glorify the name of George Lippard. One camp, including members of the town's gentry, deplored Lippard's scandalous sensationalism, much as the moral war-makers had deplored James Gordon Bennett's journalism in New York City in 1840. In the opinion of one spokesman, the novel was "a disgusting mass of filth" designed to blackmail prominent Philadelphians.[85] Another camp, including many of Philadelphia's mechanics and laborers, took Lippard's side. Derivative commodifiers placed "Monk Hall Cigars" on the local market, and the manager of the Chestnut Street Theater began rehearsals for a play based on the novel. When Lippard's detractors threatened to sack or burn the theater, the manager canceled the production, a decision that prompted another mob of a decidedly different mind to gather before the playhouse. With an armed Lippard helping city constables quell a potential riot, Philadelphians surely realized cultural work was part of their social transformation and struggle. Crime-related fiction and its cultural derivatives spoke forcefully to antebellum Americans, jarred as they were by social uncertainty.

As was the case with Poe's crime-related stories, Lippard's *The Quaker City* may be plumbed for meaning through a consideration of its general literary characteristics. The narrator of the novel, to begin with, is an orphan. His story comes not from his own experiences but rather from those of Old K—, a Philadelphia lawyer who has practiced for thirty-five years, and who, on his deathbed, turns over his papers and records to the orphan he has protected. The orphan, according to a self-conscious introductory section titled "The origin and object of this Book," works from these papers and records, ultimately offering his readers a summarizing account. However, as the account spills forth, the origins of the text disappear as does the narrator's particular social identity. In reality, we find an opinionated, third-person voice providing us with impressions and information.

Although the narrator is neither unique nor particularly articulate, his values and preferences are striking. For one thing, the narrator is ostentatiously learned, proferring impromptu critiques of antebellum art and literature, often in footnotes.[86] Yet his "taste," of which he is proud, seems less sure than boisterous, and although many readers might have seconded the narrator's attack on the genteel literary "maiden-man" of the period, our narrator registers as lowbrow. Surely the narrator is male.[87] On a dozen occasions he pauses to contemplate a sleeping, drugged or unaware woman and, in particular, her exposed breasts—in his words "snowy," "heaving" or "swelling globes." Unlike Poe's stories in which the narrator is asexual or perhaps even homosexual, the narrator in *The Quaker City* is robustly heterosexual, bordering on distressingly pornographic. Additionally, the narrator's social alignment is with the working class. He sides with the poor and with laborers and mechanics. Prompted primarily by crimes perpetrated by the well-to-do, the narrator frequently speaks with passion of social injustice.

Lippard's narrator leads readers on a tour of Philadelphia. How raw and fluid the setting seems, as people abruptly ask one another's occupations.[88] Jews, blacks and wayward southerners, all speaking in recognizable dialects, walk the streets, and social mobility has led to a new type of elite: "An Aristocracy founded on the high deeds of dentists, tape-sellers, quacks, pettifoggers, and bank directors, all jumbled together in a ridiculous mass of absurdities,"[89] Often the narrator underscores stops on the tour, an oyster house, for example,[90] and in addition to discussing specific representative locales, the narrator pauses to address particular aspects of Philadelphia life such as its fashions and press.[91] A preface informs us that the work is an "illustration of the life, mystery and crime of Philadelphia."[92]

The specific locale within the overall setting that best facilitates the illustration is Monk Hall itself. A mansion constructed by a wealthy

Englishman and one-time Catholic nunnery, Monk Hall is an elaborate structure with a tower, catacombs, and seemingly innumerable rooms and chambers. "Secrecy are the police,"[93] and the city's most dissolute, using passwords and false identities, visit the hall to gamble, steal, defraud, assault, rape and murder. The Monks themselves hail from the city's more comfortable classes, but meeting below in the "Dead-Vault" are members of another fraternity, "the Outcast Monks." Working-class thieves and cutthroats, they sometimes break into drunken song:

> A jolly band of good fellows all,
> Are the Outcast Monks of old Monk Hall!
> They dance, they steal, they drink, they fight
> And turn the shiny day into night—[94]

Undoubtedly Monk Hall is the descendant and analogue of the medieval castle, and *The Quaker City* can be placed in the international category of gothic romanticism.[95] More significantly, Monk Hall is a setting understood in the context of its particular social milieu and historical juncture. As an urban American of midcentury, Lippard did not fashion Monk Hall in order to transport his readers to a remote, exotic past. Lippard's readers found in Monk Hall a fictive embodiment of Philadelphia and of the surrounding social modernization. Like Philadelphia, Monk Hall reeks of crime, violence and injustice and betrays class division. To enter Monk Hall is to "obtain a few fresh ideas of the secret life of this good Quaker City—."[96] As the prototypical urban society, Philadelphia, in Leslie Fiedler's terms, is "a new wilderness," "a jungle of stone and glass" into which modern men and women, orphans all, venture "as into a strange land."[97]

As for plotting and characterization, *The Quaker City* is at first glance staggering. The plot gallops through three days and nights, culminating on Christmas Eve of 1842, but during the ride, the plot continually veers in oblique directions, through twists and turns almost unfathomable. We know that Lippard himself considered the story of Gus Lorrimer's seduction and rape of fifteen-year old Mary Arlington the main plot.[98] The weave of this plot line is the most extensive, stretching from an astrologer's prediction early in the novel that the seducer and Mary's brother will battle to the death to the battle itself at sunset on Christmas Eve late in the novel. Yet Lippard also says in the preface that he is "determined to write a book which should describe all the phases of a corrupt social system."[99] Accordingly, there are two other major plot lines—one involving a confidence man's defrauding of a rich merchant and seduction of the merchant's wife and a second concerning Ravoni, a religious visionary who claims to be 200 years old and manifests a strong preference for young female converts. All three plot lines abound in false leads, suspended climaxes, footnoted additions, and awkward redirections and summaries. One diligent scholar, determined to give the plot diagrammatic certainty, has outlined the three major plot lines, but he has also supplemented them extensively with a half dozen "subplots."[100] Another less energetic scholar has suggested that "nothing less than a small volume" would be required to summarize the content of *The Quaker City*.[101]

In reality, faithfulness to the reading experience the novel initially delivered is possible without complete structural clarity. *The Quaker City*'s plot is similar to those of Ingraham's and Judson's crime-related works of the 1840s; the plot is complex and sprawling. Lacking a beginning, a middle, and an end, the plot of *The Quaker City* resembles the "plot" of the antebellum daily newspaper. It is a confusing labyrinth of trails rather than a direct path, and as such, the plot is structurally homologous to the social world that spawned it. The plot does not fail but rather works superbly for a reader willing to wander through it.

Certain of the major characters in *The Quaker City*, meanwhile, are intriguing. Dora Livingstone, the merchant's wife seduced by the con man Fitz-Cowles is hardly the naive Victorian lady led blindly astray. She is instead a sharp-eyed, voluptuous adventuress, "absorbed in . . . ambition to rise"[102] and moving from lover to lover as she climbs the social ladder. Devil-Bug, the one-eyed, hunchback doorkeeper of Monk Hall, is perhaps the novel's fullest embodiment of criminality, a literary creation impressive in its wildness and horror. Talking with Monk Hall's brick pillars and creaking trapdoors, he is the essence of the building and all it represents:

> Ha, ha, ha! When I die I should feel obliged to the rowdy as un set it [Monk Hall] afire! It must go with me! When I'm gone it 'ill be like a coffin without a corpse. What's the use o' th' shell when the torkle's dead.[103]

Yet Livingstone and Devil-Bug notwithstanding, Lippard's characterization is neither full nor elaborate. The two dozen major characters—a conservative estimate—are more cardboard than human. Their motivations are single-minded and their actions are predictable. The characters are, in short, ideal for the type of work that Lippard and his readers took *The Quaker City* to be. The characters are signposts that the narrator can

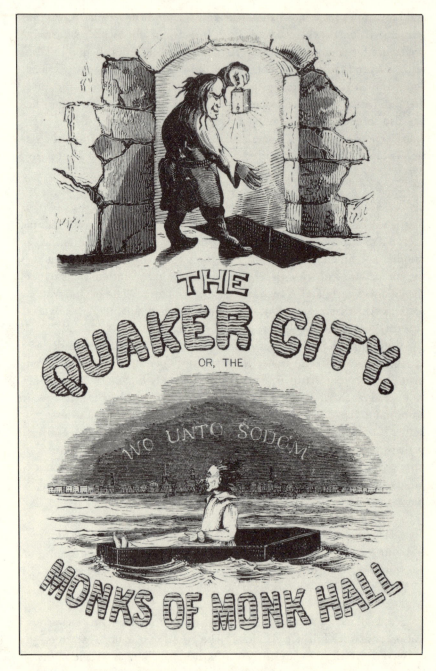

Illus. 4. Frontispiece featuring Devil-Bug, the arch personification of criminality, from an edition of *The Quaker City* (1876).

use touring the setting. They are bold markers in a stretching and extending crime-related plot. The novel's major elements pull together to produce a fascinatingly consistent popular fiction discourse.

What is the meaning of Lippard's *The Quaker City?* What did the work tell its readers? As noted in the preceding chapters of this work concerning the crime-related journalism of the nineteenth century, the designation of meaning is always difficult. Surely novels like journalistic accounts are "plural" and deliver different meanings to different readers. Still, knowing Lippard's readers were largely members of working and middle classes of the modernizing antebellum period,[104] the historical critic might at least suggest a dominant or most predictable meaning.

As the synchronized elements of the work suggest, the work has more to do with social process than precise articulation. Like the lurching, stalking Devil-Bug, who repeatedly says concerning one nefarious project or another, "I wonders how that 'ill work," *The Quaker City* asks how the new social environment functions. It answers, expansively and insistently, that modern life functions criminally. The rich and the sophisticated manipulate the poor and the naive. Society is unjust and deplorable.

Missing in this meaning is the "scientific" social criticism that Marx might have demanded and that, as noted earlier, he found lacking in Sue's works. Yet Lippard's *The Quaker City* is outraged and protesting. This should not be, the work insists time and again. Via Devil-Bug's lengthy nightmare at the end of the novel's third book, Lippard imagines an apocalyptic final judgment day for 1950 if society is not altered radically. With the Quaker City's "lordlings" installing a king, antiquarians collecting such quaint items as the liberty flag, and hordes of ghosts battling on the river in fleets of coffins, human civilization, if it deserves that name, will reach its sorry end.

After the initial furor over *The Quaker City* subsided, Lippard continued to blend literature and politics in a striking social praxis. The year 1849 was perhaps the most productive of his life. Lippard edited *Quaker City*, a journal featuring essays and articles on social issues, accounts of the exploitation of the poor, and the "Quaker City Police Court," a column in which one Justice Poe passed judgment on assorted writers and celebrities. Lippard also published five serial novels and founded the Brotherhood of the Union. Among the novels, *The Killers*,[105] an imaginative portrayal of gang warfare inspired by Philadelphia election riots, and *The Empire City*,[106] a fictive indictment of debauchery and crime among the New York elite, are perhaps the most notable. The Brotherhood of the Union, meanwhile, was, in Lippard's words, designed to "espouse the cause of the Masses, and battle against the tyrants of the Social System,—against corrupt Bankers, against Land Monopolists and against all Monied Oppressors."[107] A largely overlooked organization in American labor history, the Brotherhood grew rapidly during Lippard's life, consisted of hundreds of "circles," and prefigured the later Knights of Labor in its organization and goals.

Lippard lived until 1854, when he predicted the month and week of his death. A detailed examination of Lippard's later years must await another commentator, but in the chapter at hand Lippard's life and work stand as concluding embodiments, respectively, of the production and thrust of crime-related antebellum popular fiction.

Lippard, like Poe, Ingraham and Judson, was a cultural worker. All of these men worked in a fiction production milieu as precarious and unsettled as the modernizing social environment that surrounded it. They were victims and perpetrators of literary piracy, and they participated in and were buffeted by political agitation. Their work lives suggest not coherent careerism but rather a struggle for occupationalism and, in Lippard's case, a politicized social praxis. These lives resemble in social outlines the lives of many newspaper editors, writers and printers—men who also rode the dangerous roller coaster of antebellum cultural work. Yet working in uncertainty, the "imaginers," like many antebellum "reporters," tried in their work to understand the world in which they lived.

For Poe, Ingraham and Judson in partial ways and for Lippard in a more sustained sense, crime was central to cultural work. The writers employed crime as a cardinal motif, and they framed it aggressively and angrily. Crime told them where the limits of their social environment were and should be, and the writers imagined criminal frames offering pointed political meanings. Undoubtedly, many readers ignored or even rejected these meanings, but many, if only on an emotional or subliminal level, heard what Poe, Ingraham, Judson and Lippard imagined and said.

As the subsequent chapter of this work will suggest, writers of popular crime-related fiction came to know different work experiences as the century progressed. Popular crime-related fiction itself began to provide less pointed meanings, but prior to this transformation, the fiction of Poe, Ingraham, Judson and Lippard offered another alternative. Their work affords a critical perspective on crime that contrasts strongly with the perspective of much popular crime-related fiction from later in the century.

6.

Escapist Reinforcement:
The Detective and Crime Thriller Genres

During the final months before his death in 1854, George Lippard developed a paralyzing fear of the omnibus, a vehicle emblematic of social modernization.[1] Twenty-five years later, the publishers, editors and writers who produced popular crime-related fiction experienced no such phobia. Many rode the omnibus from their homes to their publishing concerns and offices and even to the taverns where they drained their cups with other professional cultural workers. More generally, the modern society struck them as familiar. They worked within a developed and stable fiction industry and also within more certain fictive genres. These contexts were comforting; in some cases they allowed publishers, editors and writers to achieve fame and fortune.

What impact did the new contexts and especially the new fictive frames for the criminal have on America's labeling and attributing of crime? What potential did the period's most popular crime-related fictional genres have for critical insight? No simple answers are possible. As noted at the outset of the previous chapter, fiction production and fiction conventions resist all-encompassing summaries. Yet the production processes and frames of detective fiction and the crime thriller deserve attention. Like the varieties of crime journalism that settled into place in the final decades of the nineteenth century, detective fiction and the crime thriller helped shape Americans' understanding of and reaction to crime.

The two genres can be distinguished from one another. Detective fiction, a genre produced and sold on at least three continents, offered puzzle-solving opportunities and tidy solutions that appealed especially to members of the middle class. Crime thrillers shared with detective fiction a forceful police or detective figure, but they also provided a distinctive crime story that schooled mostly working class readers in modern life. However, both genres afforded escape; both gave readers momentary, illusionary reprieves from their pressures and burdens. In providing this escape, both genres, in specialized ways, reinforced the new society.

In the thirty years since the first significant surge in fiction production, the American fiction industry had undergone what one influential scholar has called a "quantitative transformation."[2] By the 1870s, periodicals, publishing houses, editors, authors, readers and fictional works were all more numerous than ever before. Increasingly concentrated in New York and in larger publishing concerns,[3] both magazine and book publishing boasted additional and more distinct strata, more precise and permanent work relationships, and efficient systems of product development and distribution often geared to genres.

In periodical publishing, large fiction-dominated magazines were numerous. Inspired by the earlier successes of *Graham's Magazine,* similarly designed magazines such as *The Saturday Evening Post, Mirror* and *Harper's Monthly Magazine* expanded their in-house staffs, survived not months or years but decades, and attracted large middle- and upper-class readerships.[4] These periodicals, beginning in midcentury, were joined in the marketplace by the popular "story papers." Commonly an eight-page weekly including human interest news and miscellany, the story paper devoted most of its space to serialized fiction, normally carrying three or four installments per issue. Robert Bonner, the period's most successful publisher of story papers, watched the circulation of his *New York Ledger* grow from 110,000 in 1856 to almost 400,000 a decade later.[5] By way of contrast, a widely respected middle-class periodical such as *Harper's Monthly Magazine* claimed a circulation barely one-half as large.[6]

While periodical publishing thrived and differentiated into distinct sectors, book publishing experienced similar successes and changes. The more traditional publishing houses abandoned their earlier system of accepting payments from writers to publish books. Instead, the houses exercised more editorial discretion before buying publication rights. A sounder method of doing business, the new relationship between publishers and writers facilitated the growth of the largest houses.[7] At the same time, newer publishing concerns gained their share of the market. In some cases, these concerns republished as paper-covered novelettes the most successful serials from story papers, while in other cases they produced original works in the same inexpensive form. Beadle and Adams, a publishing venture that had started in Buffalo and then moved to New York, began marketing novelettes for ten cents and sold 2,500,000 copies of inexpensive fiction between 1860 and 1863.[8] While the publisher of a hard-covered novel might hope to sell 20,000 copies, Beadle and Adams routinely printed 60,000 copies of each title.[9] Occupying a middle stratum between the respected houses and the mass publishers were rapidly growing subscription houses, which relied on traveling agents to sell volumes priced between the expensive hardcovers and inexpensive softcovers.[10]

Hustling owners, some patrician and some nouveau, headed the various periodicals and publishing concerns, but even more striking were the relationships between the owners and their staffs and the increasingly specialized nature of the staff members' activities. Owners expected their editors not only to evaluate and shape works but also to convert them into a variety of marketable forms and condensations. Advertising specialists created flyers and billboards, which saturated the East and Old Midwest; they also launched expensive promotional campaigns involving complimentary chromos, sheet music and handbooks. Writers, particularly those working for the story papers and novelette publishers, perfected the practice of writing rapidly and predictably.[11] Comparable efforts had been requested and undertaken during the antebellum period, but in the Gilded Age the chains of command and work tasks became appreciably more certain and more developed.

In addition, the civil courts, particularly those in New York, stood ready to resolve any confusion concerning literary properties, work responsibilities and advertising ploys, and publishers and specialized workers turned frequently to these courts. Erastus Beadle was an especially active litigant. He asked the courts to enjoin his brother Irwin from using the Beadle name in a new publishing venture and also sought trademark protection for his "Dime Novel" products and symbols. When Irwin Beadle successfully defended against these actions, he gleefully included in an early issue of his "Ten Cent Novel" series the judge's full opinion.[12] In dozens of more prosaic rulings, free of sibling rivalries, the courts succeeded in further clarifying the ground rules for a mature American fiction industry.[13]

Genre was a crucially important aspect of the fiction industry for owners, workers and judges. The chief genres included the western, the sentimental romance, the adventure story, and the rags-to-riches fable.[14] Of this group, the western has attracted the most attention from scholars.[15] As these scholars have argued, the western genre suggests nineteenth-century American ambivalence concerning social progress and individual freedom. Yet if the western might with justification be characterized as an "objectified mass dream,"[16] it also exemplified recognizable commodity development. When Beadle and Adams sold 600,000 copies of Edward S. Ellis' *Seth Jones; or, The Captives of the Frontier,* the firm consolidated the western as a product line. Once a genre had been established and accepted in consumers' minds, publishers could and did refine its basic recipe and call on any number of professional writers to do the cooking.

Surveying the developing literary scene, Henry James was hardly delighted with what he observed. His distress was greatest when he remarked on the role genres had come to play for readers and writers of fiction. American readers, in his opinion, were "subdivided as a chessboard, with each little square confessing only its own kind of accessibility." Writers of fiction could not venture outside particular modes. The American writer, James felt, had to approach readers as "individual publics positively more sifted and evolved than anywhere else, schools of fish rising for more delicate bait."[17] Stated less metaphorically, the mature American fiction industry of the late nineteenth century, including highly specialized and industrious workers and assisted by the civil courts, had developed and was marketing strikingly standardized products. These generic products, although innovative when first developed, constricted both their producers and their readers as they came to control market shares.

One especially popular crime-related genre was detective fiction. Some American authors experimented with the genre during the Civil War years,[18] but during the 1860s and early 1870s the American fiction industry was more likely to republish and sell works of detective fiction by foreign authors. Emile Gaboriau, a master of the French *roman policier,* wrote a number of works that were in whole or in part detective fiction.[19] In England, Wilkie Collins published *The Woman in White, The Moonstone,* and a handful of shorter works employing detective fiction motifs,[20] and in the 1880s Fergus Hume and Conan Doyle followed closely on Collins' heels. Hume, today virtually forgotten, wrote *The Mystery of the Hansom Cab,* the biggest seller among all nineteenth-century detective novels, as well as dozens of other detective works.[21] Doyle of course published two dozen detective stories in the *Strand Magazine* and collected volumes,[22] stories that some scholars consider the most enduring detective fiction of the period.[23]

As suggested earlier, the original writers and readers of a body of fiction may not share the perceptions of genre that later critics develop. However, at least in the case of late nineteenth-century detective fiction, original readers and writers and subsequent critics are in agreement. All acknowledge that the writings of Gaboriau, Collins, Hume and Doyle were generic. French commentators and consumers recognized the *roman policier* in the 1860s, and newspapers of Collins' own time characterized his work as detective fiction.[24] By 1890 a review article even commented on detective fiction's various twists and degrees of popularity in different countries.[25] The writers themselves recognized one another, and they also looked to Poe as a forbear. Since Poe worked in a much less settled fiction industry, one in which genre had not been established, this recognition has an irony to it. Yet Gaboriau, who had read Baudelaire's lavish praise of Poe, determined at one point to write a Dupin series of his own,[26] and Doyle, speaking for other detective fiction writers as well as for himself, asked "Where was the detective story until Poe breathed the breath of life into it?"[27]

Among American writers of the late nineteenth century, Anna Katharine Green most successfully exploited the detective genre. Born in Brooklyn in 1846, Green was the daughter of a prosperous lawyer. After attending New York schools, she enrolled in Ripley College in Poultney, Vermont, where, like many other college students of the period, she became enamored of the work and persona of Ralph Waldo Emerson.[28] More energetic than most, Green in 1865 invited Emerson to Ripley, initiated him into a secret society, and took him on what he remembered in a later letter as "a pleasant drive to the quarries" in the vicinity of the College.[29] Following her graduation from Ripley, Green became a part of New York and Washington society before marrying the actor and furniture designer Charles Rohlfs and relocating to Buffalo.

Green attempted at several points in her life to write genteel literature, but one volume of maudlin poetry and a play in verse about Italian nobility shows that her ambitions outdistanced her poetic abilities.[30] However, in 1878 Green attracted attention with a detective novel, and during the remainder of her career, she wrote almost forty novels and collections of short stories, almost all of which were detective fiction.[31] Her most popular work, *The Leavenworth Case,* appeared initially as a 475–page volume in hard cover. As such, it was more substantial and hinted of more seriousness than the period's many shorter, paper-covered volumes. At the same time, it did not approach in length or physical impressiveness the expensively bound two or three-volume novels of the period. Initial reviewers seemed almost to use the work's physical characteristics as a key. In their minds, *The Leavenworth Case* was respectable but not distinguished; it deserved praise for its achievement within a particular tier of American fiction.[32] Reviews notwithstanding, the work was republished in at least ten different editions during the 1880s and 1890s.[33]

Presumably *The Leavenworth Case* found readers in all social classes, but sketchy information suggests that most readers came from the middle and upper middle classes. The reviews of the novel, the most influential notice of its publication, were concentrated in journals purchased and read by these classes. The novel's original and subsequent editions sold for between fifty cents and one dollar, an amount within the reach of leisured classes but in large part beyond that of family farmers or urban laborers, who tended to spend their limited disposable income on mass story papers and paperbacks that sold for a dime or less.

Opening the cover of *The Leavenworth Case,* the Gilded Age clerk, professional or housewife found fiction set in Gilded Age New York. More particularly, the majority of scenes take place in the well-upholstered home of Mr. Leavenworth, a widowed and retired merchant. His murder, via a bullet to the brain, convulses Leavenworth's two adopted nieces, Mary and Eleanor, and also his loyal Irish servants. The methodical and controlled life of the Leavenworth home, at least prior to the murder, had contrasted with the outside world of busy streets, impoverished urchins and mysterious fires. As a result of the murder, this public America seems almost to pour into the private sanctuary.

In domesticating the novel's setting, in utilizing a bourgeois American home, *The Leavenworth Case* coincides with what several commentators insist is a requirement in modern detective fiction. Namely, the setting must be easily accessible and assimilable. It should not distract the reader from the assembly of clues or from logical deductions.[34] Poe, in this sense, is an anomaly in choosing an eerie, foreign Paris, alive with both state politics and working women. *The Leavenworth Case* more clearly approaches what later commentators would consider a normal setting.

Narration of *The Leavenworth Case* is in the hands of Everett Raymond, a man well suited to address the Gilded Age's middle class. The junior partner in the law firm of Viely, Carr and Raymond, the narrator is summoned to Leavenworth's study, the scene of the murder, only because his senior partner, Leavenworth's long-time counsel, is absent from the city. Raymond's agitation at first matches the agitation of Leavenworth's family and servants. Raymond compares his confused reaction to the crime to "an enforced use of ether,"[35] but he revives and skillfully describes the murder scene and recounts the subsequent detection. Stiff for the twentieth-century reader, Raymond was for Gilded Age middle-class readers a tasteful and effective narrator. His observations and thoughts constitute the readers' primary perspective on the fictional events of the novel. Like them, he knows the stabilizing social order.

At the same time Raymond is not merely an inactive narrator recounting crime and its detection. Later in the novel Raymond intelligently reassembles the fragments of a discarded letter. He conducts excellent undercover work in the rural town of R——. Raymond is a detecting agent, heroic and recuperative. Raymond is a young professional who can act.

The chief detective in the novel, meanwhile, is Ebenezer Gryce. Employed by the New York Police Department, Gryce is portly and rumpled. He seems at first the Prefect G—— come to Gotham. But unlike the bumptious G——, Gryce is admirable and competent. His sharp eye "never pounced . . . did not even rest on you."[36] By finding burned letter fragments, a missing key, and a dropped handkerchief, Gryce early in *The Leavenworth Case* wins both Raymond's and the reader's confidence.

Skillful neophyte and experienced operative, Raymond and Gryce constitute an effective team. Neither is alienated; neither disdains the modernizing world. More significantly, Green's detecting team represents an emergent social hegemony. The industrious Raymond is a member of a prospering profession. Gryce is himself a police officer. Rather than noting the failures of social leaders and public officials, as do the narrator and Dupin in Poe's stories, Raymond and Gryce work within and for the status quo. They are indomitable agents of social order.

Initially, the detective team suspects Mary, then Eleanor Leavenworth, but Raymond in particular is hesitant to believe a woman could commit such a crime. Eleanor, after all, places an affectionate kiss on the corpse's cold lips. Eventually detection turns in other directions. The detective team finds the corpse of another murder victim, the Leavenworth servant girl Hannah, who disappeared shortly after the original murder. The team locates other clues and conducts handwriting analyses. Ultimately, Raymond and Gryce discover that Trueman Harwell, Leavenworth's private secretary, committed the heinous crime.

How tidy the successful detection proves. Gryce summarizes the clues and deductions that led him to Harwell, an explanation motif that had become standard in detective fiction. No evidence is left out of place. No questions remain unanswered. Indeed, the murderer Harwell himself takes the literary stage for twenty-five pages to detail his crime. Harwell had loved Mary Leavenworth. He hoped the murder would facilitate a liaison.

Like all cultural work, *The Leavenworth Case* offers political suggestions. Harwell, after all, had functioned in a demeaning occupational hierarchy with nonreciprocal modes of address: Leavenworth called him "Trueman," while he deferred always to "Mr. Leavenworth." Harwell's romantic hopes were made mere fantasies by the structures of social class. However, to stress these political feints would be to misstate Green's overall alignment. *The Leavenworth Case* is unsympathetic to Harwell. No justification is offered for his act. His plight does not prompt thoughts of social injustice. As a destroyer of domestic peace, Harwell is an individual who deserves detection and punishment. Reduced late in the novel to sniveling and writhing before his pursuers, Harwell experiences a severe degradation ritual. The story and the fictive society righteously label him a criminal.

Green's *The Leavenworth Case* cannot, of course, be made to stand for all late nineteenth-century detective fiction. Doyle's stories from the period, for example, betray an alienation from modern society quite reminiscent of Poe's earlier stories. Yet Green's best-selling novel does suggest the mainstream of detective fiction, a genre that at least one scholar has cast as the most recognizable literary "child of capitalism."[37] The genre invites readers to engage in delightful puzzle-solving, promising them that in the end tidy solutions will be forthcoming. Concomitantly, detective fiction deplores violations of the private sphere and the more general bourgeois order. Criminals in the end are concretely identifiable and conveniently nefarious, and as a result, detective fiction invites not new or critical insights regarding crime but rather confidence that the criminal menace can be confronted and controlled. Despite its immense popularity, the detective fiction genre has a "false bottom,"[38] one that impedes an understanding of the complex causes and varieties of crime and also obscures possible responses to it.

While Gilded Age clerks, professionals and housewives delighted in the most recent detective novel by Anna Katharine Green, working-class Americans also acquired specialized preferences in literature. Particularly noteworthy in the context of the present study was their fondness for the crime thriller. Found mostly in story papers and inexpensively covered novelettes, the crime thriller was, like detective fiction, a distinct genre.

The genre's original promoter was George Munro, a Nova Scotian who had worked as a clerk in the firm of Beadle and Adams. In 1863 Munro arranged the capital funding necessary to launch his own publishing venture, and by the 1870s George Munro & Co. had grown into one of the largest mass fiction publishers in the country. Munro published eight-page, illustrated story papers containing three or four serial installments per issue, and several series of magazine-sized novelettes. A key to the commercial success of the Munro products was the crime thriller which, in the 1870s, Munro managed not only to develop but also at least temporarily to monopolize.

The most noticeable feature of the Munro crime thrillers was Old Sleuth. Munro first marketed Old Sleuth in 1872 when he published a serial titled "Old Sleuth, the Detective; or, the Bay Ridge Mystery" in his *New York Fireside Companion* story paper. The serial was purportedly the work of Tony Pastor, a well-known Gilded Age vaudeville performer whose name Munro used as a marketing device in dozens of publications. In fact, the actual writer of the first Old Sleuth story was Harlan P. Halsey, one of the more prolific professional writers in the Munro stable. Old Sleuth himself was initially just a detective character, but when the character became popular, Munro made him into an author as well. In hundreds of publications he ostensibly recounted both his own cases and those of other fictional detectives and policemen. True authorship blended into one fiction after another, but Munro remained certain of one thing: The name and image of Old Sleuth could sell a range of literary commodities.

No complete treatment of Old Sleuth has as yet appeared, but those few scholars who have noted Old Sleuth in passing seem inclined to treat him not as a complicated literary property but rather as simply a detective.[39] The features of the noble operative most certainly prompt such a treatment. After at first appearing as a handsome young man unblushingly named Harry Loveland who wins the heart of a fair damsel, Old Sleuth aged rapidly to become a distinguished senior New York private eye. In this latter incarnation he brandishes not only guns and knives but also a card reading "Sleuth, Detective." The mere presence of the "human sleuth-hound" can cause villains to faint in their tracks. Even after settling into semiretirement in the 1880s, Old Sleuth "possessed that rare quality called magnetism—personal magnetism—a quality which gives the possessor great persuasive power over those with whom he may come into contact."[40]

The power of Old Sleuth, in fact, persuaded George Munro to fashion dozens of other characters in the same mold. Masters of intrigue and foreign languages, these characters manipulate newspapers, law enforcement officials and underworld connections. Most interestingly, a good number are older men or at least younger men who specialize in disguising themselves as graybeards and codgers, to wit: Old Terrible, Old Electricity, Old Ironsides, Old Transform, Old Phenomenal, and Old Baldy, the Weird Detective. Not surprisingly given their advanced ages, these crime-stoppers subscribe to an older moral code, drinking wine only as medicine and observing rigid puritanical ways. Their rock-ribbed morality seems to justify their proclivity not only to bash a half-dozen villains at once but also to turn somersaults on their chests and occasionally rub butter, milk and coffee dregs into their faces.

Recognizing the commercial appeal of George Munro's Old Sleuth stories, other mass fiction publishers hurried to market similar tales. Beadle and Adams, the leading marketer of westerns, began selling crime thrillers in large numbers in the early 1880s, issuing fourteen titles in 1883 alone.[41] The firms's line featured Broadway Billy, but he failed to entice away many Old Sleuth fans. More successful was the host of distinctly senior operatives who appeared on the expanding fiction market. They included Old Thunderbolt, Old Kit, Old Tabaret, Old Hawkeye, Old Cap. Ruggles, Old 16, Old Gold Eye, Old Broadrim, Old Man Martin, Old Avalanche, Old Dynamite, and Old Sledge, to name only a dozen.

Most successful at mining the lucrative vein that George Munro had struck was his own brother Norman. With the assistance of writer W. I. James, Norman Munro developed a detective and supposed author named Old Cap. Collier for his *Family Story Paper.* Old Cap. of course strongly resembled Old Sleuth, although unlike the latter, Old Cap., thanks to the freedom of fictional rendering, frequently worked on actual Gilded Age cases. In one story Old Cap. pursued the men who stole prominent New York merchant Alexander Stewart's skeleton from the elite St. Mark's cemetery, an 1878 crime that greatly fascinated the public.[42] This process of deriving fictive works from actual cases is reminiscent of Edgar Allan Poe's work in "The Mystery of Marie Rogêt" and also of George Lippard's work in *The Quaker City.* Yet while Poe and, to a lesser extent, Lippard remained generally faithful to actual incidents, Norman Munro's Old Cap. crime thrillers employed the actual cases only as marketing hooks to fascinate and attract consumers. The thrillers themselves wandered far and wide from the actual cases and concluded in ways that coincided with generic conventions rather than with factual developments.

Not only links to real cases but also violence distinguishes the Old Cap. stories. Like Old Sleuth, Old Cap. can hurl 250–lb bullies through the air or smash their heads together "with a rap that sounded like two empty cocoanuts,"[43] but the violence of the stories also exceeds this highly stylized brawling, particularly in the stories' conclusions. In *Old Cap. Collier; or, "Piping" the New Haven Mystery,* the villainous Mr. Hicks, caught once and for all in his evil ways, blows out his brains with a revolver. His bedridden mother witnesses the scene and springs up in horror:

> The effect was too much for her. The blood gushed from her mouth and there was a gurgling sound, and she fell back in the bed. Mother and son were dead. [44]

Realizing Beadle and Adams, his brother, and other mass fiction publishers were making inroads on the commercially successful genre he had developed, George Munro, like other fiction publishers before him, turned to the New York courts for assistance. In 1888 he asked the courts to enjoin several mass fiction publishers from using the word "sleuth" in their titles and on their covers, a petition complicated by the fact that Harlan P. Halsey, the originator of Old Sleuth, was himself working for one of the respondents in the case. Munro failed before a special session of the New York Supreme Court, but on appeal in 1890 he was victorious.[45] In his opinion Judge Macomber carefully reviewed the etymology of the word "sleuth," noting the Scottish or Icelandic "sloth," which meant track, and also the absence of "sleuth" in standard American dictionaries of the 1870s. George Munro, Macomber concluded, had plucked an obscure word from the fringes of American usage and given it a special fanciful meaning; Munro deserved trademark protection. As a result of the ruling, such Beadle and Adams titles as "Crowningshield, the Sleuth" and "Deep Duke, the Silent Sleuth" became "Crowningshield, the Detective" and "Deep Duke, the Silent Sharp."[46]

Despite his legal victory, George Munro failed to stem the tide of other publishers' fiction. In addition to exploiting the basic genre, publishers attempted to vitalize their chief characters and thereby gain a marketing edge. Publishers developed unlikely specialists such as Diamond Dan, the Brooklyn Divorce Detective, and Jack and Gil Alvarez, the seventeen-year-old orphan twins of a Yankee mother and Spanish circus acrobat.[47] Dart, the Self-Made Detective, embodied a popular theme, and lady detectives who disguised themselves as diminutive Frenchmen and propelled mechanical stilettos from their cuffs also entered the field.[48] Even ethnic detectives, mostly of Irish descent, showed that they too could internalize puritanical values and perform heroically.[49]

Overall, the growth and commercial success of crime thrillers involving vigorous crime-stopping characters shows how intertextuality might be not just an aspect of reading experience but also a production and marketing concern for the mass fiction publisher.[50] Old Cap. and countless other crime-stoppers derived marketability from the initial success of Old Sleuth. Conversely, the marketing and legal defense of Old Sleuth referred to other fictional products. In addition, crime thrillers related in part to the middle class detective fiction. In a sense, the mass fiction detectives and policemen were poor cousins, residing on the other side of the tracks from Sherlock Holmes and Ebenezer Gryce. Fictive commodities were linked not only horizontally in a particular sector of the market but also more obliquely to additional markets peopled by consumers of other classes.

Indeed, this web of cultural products was not exclusively fictional. As noted, crime thrillers drew from crimes reported in the daily newspapers; publishers of the Old Cap. stories in particular put their operative to work on real-life cases. Publishers also modeled operatives on nineteenth-century figures such as Eugène Vidocq and Allan Pinkerton. The latter, meanwhile, was in part moved to write his memoirs because of the popular success of the earliest Old Sleuth tales.[51] The popular success of the Pinkerton memoirs in turn encouraged mass fiction publishers to flood the market with additional fictionalized tales of Pinkerton assistants and children.[52] Crime imagining derived in part from crime reporting and remembering, and it also helped inspire both.

Against this intriguing backdrop of crime-related cultural work, the sale of crime thrillers continued. The genre was an immense commercial success, and as the century entered its final decade, the crime thriller rivaled the western as the nation's most popular mass fiction genre. Although related to the international tradition of detective mysteries, the crime thriller of the American Gilded Age with its distinctive senior operatives was also a specialized product of a particular moment in the nation's social and cultural history.

While the strong, senior operative is fundamental to the Gilded Age crime thriller, crime in the genre is much more than a simple foil for the detective. Late nineteenth-century crime thrillers presented crime in a highly subjective fashion. The collective presentation constitutes a story, and at that only one of many prototypical crime stories that could have been told. A careful exploration of the story's components reveals the normative aspects of the period's crime thriller genre.

The Gilded Age crime thriller divides criminals into two types, a simple imaginative scheme that sets the stage for the standard crime-related story of the genre. One criminal type includes the most predictable of villains, men and a few women who are a "breed," "monsters," or, from the crime-stoppers' perspective, "the game." Like Justus Rinehardt in *Old Puritan, the Old-Time Yankee Detective*,[53] these villains might have foreign blood and a concomitantly corrupt nature. They might from time to time strike the narrator as "professional" criminals. However, we in fact learn very little of these villains' pasts or reasons for leading lives of crime. With sardonic grins and glittering black eyes, they drink, gamble, plague unsuspecting damsels, and perpetrate a truly staggering array of crimes. These criminals are plotting mechanisms, standing perhaps for an evilness endemic to the new society, but they are hardly full literary characters.

The second type of criminal is more complicated and has enough depth to be thought of as a character. As was the case with George Munro, Erastus Beadle, and countless other Gilded Age Americans, this second type of criminal was born in a rural setting and then moved to the burgeoning city. Commonly an orphan, a foundling, or at least the son or daughter of a widow, this ill-fated individual may carry a Bible, memento, or set of principles from an earlier life. However, despite these armaments, he or she stands naked before the harsh winds of the new society.

Shortly after arriving in the metropolis, these individuals prove vulnerable:

> Say they take a drink, and indulge the passion, commit a little crime—pilfer a small sum from the cashdrawer. . . . With the women, love of dress leads them to the first false step, and so it goes.[54]

Jack Gameway, for example, is a nineteen-year-old orphan from Iowa who comes to New York. Following some initial success eluding "sharpers" and "city skin chaps," he is arrested for theft after helping a stranger move a trunk out of a private residence.[55] Henry Wilbur grew up with his widowed mother in a modest cottage on the outskirts of Brooklyn but takes up work in a Manhattan banking house. He becomes addicted to gambling, and, in order to cover growing debts, begins embezzling from his employer.[56] Alice Cromwell, an orphan who had been raised by a great aunt in Northampton, leaves western Massachusetts for New York. Once in the city, she joins up with a greedy gang of villains.[57] In hundreds of stories vulnerable men and women become involved in specific individual crimes as well as in larger milieux rife with crime.

The convention of waifs stumbling into criminal contacts and confidence games was also a part of more serious and diversified nineteenth-century literature,[58] but in the crime thrillers the vulnerable men and women are always saved. A detective such as Old Sleuth is present to deal with the hardened criminals. Both the detective and the reader generally learn the identity of the true villains early in the story, and as a result the detective need rarely assemble clues as does the detective in middle-class detective fiction. Instead, the detective devotes his energy to weaving "threads" around the first type of criminal, to forging "links to a chain."[59] In the end the unequivocally villainous criminals from the first category receive lengthy prison terms, are murdered, or, in the case of those with foreign blood, deservedly banished from American shores.

Criminals falling into the second category, meanwhile, are placed on the road to social legitimacy. This process frequently involves circumvention of law enforcement officials and the formal criminal justice system, as in the case of Arthur Balfour who, although guilty of burglary, is illegally sprung from the Tombs by a detective. The beneficiaries of this social redemption seem certain to reform their ways. In Balfour's words, "I once determined to be a criminal against all perils; the same determination will aid me to become an honest man—no, I have done with criminal life forever."[60]

More profoundly, the codas also include the reclamation of premodern values and social arrangements. Suddenly blessed with large inheritances or wealthy benefactors, worthy criminals are free to lead lives untarnished by the corrupt ways of the modern city. Often they begin building new families by marrying other orphans or foundlings. Women leave the work world, and men and women begin lives of countrified gentility by returning to rural wonderlands. Are these fortunate souls happy with what has transpired? In a half dozen cases they drop to the floor before the senior detective in abject thankfulness. "Oh, sir," says Mary Penham showing a sensitivity to literary form as she kneels before Old Sleuth, "this is like a romance."[61]

Like components of other mass fiction genres, the genre's crime story corresponded to certain needs and anxieties among its readers. This is not to argue, as did Merle Curti in an important article, that nineteenth-century mass fiction was a type of "proletarian literature," that is, a literature created by the working-class populace.[62] Sophisticated entrepreneurs and cultural workers produced and marketed the stories with an eye to profit. However, George Munro and his imitators were acutely sensitive to what would sell. They tailored their works accordingly, and only in this *indirect*, administered sense was the crime story an indicator of Gilded Age preferences.

One example of the way crime thriller publishers and writers sold what their readers would buy involves the escapist character of the genre. While middle class readers of *The Leavenworth Case* and other detective novels could escape into the pleasures of problem solving, working class readers of the crime thriller could escape in another way. In the crime thriller story, the average reader found a dozen literal escapes from secret dungeons, torture chambers, cemetery vaults and even the dreaded Tombs. Although each escape except the last was followed by another imprisonment in the next chapter or installment, each escape in and of itself was dramatic, suspenseful and successful. At the end of a crime thriller a lasting and complete liberation took place. As previously noted, the worthy criminals, that is, the orphans and foundlings with whom the readers identified, were sprung from the working world of modern society. Free to travel backward in time, they reached a fantasy utopia of wealth, country ways, cohesive families and traditional gender roles.

In addition and concomitantly, the manufactured crime thrillers were instructive. Readers could garner from the tales information regarding the new way of life. Interwoven in a work of fiction, this information was sometimes skewed, but to remind readers that the stories had informational content, editors sometimes provided footnotes declaring that a statement was indeed "*A fact."[63] For the American confronting the modern city, it was valuable to know how to open a bank account, secure an inexpensive room, shop in a ready-made clothing store and raise a citified mustache. For others, content to remain on the farm but curious about the new society, it was fascinating to peek at banking houses and masked balls, at gambling dens and Fifth Avenue mansions.

It was in fact the crime story within the genre that conveyed information in a particularly effective way. As they traveled with any number of orphans and foundlings through the Gilded Age city, readers could not only learn of city ways but also vicariously experience them. When fictional neophytes fell victim to unequivocal villains, when they failed to navigate the new society's channels of legitimacy and illegitimacy, readers could recognize ways they in the same situations might have better preserved reputations and nest eggs. As was the case with instruction provided more straightforwardly, writers and editors hastened to alert readers to the instructive potential of the crime story. After all, Jack Gameway, himself a faithful reader of story papers during his Iowa youth, "had become well posted in all the schemes of city swindlers, so that he was prepared to 'smell around before he fingered for the bait,' as he expressed it."[64]

The impact of the crime thrillers on their readers did not amount to a full and successful brainwashing. The cultural workers who produced the genre were not engaged in a political conspiracy, and indeed, even had they been inclined to execute a conscious political program, the period's other available cultural experiences precluded control of the readers' consciousness. The readers, meanwhile, even though enthralled by the story and the whole genre, realized the works were not reality. They recognized the tales as fiction for a price, and depending on their individual characteristics and preferences, readers might even have used the stories to mount a social critique.

Yet the possibility of a crime thriller–generated social critique notwithstanding, the prototypical crime story of Gilded Age crime thrillers in general supported the stabilizing social system. The crime story afforded escape from the new society, both in the titillating episodes that made up the genre's narrative spine and in the virtually codified concluding fantasies. Simultaneously, the crime story introduced its readers to the new society; the story taught modern life. The crime story was a nostalgic, socially unreal way out of the modern society and also a collection of lessons in its norms and attitudes. Crime thriller publishers, editors and writers provided readers the opportunity, literally, to buy into modern America.

As the century drew to a close, the fiction industry continued to develop and market detective novels and crime thrillers. To be sure, these genres were not the only available varieties of crime-related fiction. Samuel Clemens, to cite one example of an individualistic popular writer, published a half-dozen works with provocative crime-related themes,[65] and a group of journalists turned literary naturalists creatively plumbed the meaning of crime in the urban setting.[66] Yet for every Clemens, there were dozens of cultural workers who worked within the period's most popular genres. For every work of naturalist fiction, there were hundreds of detective novels and crime thrillers.

Developments in the two core genres carry this chapter not only into the twentieth century but also to its conclusion. In the case of detective fiction, Anna Katharine Green continued at the turn of the century to be America's most successful and representative writer of detective fiction. Her settings, as was true in *The Leavenworth Case,* remained for the most part private and domestic. If sacrosanct, the private family sanctuary was also sometimes uniform. In *The Doctor, His Wife and The Clock,* an 1895 novel, a blind murderer mistakes a neighbor's home for his own adjacent and architecturally identical Lafayette Place townhouse.[67] Green's narratives, meanwhile, rarely involved introspective questioning. Henry Raymond of *The Leavenworth Case* was at least a sometimes uncertain detective, but in Green's subsequent novels Ebenezer Gryce is more commonly the narrator. He ages to the point where his sharp detective's eyesight begins to fail.[68] In one of Green's final novels he is an octogenarian who arrives at the scene of a crime in an automobile.[69] Most importantly, however, he is never an outsider to law enforcement. His narrator's perspective is neither distant nor critical. The reader who sees a fictive world through Gryce's failing eyes sees that world from the perspective of a professional detective.

In *The Leavenworth Case* Gryce's only professional assistant is the curious Q—, a minor operative who can expertly disguise himself as a woman, but in later stories Gryce works with a growing bevy of specialists: ballistics experts, police psychologists, eager beginning operatives, and shady figures skilled at underworld dirty work. Added together, Gryce and his assistants come to resemble the growing detective bureaus of late nineteenth-century police departments or perhaps the Pinkerton National Detective Agency, the subject of a subsequent chapter in this work.

In addition, Green sometimes places specialized female operatives into the fictive detective's role. They include the genteel Miss Amelia Butterworth and also Violet Strange and Rita Van Arsdale.[70] A resident of Gramercy Park and a spinster, Miss Butterworth fears dogs, banters with Gryce, and is always acutely sensitive to the standards of the private domestic sphere and also devoted to preserving them. In one novel her knowledge of stylistic changes in bonnet strings provides a breakthrough in a difficult case.[71] Less intriguing than Miss Butterworth, Strange and Van Arsdale seem attenuated versions of the Butterworth character.

Green, the only American woman among the major writers of nineteenth-century detective fiction, must be credited with helping to initiate the string of female detectives that subsequently stretches from Jane Marple to Kate Fansler. Yet at the same time her female operatives do not bring critical alignment to detective work or to detective fiction. They are products of the Victorian private sphere, itself a variety of social encirclement, and they work to restore and perpetuate the decorum of that sphere. Frequently, Green's female detectives work as assistants to male operatives. Like Gryce, they are agents of the status quo.[72]

In a number of ways Green's crime fiction resembles the crime reports in the period's daily newspapers. Most obviously, both varieties of cultural work are imbued with a detective's élan. Green fuels the vicarious detection by including fictional tidbits resembling the reportorial tidbits from the newspapers: maps of the scene, coroners' reports and facsimiles of written documents. Green's novels provide a wide range of crimes, but as was the case with the yellow newspapers, the novels emphasize crimes involving personal violence. A product of neither a swirling public world nor state politics, the core crimes in Green's novels are murders in the private sphere.

In the crime thriller area, story papers in their traditional format disappeared from the market, but mass publishing firms expanded their production of quarto-sized novelettes. Individual titles in these "libraries" were roughly 16,000 words in length, only half the length of the earliest

Old Sleuth stories. Issued on a regular basis, the libraries sold primarily from newsstands, and their gaudy covers, after 1896 in three-color, helped catch the eye of the newsstand shopper.[73]

Both Old Sleuth and Old Cap. Collier still pursued criminals during the 1890s, but the most popular turn-of-the-century crime-stopper was Nick Carter. Although a number of professional "hacks" wrote Nick Carter stories, the originator was John Russell Coryell. The son of a shipbuilder who had worked for the Chinese government, Coryell learned to write as a California journalist. According to a loving memoir by his son, Coryell was the prototypical mass fiction writer.[74] Under contract to the publishing firm of Street & Smith, Coryell wrote 20,000 words of fiction per week. Customarily, he conceived the climax of a Nick Carter story first and then worked his way, situation by situation, backward to the beginning. His characters did not in a creative sense generate their adventures but rather, under Coryell's guidance, accommodated themselves to what they found. On one occasion when Coryell wandered away from the Nick Carter formula, his irritated Street & Smith editor asked, "My God, Coryell, can't you curb that damned imagination of yours?"[75]

The original Nick Carter character was the son of Sim Carter, himself an extraordinary detective who had trained Nick in the family calling. Like his fictional father and the fictional senior detectives who had preceded him, Nick disdained cigarettes, liquor and profane language, but, in both a literal and figurative sense, Nick as a second-generation detective was inclined to chart his own course. While Old Sleuth and Old Cap. Collier worked as senior New York operatives, Carter was a young man, dashing and bold. He performed his heroic deeds everywhere from Gotham, where he was vaguely affiliated with Thomas Byrnes' detective bureau, to the wild west and dozens of foreign lands. Carter is an attenuation of the distinctive mass fiction detective of the Gilded Age, much as the cowboy character of the 1890s is an attenuation of the more complicated western hero of earlier years.[76]

As the crime-stopper character attenuated in the 1890s, the unique Gilded Age crime story that had distinguished the Old Sleuth and Old Cap. Collier product lines also began to disappear. If a man from the country appeared at all, he was more likely to be a cliched hayseed prone to such expressions as "crickety junebugs" than a lonely soul vulnerable to urban crime.[77] Criminals in the Nick Carter stories perpetrate their evil deeds in a variety of urban, rural and nautical settings and rarely manifest more than one-dimensional badness. In the convoluted and often surprising endings of the stories, these criminals rarely deserve or receive redemption.

Both the later detective fiction of Anna Katharine Green and the evolution of the Nick Carter tale deserve attention from scholars of twentieth-century mass culture,[78] but for present purposes the two bodies of crime-related fiction are concluding indicators of what happened to crime-related popular fiction in nineteenth-century America. As was the case with urban crime reports in daily newspapers, crime-related fiction set in the urban surround first achieved prominence and wide distribution during the antebellum period. Questioning and politicized, the crime fiction of Poe, Lippard and others invited readers to reflect critically on crime in a period of rapid modernization. However, by the end of the century crime-related fiction had grown more generic and specialized. While crime reporting became encased in large daily newspaper operations and, more specifically, in the bourgeois and mass newspapers, crime imagining became part of a sophisticated fiction industry and evolved into detective fiction and the crime thriller. The two genres attracted, respectively, middle-class and working-class readerships, much as the bourgeois and mass newspapers did. Meanings remained plural. Crime imagining had not become merely propaganda, but in providing readers puzzles with tidy solutions and informative escape, detective fiction and the crime thriller framed the criminal in noncritical ways. In the late nineteenth century crime imagining not only reflected but also helped reinforce a normative social order.

III.

REMEMBERING CRIME

7.

From Memoir to Ideology:
Gilded Age Police Writings

In the late nineteenth century Lincoln Steffens was a young journalist assigned to police headquarters by the *New York Evening Post*. He one day found himself and other journalists listening to Thomas Byrnes, the head of the Detective Bureau, recall assorted criminal capers and investigations. Somehow these recollections, this "remembered crime," struck Steffens as familiar. Steffens then realized that Byrnes was combining and embellishing his recollections with material from assorted detective stories and crime thrillers, works of fiction that Steffens had himself read.[1] A crime rememberer was relying on crime imaginers and simultaneously inviting a group of journalists to use his fiction-inspired rememberings in their crime reporting.

Steffens' experience with Byrnes, of course, was only an isolated episode, but in more extended ways as well American crime remembering of the nineteenth century intersected with the period's crime reporting and imagining. The chief rememberers of crime were police, detectives and criminals, and their memoirs, histories and miscellaneous works are the subjects of this chapter and the two that follow. Although these works were less numerous and less widely read than works of nineteenth-century crime journalism and fiction, they illustrate as clearly the loss of critical perspective in nineteenth-century criminal portraiture. The works appeared primarily in the final decades of the century, and even though a handful assumed critical stances, the great majority and the most popular of the works were supportive of the modern social order.

Contemplators of antebellum urban life might have been surprised to learn that American policemen and police departments of later years had the composure to generate memoirs and police histories. In the midst of antebellum modernization traditional approaches to policing, approaches that had worked well in smaller communities with common values, seemed woefully inadequate. Part-time and unsalaried day and night watchmen, Sunday officers, procession officials, constables and aldermen competed for fees and rewards. However, they failed to rein violent individuals, riotous mobs and roving gangs or, more generally, to suppress the behavior that dominant groups considered criminal. Modernization had begun abruptly, and those charged with preserving social order were unequal to their suddenly expanded task.[2]

The larger European cities had faced comparable social complications several decades earlier, and Americans looked to the histories of those cities for solutions to their own problems. One possibility was the private police force, and inspired by a similar step in several European cities, wealthy American families and merchants hired policemen to patrol downtowns.[3] Even more encouraging was the successful organization in London, Liverpool and elsewhere of uniformed metropolitan police forces. By the 1840s influential American patricians and ministers as well as business leaders became convinced this new approach to policing could be profitably adopted in the United States. New York City acted first; in 1845 it organized the nation's first modern police force. Boston and Philadelphia established forces in 1854, and Baltimore followed suit in 1856. By the early 1860s the police movement had swept most American cities. Each of the new forces had salaried officers and patrolmen, citywide authority, and a hierarchical and bureaucratic structure. Chiefs of police—men newly appointed to positions that were in themselves new—promised to provide social decorum. In keeping with the so-called "London model," their forces would not only respond to crime but also through a robust, strapping presence actually prevent it.[4]

As the next twenty years would illustrate, the mere adoption of the London police model would not in itself solve all the problems. The patrolman on the beat and the captain in the station house received the difficult assignment of carrying theories of policing into action, and uncertain, sometimes disastrous practices resulted.[5] Police used dragnets and shocking brutality to sweep up those deemed likely to commit crimes, and as the first major providers of municipal services, they tackled everything from housing transients to inspecting fat-boiling establishments. Troubled by these developments, city fathers and the leaders of state legislatures, which wrote city charters, sought ways to supervise police departments, but here too steadiness proved elusive.[6] In New York in 1857, for example, the state legislature replaced the city's police with a state-supervised police department, but Mayor Fernando Wood refused to disband the municipal department. With state and local officials disputing fundamental responsibility for local affairs, New York's rival forces literally battled for possession of station houses.

Indeed, well after the formal establishment of American police departments average citizens as well as city fathers were profoundly perplexed by the new institution. As Allan Silver has argued in his influential essay concerning the novelty of nineteenth-century police departments, organized police stood for much more than a response to crime. The police "represented the penetration and continual presence of central political authority throughout daily life."[7] Except in certain areas occupied by British troops during the Revolutionary War and the War of 1812, such a presence was unprecedented in American life. Some Americans looked upon the establishment of police departments not only as a necessary reaction to urban, industrial life but also as an ominous commitment to a new, perhaps undesirable type of society.

Only in the years immediately following the Civil War did the police attain operational and administrative maturity. Mugwumps of the period would have been loath to admit it, but police forces steadied their identities largely through a conscious integration with urban politics. By the 1870s all major cities other than Philadelphia had boards of police commissioners ostensibly supervising the local departments, but the boards and the police forces themselves were usually parts of the systems of ethnic give-and-take called machines. Hardly as mechanized as their generic name suggests, machines were too loosely organized and vulnerable to intramural disagreement to exercise complete control over day-to-day police operations. However, the machines did provide matrices of institutions and procedural norms within which police departments could develop. Local variations remained, but from roughly 1870 until the progressive reforms at the end of the century, a thirty-year period that historians treat as a distinct stage in American police history, police departments were stable institutions.[8]

This period was in a sense launched in October of 1871 when policemen from twenty-two states congregated in St. Louis for the nation's first police convention. Bursting with self-assurance and seriousness of purpose, the delegates smoked cigars in the Southern Hotel lobby and inspected the harbor aboard the steamboat *Commonwealth*. At the convention's work sessions the delegates debated their host city's experiments in the legalization of prostitution or, as the delegates gingerly dubbed it for purposes of the official record, "the social evil." They listened to reports on the telegraphing of information and on the fascinating new practice of photographing criminals, and they contemplated pleas for not only a permanent police association but also a national police. As the three-day gathering drew to a close and the pleased delegates began departing for Hartford, Baltimore, Detroit and dozens of other cities, St. Louis Chief of Police James McDonough offered one last earnest commendation, "I have noticed with the greatest pride of my life that, of the one hundred and thirty delegates to this convention, assembled here in St. Louis, there has been no excessive worship at the shrine of Bacchus."[9]

As the police convention suggests, new attitudes and confidence accompanied the maturation of police departments as social institutions. In addition to growing in size and achieving new organizational certainty,[10] police during the post-Civil War years also developed a recognizable police superstructure. Spawned in large part by a sense of professionalism and marked by an unusual degree of occupational solidarity, the police superstructure differed from actual police institutions and practices. Police of the period, influenced by the military spirit of the Civil War, not only donned blue uniforms but also took pride in them. They sang of their bravery in the Boston, Detroit and New York draft riots of 1863. And they generated powerful rituals such as the martial funeral for an officer slain on duty and the annual policeman's ball supported by gently coerced contributions. Once the police superstructure began to appear, it naturally factored back into police institutions and practices, creating greater stability and affecting their development. When police gathered in 1871 for their first national convention, they did so as self-conscious experts. Striding about St. Louis with white silk badges pinned to their chests, they surely felt themselves more competent than others to discuss crime and the criminal.

Of particular interest in the study at hand is the surprisingly large body of police writings that appeared in the late nineteenth century. Consisting of several dozen books, a few of which went through multiple printings, the writings constitute a unique and particularly accessible portion of the police superstructure. The writings include several memoirs in which prominent policemen juxtapose themselves with what they take to be significant events.[11] They also include police histories in which the personal juxtaposing gives way to institutional positions and projections. Both types of police writings, like other parts of the police superstructure, are of course grounded in the social practice of policing, but neither type merely reflects this practice. The police writings are instead symbolic, creative renderings of policing, renderings in which the treatments of crime vary significantly and are particularly illustrative and provocative.

The two most prominent American police officers to pen their memoirs were Edward Hartwell Savage and George Washington Walling, authors, respectively, of *Police Records and Recollections* and *Recollections of a New York Chief of Police*.[12] Like their nation, both men had roots in a simpler past. Savage immigrated to Boston as a young man, but he was raised on a family farm near Alstead, New Hampshire, in the years following the War of 1812. In his memoirs he often departs for a comparable setting, using as vehicles a lock of his deceased child's hair, a seventeen-year-old gray cat, the foundations of old buildings, and an aged elm on the Boston Common. At one point Savage literally travels home. He gawks at wintry scenes that forty years earlier would barely have caught his eye. He exchanges quips with a country sage, joins a maple sugar party, and boards still another vehicle—a sled. Savage, in the midst of a coltish reverie, imagines a course winding "around among the hills . . . til you arrive back almost to your first starting-point, where you can commence your journey anew."[13]

Walling's nostalgia is less literary but still palpable. He was born in 1823 near Keyport, New Jersey, where his grandfather was an honored Revolutionary War veteran and his father captained both an oyster schooner and a country store. Ambition called Walling to New York, but he never forgot the warm waters and familiarity of his Raritan Bay home. As a grown man, he tramped frequently through the New Jersey meadowlands, and he empathized with the men from the country who, in the immutable tale of modernization, lost savings and innocence in the big city. "Comparatively little is known of the lives of many persons in New York," he notes sadly. "Acquaintances are formed which ripen into intimacy among men and women who know nothing of one another's past history."[14] Surely things were different in the Keyport of Walling's boyhood.

However, for men with more than a trace of country in their hearts, Savage and Walling did extremely well in the urban setting. Edward Savage joined the Boston police force in 1851, and in ten years climbed the ranks to captain and then to deputy chief. In 1870, when scandals led to the abolition of the detective bureau and the firing of the Chief of Police, Savage received the support of all divisional captains and became the new commanding officer. He served for eight years, watching the force grow to almost 600 men and earning unusual esteem for a Gilded Age police chief. In New York twenty-four-year-old George Washington Walling joined the force in 1847. He was a captain by the time of the 1857 battles between the state-appointed Metropolitan Police and Mayor Wood's Municipals, and siding with the former, Walling took powerful symbolic action. Cocksure and bold, Captain Walling served an arrest warrant on Wood himself. In 1863 Walling ordered his men to kill armed

draft rioters and, as a result, was lionized in elite circles. He became chief
of the New York force in 1874, and during his eleven-year tenure the
force grew to over 2000 men. Walling resigned in 1885, but he did so
with dignity and of his own volition.[15]

When late in life Savage and Walling laid down their badges and
picked up their memoirists' pens, they were able to make the transition
from police executives to writers smoothly. Indeed, both displayed a
surprising degree of aggressiveness as self-styled cultural workers. Savage,
who also authored a work of local history titled *Boston Events*,[16] notes that
while fictional works concerning police practice and crime are tempting,
readers should direct themselves instead to a factual work, such as his
own, which makes "no attempt to draw upon the imagination."[17] Walling
warns that newspaper accounts are unreliable and urges readers to accept
instead his own "unvarnished statement of indisputable fact."[18] However,
lest anyone think them lacking in gentility, the police memoirists show a
lyricism as well. Savage, in particular, is self-consciously literary and even
appends several poems for his readers' amusement. Most deal with the
deaths of mothers and children, but in one Savage chastises an overly
zealous police captain:

> Now tell me plainly, as your friend,
> What right you have down at North End,
> To pick up strangers, just for sport,
> To worry and perplex the court;
> Should you not strive its cares to lighten,
> When sleighing's tip top out to Brighton?[19]

As the Savage poem suggests, a police memoirist is quite likely to be
concerned with the essential and correct features of police work. Savage,
always the more whimsical of the two, provides a chapter titled "Advice
to the Young Policeman" but of course allows the layman to peek. He also
complains about the public's failure to understand police work and the
legal technicalities that hamper effective policing. For his part, Walling
veritably bristles:

> A New York police officer knows he has been sworn in to
> "keep the peace," and he keeps it. There's no "shilly-shally-
> ing" with him; he doesn't consider himself half patrolman and
> half supreme court judge. He can and does arrest on suspicion.
> In times of turbulence or threatened rioting, he keeps people
> moving.[20]

Yet despite writing confidently of police work, Savage and Walling eschew the perspective of police executives. Both are more inclined to recall their days on the beat than their days in police headquarters. They sketch the wide range of challenging situations a patrolman encounters in an anecdotal manner and ignore for the most part the categories and abstractions of police bureaucrats.

When the memoirists turn to the subject of crime, their anecdotalism continues. Savage counts himself among the "jolly policemen" who encounter "numerous specimens of human oddities" and "like the ingenious sculptor who sees symmetry and beauty in the rough block, are often successful in drawing out a comical figure to suit their taste."[21] He sketches a half dozen shoplifters, pickpockets and sneak thieves, and although his position dictates disapproval, Savage betrays amusement when a shoplifter converts the entire front of her Florentine silk dress into a bag for pilfered goods. Even Chauncey Larkin, a sophisticated swindler who makes his way through life with military outfits and bogus letters of introduction, heightens not Savage's ire but rather his appreciation of All Fools' Day.

At other points Savage writes more somberly of Boston's "roughs." His tone is tight-lipped, almost clinical, as he tells of maniacal Dick O'Brien, who stations himself on a street corner and without warning knocks senseless all passers-by or of Shoddy and Mary Lovina who repeatedly abuse their street's tranquility as well as one another. Often these "tough customers" are besotted with rum, but Savage is less interested in pleading for temperance than in noting the rage that burns in some of us. When attempting to arrest the brutal, 200–lb John Welch who beats his wife and girls, Savage is sickened to think a blow from his lignum vitae billy may have broken Welch's skull. The city contains its share of criminal horrors, and the policeman need not add to them.

Most unsettling to Savage are those individuals who stumble impulsively into lives of crime, and he treats their lives in greater detail than he does those of the tricksters and psychopaths. These individuals resemble the innocents in the Old Sleuth and Old Cap. Collier crime thrillers, but unlike the characters from Gilded Age mass fiction, the wayward souls in Savage's work for the most part do not find exoneration and redemption. When Savage tries to draw conclusions, his voice rises:

A false step, perhaps, at the beginning, and the tide of adversity has borne them onward and downward. Former friends forsake them, strangers ridicule and despise them, no helping hand is outstretched to save, and the victim, writhing

CONFIDENCE MAN.

Illus. 5. Portrait of Chauncey Larkin, an amiable confidence man, from *Police Records and Recollections* (1873).

PICKPOCKETS.

Illus. 6. Drawing of pickpockets at work from *Police Records and Recollections* (1873).

under the sense of its wrongs, seeks refuge in the haunts of dissipation and licentiousness, and perishes in misery and degradation, uncared for and unknown.[22]

A tone of desperation does not dominate Savage's *Police Records and Recollections,* but his deepest thoughts on crime are profoundly melancholy. How sad it is to see lives frittered away.

With literally hundreds of brief criminal reports and a chapter titled "A Pot Pourri of Crimes," Walling's *Recollections of a New York Chief of Police* is even more anecdotal. Like Savage, Walling notes the urban tricksters and pathetic psychopaths, although, unlike Savage, he has little time for amusement or sympathy. He pauses only when he discusses the men and women who slipped into lives of crime, the same individuals who most distressed Savage. Walling tells the story of a young laborer who settled in New York, became a burglar almost by accident, and is now serving a long sentence in Sing Sing. This representative story challenges Walling's capacity for comprehension, and he is dissatisfied with his own suggestion that the laborer drifted into crime due to want. He contemplates the word "drifted" and complains, "I can find no better word in the English language."[23]

When Walling consciously attempts to categorize criminals, his efforts also fall short. He endorses the assignment of different types of criminals to different floors of the Tombs, but he fails to share with the reader the thinking behind these assignments. At another point Walling remarks on the correlation between types of criminals and party affiliations. Sneaks, forgers and the higher grade of criminals, he asserts, almost invariably belong to the Republican party, while robbers, muggers and pimps are Democrats, but once again Walling cannot decide what to make of his observations. "I will not pretend to account for these remarkable phenomena, but leave them to future philosophers and scientists, who will doubtless enlighten humanity."[24]

As is the case in most crime-related cultural work, the authors wander from a discussion of crime to broader comments on society. The likable but still irritable Savage is distressed by the larger social story unfolding around him; his image of the Boston cityscape brutalized by a fire during a blizzard conveys his dismay. Walling, writing at a later date and in a testier frame of mind, argues at one point that much crime "springs peculiarly from society."[25] Like the journalist and editor James Gordon Bennett, Sr., Walling is detectably uneasy about Wall Street procedures and business speculation in general.[26] However, Walling, like Savage, cannot articulately analyze the relationships between the new society and the personal violence, civil disturbances and property crime he has devoted his life to stopping. Expert as they might be, the police chiefs are unable to stand apart from their world and mount the critiques it so desperately required.

While several scholars have argued that nineteenth-century American policemen lacked the systematic knowledge and expertise to be professionals,[27] Savage and Walling are special cases. Unlike the very first generation of American police chiefs from the 1840s and 1850s, Savage and Walling were not men who had made their marks in other occupations before accepting a horizontal call to be police chiefs. Savage and Walling spent the major portions of their adult lives in police work, moving vertically through police ranks, literally from patrolman to chief. Police work constituted for them a coherent professional career. It was in fact an extended experience, which could inspire the feelings of importance and significant placement necessary for the cultural work of memoir writing.

But if Savage and Walling are police professionals, their memoirs suggest they are also especially intriguing ones. Neither manifests the precise, rational perspectives that we today expect from our police chiefs. Sensitive to the massive social restructuring of their time, they perceive crime as countless individual episodes. Attempting with mixed success to group and analyze the episodes, the memoirists—particularly Savage— respond sympathetically to the criminals' plight. Their works would have been impossible without the Gilded Age maturation of American police departments, but the authors reflect a moralistic, sensible Christianity rather than the rigid self-confidence that contemporary Americans take as the mark of "true" professionalism.

If the Savage and Walling memoirs charm the modern reader, they are hardly the dominant works among Gilded Age police writings. More prevalent were the numerous local police histories, which, one hundred years later, still seem grand what with their ornate covers, abundant illustrations and lengthy texts. While the memoirs have one leg in an earlier America, the histories rise to their feet in a period of full modernization. While in the memoirs individual policemen attempt to juxtapose themselves with events and emerging institutions, in the histories the police institutions themselves express preferences and biases. Aggressive and almost boisterous in tone, the histories frame the criminal confidently and with harsh, misleading objectivity. In this regard and in others as well, the police histories are ideology produced close to the bone of the urban, industrial society.

Police boards and other police organizations planned and commissioned the histories in dozens of large and medium-sized cities in the final decades of the nineteenth century. The actual authors, who sometimes go unnamed, are professional cultural workers who in a few prominent cases worked primarily as newspaper journalists before becoming, at least temporarily, police historians. For example, John Flinn, the author of *History of the Chicago Police from Settlement of the Community to the Present Time,* had been a Chicago police reporter, and Augustine E. Costello, author of *Our Police Protectors—A History of the New York Police,* had worked for *The Herald.*[28] In the space of only eight years Costello wrote the histories of the New York, Minneapolis, Syracuse, Jersey City, Paterson and New Haven police departments as well as that of the New York fire department.[29] Other writers were less prolific, but they too wrote quickly what their employers wanted.

Like the Savage and Walling memoirs, the police histories pause to condemn escapist fiction and sensational journalistic accounts, but the histories themselves hardly deliver on their claims to superiority. The form of the works never varies. Each work begins with a brief account of the given city's antebellum police developments, sometimes sloppily repeating episodes. The work then switches to an almost completely synchronic mode with sections reflecting the organization and hierarchy of the department: each precinct receives a chapter and officers are sketched at length, while patrolmen are merely listed by name. Unimaginative and deadening, the form of the local police histories suggests a distended, frozen present.

The content of the works provides little relief from the form. The works are history of the most prosaic, unscholarly sort. Modern historical analysis would be too much to ask of a nineteenth-century work, but also lacking is anything comparable to Savage's poetic flair or Walling's personal feistiness. When the Denver Policemen's Mutual Aid Association published under one cover Walling's memoirs and a history of the local force, the uncomfortable coupling revealed clearly the latter's weaknesses.[30] The Denver police history, like dozens of others, is a dogged, uninspired recording of facts.

The histories' facts are invariably presented as positive developments, an approach quite consistent with the works' promotion of cities on the make. Precise language varies, but in general the histories credit the cities with excellent "blue-coated conservators of the peace . . . who watch while other men sleep, who keep the social wolves at bay or track them to their lair."[31] Each police department is cast as efficient and well organized. Committees on improvement and economy, it seems, have standardized procedures and terminated wasteful, unspecialized activities such as the lodging of tramps in station houses. Distinguished Union Army veterans have taught patrolmen soldierly bearing and precision drilling. With a given police department so close to perfection, each department's host city is shunned by criminals "with a wholesome dread."[32] Such protection was no doubt a special comfort to what the histories cast as the other pillar of local prosperity: boards of trade and the general business community. By the time the police histories appeared in the 1880s and 1890s, downtown merchants had abandoned their experiments with private police forces, but a close relationship between business and police remained, a relationship extolled not only in the police history texts but also in the expensive business advertisements that fill the works' final sections. Police and business, working hand in hand, produce the ideal city.

The only dark clouds that pass through the unremittingly positive civic utopia of the police histories take the shapes of riotous mobs. As was the case for Gilded Age newspaper reporters who, in their desperation to cover pointed social disorder crime, resorted to the war dispatch form, the police historians portray the rioters as an enemy army. The histories deplore rioters with a "thirst for violence" and "craving for plunder" hurling not only missiles but also "vile abuse in Sclavonic [sic] and broken English."[33] Foreign radicals are the generals leading the rioters, and while the rioters may lack platoons and companies, their trades provide militaristic organization:

> Workingmen who had no earthly cause to complain, who could not call to mind a grievance, threw down their tools, tore off their "overalls," snatched up their coats and hats, shook their clenched fists at the employers, and—joined the nearest mob. The railroad employees, the lumber shovers, the saw and planing mill men, the iron-workers, the brass finishers, the carpenters, the brickmakers, the bricklayers, the stone-masons, the tailors, the painters, glaziers, butchers, bakers, candlestick makers—all went out without motive or reason.[34]

Faced with such disrespectful horror, the police, with the support of the business community, have no choice but to respond forcefully. According to the Syracuse police history, "It is only when the heavy hand of the law smites those malefactors that they crouch and stand still."[35]

In the midst of the police histories' extended exercises in self-praise

134

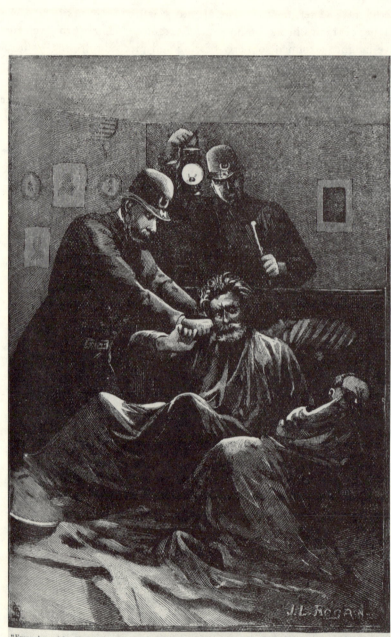

"Every Anarchist Hole was Entered and the Assassins in Some Instances were Dragged from Their Beds."

Illus. 7. Drawing of an anarchist being arrested from *History of the Chicago Police* (1887).

Illus. 8. Drawing of animalistic rioters in flight from *History of the Chicago Police* (1887).

and figurative warmaking, the histories also devote significant attention to criminals of a daily variety. Stated simply, the histories tabulate criminals. They count arrests and convictions by precinct, by year and by type of offense. The overall presentation is consistent with the work's emphasis on efficiency and organization, but the similarity between the criminal tabulations and those for uniforms, precinct houses, city piers and other material items gives one pause. Where is the sense that crime is a complex human phenomenon with social and political meanings?

One should beware of making too much of this type of criminal portraiture. However, as Savage and Walling's conception of the criminal presumably interrelated with their social practices, so too did the police institutions' tendency to reify. All is well and good, according to *The Philadelphia Police, Past and Present,* when a watch snatcher can be arrested on Sunday afternoon, convicted on Monday morning, and sent to the penitentiary for a four-year term by Monday afternoon.[36] When criminals are merely statistics, one need never worry about their families and lovers, their hopes and dreams. When criminals are objectified facts, the quality of their social existence is irrelevant.

A related, particularly intriguing example of the late nineteenth-century police departments' tendency to reify involves the rogues' gallery, the assembly of criminal photographs, which had originated in Belgium in the 1840s. Each of the police histories from large cities boasts of the size and usefulness of the home gallery, customarily concluding it is the nation's best. The works present photographs of the galleries themselves as well as representative criminal portraits. We can see both our own operations and the criminals with whom we battle, the police histories bray. We can capture them on film.[37]

On a practical level only urban police departments and other large social control institutions had the resources to maintain rogues' galleries. However, in their references to these mechanisms, the police histories do not simply mirror practices of large police departments. The histories are composed cultural artifacts. As such, they possess an alignment; they speak normatively and ideologically. Through a particular handling of the rogues' galleries and the like, the police histories attempt to change or confirm opinions, teach lessons and affect sensitivities.

Contrast the efforts of Savage and Walling with the police histories. The former, although inspired by feelings of police professionalism, at least in part maintain the perspectives and moral sensitivities of an earlier America. The memoirists, although the chiefs of large urban institutions, echo a large body of contemporary works that also toured the city in a melancholy mood.[38] In particular, Savage and Walling as individuals

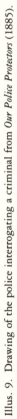

Examining a " Crook."

Illus. 9. Drawing of the police interrogating a criminal from *Our Police Protectors* (1885).

137

138

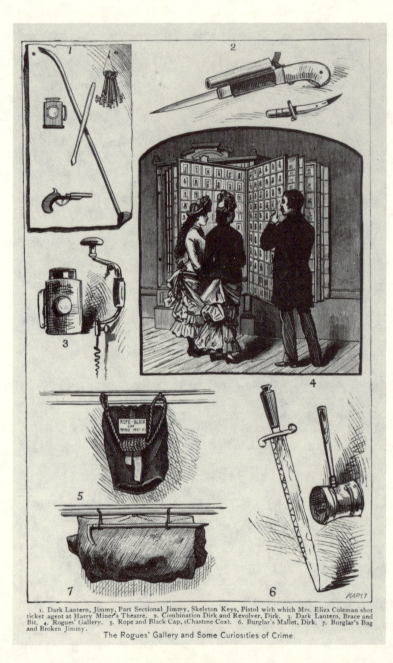

1. Dark Lantern, Jimmy, Part Sectional Jimmy, Skeleton Keys, Pistol with which Mrs. Eliza Coleman shot ticket agent at Harry Miner's Theatre. 2. Combination Dirk and Revolver, Dirk. 3. Dark Lantern, Brace and Bit. 4. Rogues' Gallery. 5. Rope and Black Cap, (Chastine Cox). 6. Burglar's Mallet, Dirk. 7. Burglar's Bag and Broken Jimmy.

The Rogues' Gallery and Some Curiosities of Crime.

Illus. 10. Composite drawing of the New York Police Department's rogues' gallery and collection of criminal memorabilia from *Our Police Protectors* (1885).

ponder crime and the criminal sympathetically. The police histories, meanwhile, are of a decidedly different cast. As cultural artifacts actually generated by late nineteenth-century police institutions, the histories create images and express attitudes consistent with the interests of these institutions. The histories' tabulations of crimes and criminals, their reductions of criminal acts and perpetrators to numbers on charts, lack sympathy, but they do bolster institutional claims of productivity and efficiency.

The histories' crime-related tabulations as well as their proud invocations of the rogues' galleries are confident criminal frames. By printing the tables and the rogues' gallery information and actual photographs, the writers of the histories confirm and sanction the perspectives and activities of the urban police departments that employed the writers. The departments can conceive and contain criminals. According to the writers and their historical works, the police have the criminal clearly in sight and firmly under control.

8.

Looking Through Private Eyes:
Late Nineteenth-Century Detective Writings

Late nineteenth-century detective work could inspire a devotion and respect for authority almost religious in nature. The files of the Pinkerton National Detective Agency record the story of an agent who had fought proudly in the Civil War as a member of the Mulligan Guards, the 23rd Illinois Infantry. After the war, the veteran's taste for discipline and service led him to join the agency. A crack operative, he rose quickly through the detective ranks, and when Allan Pinkerton, the director and founder of the agency, died in 1884, the faithful agent transferred his loyalty to Pinkerton's son William. Well after old age had prevented him from working in the field, the senior agent trudged to the office, and even in his final years he did paperwork in his home. When the agent finally passed away, relatives found in his bedroom a pristine shrine centered around a yellowed newspaper picture of William Pinkerton.[1]

A half-century earlier, American detective work was much less consecrating. With antebellum urban police departments still small and fragmented or unable to live up to the hopes that prompted their reorganizations, thefts were a concern of commercial interests and the well-to-do. In addition, as family ties loosened in conjunction with urbanization, clandestine affairs and infidelities grew increasingly common. Detectives were useful operatives in both situations. Often called constables or private police, they worked part-time, cultivated contacts with urban gang members and other criminals, and customarily employed the shadiest and roughest of methods.

Since their compensation was a percentage of the value of returned property or depended on the strength of the evidence they collected, American detectives of the antebellum period are perhaps best thought of as entrepreneurs marketing services. They advertised in assorted newspapers and journals, notably in the *National Police Gazette,* and in keeping with an entrepreneurial model, they often launched side ventures, some of which were illegitimate. Certain detectives concocted workplace and domestic infidelities, confided them to the appropriate parties, and were then hired to investigate. Detectives also alerted underworld contacts to criminal opportunities and, on occasion, either masterminded or cooperated in the perpetration of property crimes.[2]

In the years following the Civil War, detective work maintained a tawdry cast. The journalist Edward Crapsey called detectives "harpies,"[3] and Matthew Hale Smith, another reporter on midcentury life, found it discomforting "to know that such shadows are on our paths."[4] When Boston detective George Chapman was arrested for conducting pickpocketing operations that stretched from Boston to Hartford, Connecticut,[5] the impressions of the public were prominently confirmed. Yet at the same time detective work became a more fixed and sizable feature of modern life. In New York, dozens of detective offices dotted Broadway, and the discriminating consumer could choose the office, services and fees that seemed most appropriate.[6]

In conjunction with the post-Civil War stabilization of detective work, the occupation gradually differentiated into public and private branches. The public branch included federal agents affiliated with the Post Office and Treasury Department. They worked to stop mail frauds and counterfeiting, but in comparison to late twentieth-century federal investigation activities, the operations of these federal detectives were small and limited. More significant were the public detectives who worked in the detective bureaus of municipal police departments. In New York, Chief of Police George Matsell, who subsequently purchased the *National Police Gazette* from George Wilkes, had made a small group of detectives regular members of the department, and in 1857 a distinct squad of public detectives was established.[7] As large criminal capers spread to other cities in the 1860s and 1870s, these cities followed New York's lead. Often a department's top detective was second in command to the police chief himself. Yet due to higher salaries and frequent opportunities to garner rewards and illegal payoffs, most detectives still stood apart from their police brethren. While many public detectives had moved from the uniformed to the plainclothed ranks earlier in their careers, few moved in the opposite direction.

Private detectives, meanwhile, had a veritable monopoly in interstate matters due to the nascent state of federal investigation and the jurisdictional restrictions faced by local police department detectives. Private agencies grew rapidly in the 1870s, with work tasks ranging from the surveillance of wayward spouses to the tracking of bank robbers and the infiltration of workers' organizations.[8] Large private agencies boasted dozens of operatives, and one, the Pinkerton National Detective Agency,

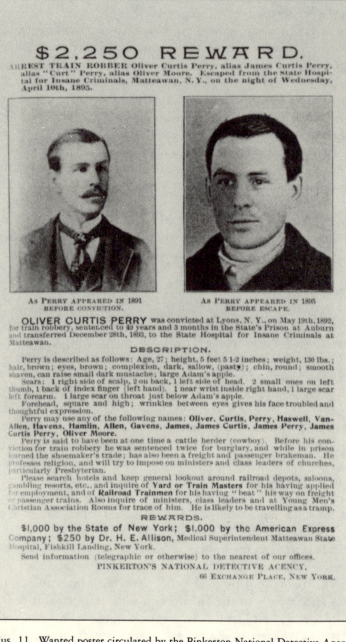

Illus. 11. Wanted poster circulated by the Pinkerton National Detective Agency (1895).

was a national concern that came to dominate the field.[9] Between 1866 and 1892 the Agency guarded property and strikebreakers in seventy-one labor strikes, and during the same years it began to provide nationwide protection for the Jewelers' Union and the American Bankers' Association.[10] The agency widely distributed wanted posters, developed the largest rogues' gallery in the world, and played a leading role in convincing the International Association of Police Chiefs to pool its criminal photographs.[11] The agency also adopted, as a supplement to the rogues' gallery, the French detective Alphonse Bertillon's ambitious system of criminal identification.[12] First utilized by the French national police in 1882 and then accepted in Belgium, India and Switzerland, the Bertillon system measured assorted parts of the criminal's body and, according to its promoters, forever and unequivocally placed the criminal "on file."[13]

As was the case with the police, detectives eventually achieved a stability and professionalism conducive to the development of a superstructure. This superstructure not only grew out of the social practice of detective work but also contributed to it. The superstructure's central premises became public service in the public branch and loyalty to the client in the private branch. When members of the occupation's private branch named themselves, they chose the phrase "private eyes"—a self-designation derived from the Pinkerton National Detective Agency's trademark. Detectives in both the public and private branches lionized detectives such as Allan Pinkerton and Thomas Byrnes, both of whom will be discussed shortly, and while police looked back proudly on their efforts during the draft riots, detectives recalled their heroism and sharp thinking in subverting a plot to assassinate Abraham Lincoln when he passed through Baltimore on his way to the 1861 inauguration.[14]

The poignant story of the Civil War veteran, firmly stationed in the Pinkerton hierarchy and devoted to his job, is a representative tale of late nineteenth-century American detective work. The occupation had solidified and garnered respect, so much so that a man or, in isolated cases, a woman could build a career as a detective. The occupation's superstructure had grown rich and self-aggrandizing, helping detectives to be proud and aggressive in their work. It was in this context that the detective, as social and cultural worker, attempted to frame the criminal.

Of particular interest are the written works by detectives that appeared in the late nineteenth century. Consisting of dozens of books, many of which were republished time and again, these writings are a revealing part of the detective superstructure. Like the publications of

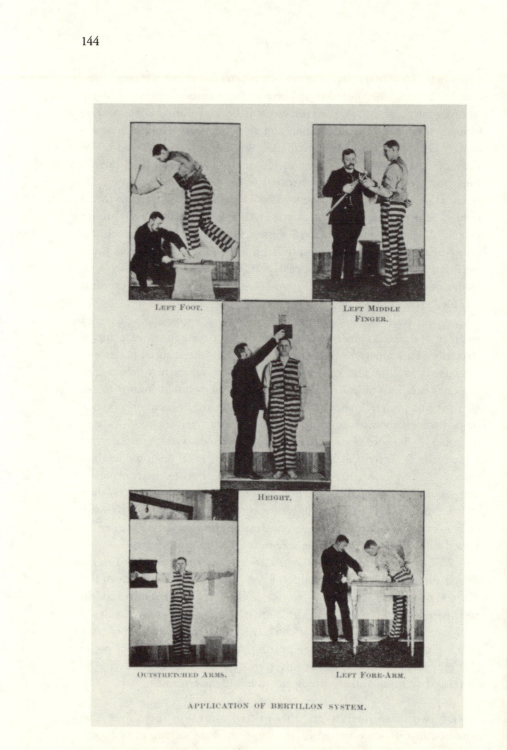

Illus. 12. Photographs of a criminal's measurements being taken in keeping with the Bertillon System of criminal identification from *Our Rival, The Rascal* (1897).

individual policemen and of police departments, detective writings do not merely reflect social practice but rather constitute a creative remembering of detective work. The detectives' views of crime and the criminal change over time in ways that suggest the increasing stability of the modern social order.

As is the case with nineteenth-century American crime journalism and crime-related fiction, works by American detectives were to a certain extent prefigured by European works. Throughout much of the century, social development on the eastern rim of the Atlantic was several decades ahead of that in the United States. Detectives emerged earlier in Europe, and European detectives produced a small body of writings in the first half of the century. Most strikingly, the French criminal and convict turned detective Eugène Vidocq published his highly fictionalized memoirs in 1828.[15] Poe, as noted earlier, was familiar with an account of Vidocq's life, and this account arguably influenced Poe's Dupin stories. The reckless but provocative twentieth-century historian Michel Foucault has cast Vidocq's life and writings as a significant divide in French history. "Vidocq," Foucault says, "marks the moment when delinquency, detected from other illegalities, was invested by power and turned inside out."[16]

The first examples of American detective writings trailed the works of Vidocq by roughly forty years. Predictably, the American works were also reminiscences and recollections, memoirs in which the author recalls his juxtaposition with events, but more surprisingly, the first American detective memoirs divide into two parts. Each work begins with a section written in a third-person voice. Sometimes stretching through the first quarter of the whole work, the section chronicles the formative experiences and most noted operations of a detective. Customarily the operations are more covert and more elaborately engineered than the actions recounted in the police memoirs, although accounts of the operations in this first section are in themselves brief and selective. Particularly noteworthy is this section's invariable endorsement of tough-minded crime control. A book concerning a detective, it seems, cannot be allowed to stand alone without another voice, one closely affiliated with social stability, enunciating the true value of detective practice. In fact, in the first of the detective works the publisher complains because the detective subject refused to cooperate in the preparation of the opening section. The introductory section, the publisher asserts grumpily, is a crucial part of the work.[17]

When the first section concludes, a break occurs, and the work begins anew. Either a different third-person narrator who is recording the detective's recollections or, more commonly, the first-person detective himself replaces the original third-person narrator. The new narrator then presents the remaining chapter-length accounts. Although lengthier and more shaped than accounts in the police memoirs, these accounts hardly consume the reader or invite a sustained vicarious involvement. Instead, they burst into the reader's consciousness as small, individual salvos. Most importantly, these accounts differ significantly from those in the works' first sections. The voice is less formal, less enamored with detective work and less fiercely committed to crime control. In the end a striking ambivalence results from the divergent first and second sections.

The precise nature of the ambivalence varies from work to work. In *Three Years with Counterfeiters, Smugglers and Boodle Carriers,* for example, journalist George Burnham announces plans in the opening section to recount the exploits of United States Secret Service Division Chief Hiram C. Whitley—a worthy endeavor since Whitley between 1869 and 1872 supervised no fewer than 1220 arrests. However, shortly after beginning the work's second section, the reader realizes Burnham is much more beguiled by the nation's criminal foes than by Whitley and his men. Burnham even supplies a glossary of the criminal vernacular, one that informs those wondering about the work's title that counterfeiters often "shove" large bundles of their "boodle."[18] In *Hands Up,* the opening section promises a report on the activities of David Cook and his semicovert detective association. The second section, meanwhile, reveals the author's predominant interest not in crime control but in violence perpetrated by criminals, detectives and citizens' mobs. Writing of the 1875 murder of four Italian immigrants in Denver, the author reports with perfect aplomb, "The four throats had been cut from ear to ear, and the sickening wounds gaped wide, like the mouths of some huge fish."[19]

The Gilded Age detective who most successfully exploited the disconnected and compartmentalized genre was George S. McWatters. Born in Scotland, McWatters lived in Ireland and London before immigrating to the United States. He apprenticed with a Philadelphia lawyer, but like George Lippard who also walked the streets of the Quaker City during the same years, young McWatters was unable to "harden his heart to the practice of a profession which often requires much of unscrupulousness of conscience and such mercilessness."[20] McWatters abandoned legal work. He moved to New York, worked briefly for actress Lola Montez, and from 1858 to 1870 served as a detective in the New York Metropolitan Police Force. During his detective years McWatters contributed letters and sketches to assorted journals and frequented Pfaff's, a Broadway saloon favored by actors, artists and bohemian writers such as Walt Whitman. In the eyes of some New Yorkers, McWatters became "the

Literary Policeman," a sobriquet he confirmed with his 1871 publication of *Knots Untied*.

The first section of *Knots Untied* is the customary third-person account, in this case by a writer identified only as "S," but in the second section McWatters himself takes over. His literary tools and critical eye, it quickly becomes obvious, are sharper than those of other detective authors, and the second section so overpowers the first as to relieve the generic ambivalence. When McWatters exposes a group of swindlers selling interests in nonexistent English estates, he not only condemns the criminals but also comments on the greediness and need for ancestry among the pathetic defrauded. When McWatters finds the somnambulist proprietress herself responsible for a rash of petty theft in an established Knickerbocker home, he gracefully explains that women of means are especially susceptible to kleptomania. In virtually every chapter McWatters wins the reader over through his sensitivity to social subtleties and special ironies.

McWatters' most pointed reflections appear when he contemplates detective work. He views detective work as hard, physical labor and believes it cannot be delegated to any great extent. The detective must travel often, and while hurtling across the desolate countryside in a train car, McWatters as detective must fight off a paranoia that imagines crime in everyone's eyes. His office is located in an undesirable area and slovenly kept, and McWatters notes that distinguished clients are uncomfortable when they come to see him. Occasionally McWatters dons the pleasing disguise of an artist or enjoys expertly reconstructing a crime, but he more frequently considers himself "a miserable snake, not in paradise, but in a social hell." "The duties of my position," McWatters sighs, "were frequently obnoxious to my taste and—perhaps I will be pardoned for so expressing myself—to my better nature."[21]

While his police colleagues dealt with a wide range of criminals, McWatters, as the typical detective, concerned himself with a particularly sophisticated subgroup: forgers, bank and train robbers, confidence men, and embezzlers. Many of these criminals purportedly looked upon their careers with a displeasure similar to McWatters' own, and McWatters is sensitive to their melancholy. In his mind both criminals and detectives reside in a deterministic universe, the criminal compelled by "the very conspiracy of circumstances" and the lonely detective plagued by "fore-ordination."[22] The proverbial "honor among thieves" provides one small prop in the dreary struggle of life, and detectives often abide by the same honor code as criminals. When McWatters, using a false identity, crosses paths in a New York beer garden with a criminal who is also incognito, quick winks signify both a willingness to protect covers as well as more fundamental bonds.

With detective and criminal almost one, it is hardly surprising that McWatters' conceptions of criminals lack anger or hatefulness. To be sure, he finds "himself frequently among the vilest characters—thieves, gamblers, highway robbers, unfortunate and lost women, and wretches too low and vile to be named here," but in general the lawbreakers about whom McWatters chooses to write are sympathethic and even admirable souls.[23] Who could be angry with Hattie Newberry, "the Vermont Beauty" who flirts with both prostitution and danger, or with Lewellyn Payne, a young gentleman from Kentucky whose plunge into the urban depths includes illegal gambling? And who could hate the elegant Colonel Novena, who uses part of his income from real estate and loan frauds to pay for the schooling of poor children?

Certainly not McWatters. Criminals, he feels, are a diverse lot created by a society whose highest moral prescription is "buy at the lowest possible price, and sell for as much as you can."[24] They make their way through life the best they can, struggling to be among "the successful and proud, who govern everything" rather than among "the unsuccessful and the wretched, who have nothing but woes and toils."[25] If anything, McWatters prefers criminals to traders, manufacturers and Wall Street speculators, who in his opinion cheat society under the rubric of profit and occasionally turn to detectives to recoup certain of their losses.

Like Savage, Walling and most of the other early police and detective memoirists, McWatters uses his law enforcement experiences as a springboard to cultural work. Had McWatters never become a detective, he most likely would never have written his memoirs, but as one of the very first American detectives to establish himself prominently, he is hardly an ideologue for the new social order. Even after becoming successful, McWatters remains uneasy with his calling. Time and again he expresses a sad comradeship with the men and women he pursues and also a pronounced melancholy regarding the society in which he finds himself. His voice is a powerful counterpoint to the more rigid detective voices that follow.

The era's most prominent detective was Allan Pinkerton. In his life and his memoirs, Pinkerton understood himself quite differently than did the police and detective memoirists previously discussed. He considered himself the complete professional, and his views on crime and the criminal were concomitantly more rigid and less sympathetic. Additionally, in the whole body of late nineteenth-century American police and detective memoirs, Pinkerton's voice is the one that eventually drowns out the others.

The son of a police sergeant, Allan Pinkerton grew up in Glasgow during the Chartist campaigns. In 1843, at the age of twenty-four, he emigrated to the United States and settled in the Scottish community of Dundee, Illinois. He prospered as a cooper, soon employing eight men, and was known as both the town atheist and the town abolitionist. The cooperage became an active stop on the Underground Railroad, and if Pinkerton's biographers are to be trusted, John Brown himself once spent the night with a group of slaves he had liberated from Mississippi plantations.[26]

In 1850, after working briefly as a security guard and as a sheriff, Pinkerton founded the Chicago-based North Western Police Agency, which later became the world-famous Pinkerton National Detective Agency. However, just as the agency began to attract attention, the Civil War intervened. Pinkerton, a personal acquaintance of Lincoln from the days when they had worked, respectively, as a detective and as a lawyer for the Illinois Central Railroad, traveled to Washington to aid the Union cause. He worked to rid the local police force of secessionists and also conducted surveillance and intelligence operations for General George McClellan, himself the former president of the Illinois Central. However, even Pinkerton's adoring biographers admit that as an intelligence officer he proved inept, at one point estimating the number of rebel troops defending Richmond at 200,000 when they in fact numbered only 68,000. When Ambrose Burnside replaced McClellan as commander of the Union army in November, 1862, Pinkerton resigned, claiming a great injustice had been done to "Little Mac."

Pinkerton returned to Chicago and redoubled efforts to remove the tarnish from detectives' reputation. Recalling the positive chord he had struck prior to the Civil War by declining a $10,000 reward for the capture of the Adams Express Company robbers, Pinkerton began to emphasize a "professional" mode of operations. As a matter of policy, his agency refused rewards and compromises with criminals and turned away all cases involving public officials, political parties, vice crusaders and divorcing spouses. Pinkerton's operatives were expected to dress like business clerks and abstain from excessive drinking, smoking, swearing and card playing. David Cook, to cite only one rough-and-tumble detective, was no doubt amused, but the expanding business community heartily approved. Banks and express companies, anxious to regain stolen or embezzled cash and securities, became devoted customers, so much so that Pinkerton soon opened a half-dozen regional branch offices.

In the 1870s, with the Pinkerton National Detective Agency's cash registers ringing merrily, Pinkerton also found time to delight in his personal wealth and prominence. He imported thousands of Scottish larch trees for the 250–acre estate he owned in Onarga, Illinois, and he further embellished his personal domain with an artificial lake, swimming pool, private railway siding, and castle. With the sweet smell of larch blossoms recalling his humble Glasgow boyhood, Pinkerton triumphantly returned to Scotland. Glasgow's mayor hosted the city's prodigal son, and Pinkerton addressed a Queen's Park assembly on the opportunities available in America.

With his busy and successful life at last winding down, Pinkerton in the eleven years prior to his death in 1884 produced no fewer than eighteen volumes of memoirs. As noted in an earlier chapter, Pinkerton was in part moved to write his memoirs because of the popular success of the Old Sleuth tales. Remembered crime and criminal detection, he reasoned, would be even more interesting than imagined crime and criminal detection.[27] However, Pinkerton did not view positively the crime fiction that in part prompted his memoirs. The spate of fictional works purportedly concerning Pinkerton agents, relatives and Pinkerton himself became a source of irritation. Shortly before his death, Pinkerton's lawyers even argued in court that a fiction publisher had stolen a plot from a volume of Pinkerton's memoirs.[28]

Given Pinkerton's energy and ambition, one could imagine that the memoirs were completely his own work, a position taken by his biographers. In the opinion of the earliest, "It would appear that, still proud of his great capacity for work, Allan Pinkerton imposed on himself a fearful amount of remembering to attend to, and either wrote or dictated the last of his years away."[29] Another claims, "No modern author describes people with more skill than Allan Pinkerton showed in his portraits of honest men and criminals."[30] Even the single biographer who admits Pinkerton had assistance correcting proofs and rewriting chapters concedes only the most intimate of helpmates, namely, Pinkerton's own wife Joan.[31] However, popular biographers of this variety are hardly known for casting their subjects in human scale. Surely Pinkerton read, approved and contributed to his memoirs; surely they can be attributed to him. However, a comparison of passages in selected volumes reveals several distinct prose styles, the work of at least two and perhaps three or four writers.[32]

Each of the eighteen volumes has a preface and body. The form of all of the prefaces is largely the same, but the form of the bodies varies tremendously. *Bucholz and the Detectives* and *The Spiritualists and the*

Detectives are book-length accounts of single investigations, but other volumes consist of short accounts, sketches or even chapters devoted to particular criminal specialties. While in the earlier detective memoirs an ambivalence results from the discordant first and second sections, the Pinkerton memoirs are literary echo chambers. The booming voice one hears in the prefaces and takes to be the purest expression of Allan Pinkerton himself is followed by the attempts of employed writers to mimic their master.

Just as Pinkerton selected policies and practices designed to connote detective professionalism, he employs in his memoirs language designed to convey a similar impression. Most obviously, he flaunts the term "professional," asserting time and again that he and the men who work for him are indeed "professionals." In the nineteenth century, given changes in American usage, Pinkerton's repeated use of the term had a decidedly normative thrust. In the course of the century the term "amateur" had for the first time acquired pejorative connotations. A "professional," by way of contrast, was dependable, skillful and committed.[33]

Burton J. Bledstein, the historian who has noted these developments in nineteenth-century usage, has also suggested that professionals from this period were particularly likely to credit themselves with character and careers.[34] In his memoirs Pinkerton manifests both proclivities. Even as a young immigrant who had never seen a ten-dollar bill, Pinkerton tells us, he was able to resist bribes. Throughout his life he was a pillar of internal strength and moral firmness for his employees and acquaintances. His work life, meanwhile, was coherent. Perhaps it was necessary to include in his memoirs a volume such as *Professional Thieves and Detectives,* which consists of a preface, a forty-page section titled "How I Became a Detective," fourteen criminal sketches, three longer accounts, and five criminal reminiscences. But with a stable of writers at his command, Pinkerton was determined to assemble the bits and pieces of his life into a career.

Unlike other police and detective memoirists who emphasize their days as streetwise operatives, Pinkerton writes primarily as an organization executive. Whenever he surveys the Pinkerton National Detective Agency, he finds himself at the top of the pyramid, flanked a step lower by sons Robert and William and by General Superintendent George Bangs. When a case appears on his desk, he considers costs and service options before assigning it to the appropriate number of specialized operatives. In *The Expressman and the Detectives,* a typical work, the operatives include "spotters," "shadows," "anglers" and one "worm," namely, a woman adept at extracting a criminal's secrets who resembles and precedes by thirty years Anna Katharine Green's Violet Strange.[35] Although Charlie Siringo, a disenchanted Pinkerton agent who later authored a pointed exposé of the agency, certainly did not fit the model,[36] Pinkerton maintains that his operatives are unflinchingly loyal. When Pinkerton tells operative James McParlan he need not accept assignment in the dangerous Mollie Maguires investigation, Pinkerton remembers McParlan responding with brisk associational devotion: "I am not in your Agency to object to such a thing as this seems to be; on the contrary, I am anxious to go and ready to start at the word of command."[37]

With Pinkerton in control and dozens of operatives ready, literally, to be "Pinkertons," the large operation easily surpasses its competitors. In each volume Pinkerton denigrates the competition and brags shamelessly. Recalling his organization's pursuit of a forger who victimized railroads, Pinkerton boasts:

> The fact, however, that the devices I employed, and the skill and aptitude of my agents, enabled me continuously to rectify our course, and conduct it to a victorious issue, is but one more testimony to the merits of my system. The detective methods of the past days and other countries, would certainly never be competent to the work which is performed by the Modern Detective Agency.[38]

Indeed, even without Pinkerton's repeated self-aggrandizement, the cynically minded might note that all but one of the memoirs' titles include the words "detective" or "detectives," as if to remind the reader and consumer of the commercial crux of the matter. Covers and title pages, meanwhile, display the ever-open eye, the business trademark that Pinkerton adapted from Philip Schuyler's early nineteenth-century American currency design.

Pinkerton, of course, has more to hawk than just professional detective services. His true products are an attitude and a way of life, products best embodied by gentlemen business executives of Pinkerton's own ilk. More so than the new fickle middle class of American cities or, most certainly, the bohemian crowd at Pfaff's, these men are Pinkerton's people. In virtually every volume Pinkerton stands beside them in sumptuous offices joking, affirming Victorian morality and commiserating about the imperfections of the transportation and communication systems. Rather than merely advertising in a strictly commercial sense, Pinkerton is making a pitch for life at the top of American capitalism.

"All the officials of the Pennsylvania Railroad Company," Pinkerton tells his colleague George Bangs, "are my friends."[39]

Pinkerton becomes most detectably propagandistic in *The Mollie Maguires and the Detectives* and *Strikers, Communists, Tramps and Detectives*, two relatively atypical volumes in his eighteen-volume memoirs. In the two volumes Pinkerton and his writers address big business' most obvious opponent: workers' organizations and unions. While supervising a large-scale investigation on behalf of the Philadelphia & Reading Railroad Company, Pinkerton concludes the Mollie Maguires "were, with some exceptions, assassins, murderers, incendiaries, thieves, midnight marauders, gamblers, and men who did not scruple to perform almost any act of violence or cowardice that a depraved nature or abnormal criminal instinct might conceive."[40] Not only do the Mollie Maguires nail men to trees and leave them to be eaten by wild animals, they also force at least one woman to participate in an "orgy" and then place her face downward on a red-hot stove. The founders of the Trainmen's Union, meanwhile, are "confirmed tramps, disgusting drunkards, and miserable communistic outcasts," and Pinkerton reports union signs, grips, passwords and rituals as if he had plumbed the most nefarious of workers' collectives.[41]

When workers involve themselves in strike and riot activities, the tone of the two Pinkerton volumes becomes even more strident. Pinkerton and his writers report that anarchy nearly triumphed in the riots of 1877, particularly since treasonous communists were pulling the strings. "Constituting the real and effective force in all riots," communist radicals in Pinkerton's opinion, "swarm to the theater of fresh troubles and hang about the purlieus of threatened cities, like unclean beasts and birds which sniff the scent of carrion in the air."[42] As the proprietor of a profitable detective business, Pinkerton is horrified by this threat to the status quo. With thoughts of communist workers and radicals meanly dancing in his head, Pinkerton blurts, "Out upon them!"[43]

Pinkerton's more standard treatment of the assorted embezzlers and burglars with whom detectives more customarily dealt is less rabid but still aggressive. While other police and detective memoirists believe they are serving the public by discussing crime, Pinkerton is in the throes of messianic self-delusion. When in "From the Bank to the Prison" a young newlywed becomes enthralled with a beautiful sunset over the Callao harbor and falls into the water, vicious sharks instantly devour him.[44] Crime, hungry and mean, lurks beneath the surface of the social order. Only expert detectives, like Pinkerton and his operatives, can protect us from this snarling, ever-present menace.

As *A Double Life and the Detective* illustrates, property criminals divide in Allan Pinkerton's mind into two groups. One group is simply villainous. Its representative in this volume is Vernon Barber, a young man from Rome, New York, who allowed his unmarried lover and child to die in childbirth and now drinks, swears, steals and never knows a pang of guilt. The other group consists of respectable citizens who are pulled down by personal weakness. It includes in this volume Archibald MacDonald, an ambitious Scottish immigrant like Pinkerton himself, who chases the dream of luxury, education and contentment across the Atlantic and from Pennsylvania to Indiana. When the dream continues to elude him, he joins forces with Barber to steal horses, rob banks and pursue a secret life of crime.

In dividing property criminals into two groups and stressing men like MacDonald who fall into the second group,[45] Pinkerton resembles other police and detective memoirists and also crime thriller writers of the period. Like the wayward urban dwellers who bewildered police chiefs Edward Savage and George Walling and who struck a chord of self-recognition in George McWatters, the MacDonalds of Pinkerton's memoirs are the products of good families and communities and often blessed with social standing. Like the orphans and foundlings traveling to the city in the Old Sleuth and Old Cap. Collier stories, the MacDonalds are men and women buffeted by the winds of modernization. The criminal frames have categories and motifs that cross the lines dividing police and detectives and, more generally, those separating rememberers and imaginers.

However, unlike other cultural workers employing the same bifurcation and focus, Allan Pinkerton has no time for sympathy. His mission is inspired by neither Christianity nor humanitarianism. An efficient, elite professional, Pinkerton is a man of the new society. His fix on criminals is hard and unyielding. "The greed of gain, the desire to possess themselves of the property of others, without the labor required for honest accumulation, have led them to adopt the nature of the vulture and to prey unscrupulously upon the community at large."[46] Once they have chosen lives of crime, criminals decline precipitously. Even the abstinent begin drinking and gambling. Even the confident stand one day before a judge for a gruesome degradation ritual:

> Byron's [a train robber] face changed in a moment from vivid
> life to ashy paleness of death. His eyes seemed to dilate as if
> they would burst from the sockets. . . . Indeed he looked like a
> lost soul, shivering with terror on the margin of eternity.[47]

These men and women need not have chosen criminal pursuits but, Pinkerton insists and his writers elaborate, they did!

More so than the other nineteenth-century police and detective memoirists, Pinkerton is the fully shaped professional. With a father on the Glasgow police force, Pinkerton was in a sense born into law enforcement. While Christianity invigorated Edward Hartwell Savage's work as a police chief and then as a probation officer, self-interested professionalism invigorated Pinkerton. Unlike George McWatters who lamented the career he had chosen, Pinkerton saw himself scaling the careerist heights. Imbedded in a detective professionalism that he himself was fashioning, Allan Pinkerton offers in his memoirs a view of crime and the criminal less humane than those offered by earlier policemen and detectives. One hundred years later, the statements from contemporary police and detectives frequently resemble those of Allan Pinkerton, but are the similarities comforting?

If the contrast between the voices of first-generation professionals with ties to antebellum America and more stiffly shaped late-century professionals is the most striking feature of the police and detective writings, the eventual dominance of the latter is the most ominous. The characteristics of these writings, of course, cannot be graphed as if they were quantifiable variables, but as police departments and detective agencies became larger and more established in the 1880s and 1890s, police and detective writings changed. Memoirs gave way to local police histories and even more curious artifacts yet to be discussed, and the attitudes of police and detective authors toward crime became tough-minded and harsh. Late nineteenth-century American ideology is too complex for simple schematization, but one area of the ideology, that articulated in written portions of the police and detective superstructures, clearly shifts and rigidifies as police and detective institutions age and the new society comes fully into operation.

The most audible voice in late nineteenth-century police and detective writings is Allan Pinkerton. More so than most other police and detective writings, the Pinkerton memoirs were best-sellers, and between Pinkerton's death in 1884 and the end of the century, both G. W. Carleton's and Dillingham's reissued expensively bound, illustrated collections of Pinkerton's entire oeuvre. When George McWatters, "the Literary Policeman," lent his name to a second volume of detective reminiscences, *Detectives of Europe and America or Life in the Secret Service,* it had little in common with his earlier *Knots Untied.* Lacking introspection and irony, McWatters' second volume abandons any suggestion of comradeship among detectives and criminals and casts criminals simply as bad people deservedly sent away for long prison terms. In the last twenty years of the nineteenth century *Detectives of Europe and America or Life in the Secret Service* appeared in at least five editions, the last appropriately enough bearing the imprint of "The Pinkerton Detective Series."[48]

Even more striking illustrations of what became of the police and detective writings in the final years of the century are *Our Rival, The Rascal* by Benjamin P. Eldridge and William Watts and *Professional Criminals of America* by Thomas Byrnes. The authors of the latter works, either as a pair in the case of Eldridge and Watts or individually in the case of Byrnes, have links to both the police and detective professions, but ultimately they seem to affiliate with neither one nor the other. They represent instead a more basic commitment to crime control, one frequently untempered by notions of public service or loyalty to a client. By virtue of their subscription to the fiercest of crime control attitudes, these works constitute the distressing culmination of the century's police and detective writings.

Eldridge and Watts hailed from towns within what, as early as the late nineteenth century, can be called the Boston metropolitan area, and both went on to make their marks in the Boston Police Department. Born in 1838, Eldridge was raised in Dorchester, a township annexed by Boston in 1870. He joined the Boston Police Department in 1875, and by the time *Our Rival, The Rascal* appeared in 1896, he had become Superintendent of Boston Police as well as President of the National Union of Police. Watts, his co-author and professional colleague, grew up across the river in Cambridge. He joined the Boston Police Department in 1877 and in 1894 became the Chief Inspector of the Bureau of Criminal Investigation, the police force's detective branch.

Thomas Byrnes, meanwhile, found similar, if more controversial, success in New York. Born in Ireland in 1842, Byrnes immigrated to America as a boy, fought with the Union army and then rose rapidly through the police department's ranks. In 1880 he became chief inspector in the detective squad, and in subsequent years he successfully lobbied for higher pay for detectives and a centralized detective bureau.[49] According to one commentator, Byrnes was "one of the most skilled thief-catchers we have ever had in America,"[50] and business and banking interests were pleased when Byrnes began arresting on the spot any known criminal who went south of Fulton Street into the Wall Street area. At the same time, however, others condemned Byrnes for his brutal handling of suspects. Lincoln Steffens, who, as noted earlier, had found Byrnes borrowing from fiction when recalling criminal investigations for reporters, considered

Byrnes "a man who would buy you or beat you, as you might choose, but get you he would."[51]

Our Rival, The Rascal and *Professional Criminals of America* are strikingly similar works. Large and impressively bound—the Byrnes work is in fact a folio—the works are even grander than the ornately decorated police histories. They contain great potpourris of crime-related items. Eldridge and Watts provide, among other things, chapters on types of criminals, discussions of specific crimes, an analysis of "the criminal woman," a review of criminal implements, and consumer guides to locks and safes. Byrnes, hardly to be outdone, adds sketches of fifteen forgers, a report on international crime, profiles of men and women executed at the Tombs between 1851 and 1866, and elaborate tabulations of bank robberies, prison commutation laws and state penitentiaries. In addition, both works utilize a large number of illustrations and photographs, most of the latter coming from rogues' galleries. Overall, each work is not so much a book to be read as a bound crime-stopper's kit.

And indeed, crime-stopping is exactly what the authors have in mind. They are concerned about a wave of criminal villainy, one that extends far beyond their own bailiwicks of Boston and New York. They perceive policemen and detectives struggling desperately to maintain order. More so than even the writers of the police histories and Allan Pinkerton, they are anxious to enlist laymen in the battle against crime. "It has been our aim in the preparation of this book to make not only a graphic and faithful portrayal of the criminal classes and police of today, but also to supply a work of practical every day service to the public at large in the suggestion of precautions for the better security of life and property."[52]

In their comments on criminals, Byrnes, Eldridge and Watts propose a curious version of their own professionalism and institutionalism, one derived more from narcissism than social reality. Byrnes includes a peripheral chapter on "Mysterious Murders" and another condemning gigolos and bohemians, but he devotes three times as much space to a discussion of eleven types of professional criminals.[53] Eldridge and Watts are even less willing to consider amateur criminals:

> Nor does our discussion and review of the rascal extend to cover the crimes that are committed on the spur of some uncontrollable passion or frenzy. In such cases murder and other outrages are simply dreadful incidents and not regular pursuits against which society may be well armed and cautioned.[54]

True professionals, by way of contrast, are a well organized social force. The individual criminal, the authors maintain, enters the underworld as an apprentice on the lowest rung. Advancement is slow, "from round to round on the ladder of crime and not by a single spring from the ground to the top," but eventually, the criminal develops a specialty, theft from boarding houses perhaps, confidence work, or one of many others.[55]

Prominent in both works, this nineteenth-century vision of organized crime serves as a backdrop against which the authors can securely place individual criminal foes. Eldridge and Watts provide representative wanted posters, and Byrnes provides the place of birth, age, build, height, weight, body markings, *modus operandi,* current status, and, most importantly, rogues' gallery photographs for 204 criminals. He boasts of the quality of his photographs, recalls tricking criminals into being photographed, and even supplies a posed yet gruesome picture of four policemen holding a recalcitrant prisoner for the photographer. Byrnes believes his book, in many ways a portable rogues' gallery, to be a crime control device every crime-stopper—lay or professional—can employ.

Indeed, this crime-stopping photography even takes on scientific pretensions. In perhaps the strangest and most troubling attempt to capture the criminal in the whole body of late nineteenth-century police and detective writings, Eldridge and Watts combine photographs in hopes of obtaining composite criminal types. Man blends into man until the visage of the "forger" and the "hotel thief" emerge. In the process, the criminal's motivations, his spirit, or her dreams disappear completely. The crime control animus, the drive to identify rather than to know, results only in caricature. As Eldridge and Watts complete their effort, even they become leery of the undertaking.

While less prevalent and popular than the crime reporting and imagining considered in the first two parts of this work, crime remembering by police and detectives manifests a developmental pattern that can be coordinated with the patterns for journalism and fiction. During the years preceding the Civil War, with the modern police and detective professions still in formative stages, police and detective writings did not appear in the United States. However, after the war, as daily newspapers and fiction publishing enterprises grew massive and increasingly generated generic products, police departments and detective agencies also grew, stabilized, and eventually generated specialized cultural works. Police and detective memoirs and also police histories and assorted crime-stopping volumes became in the final decades of the nineteenth century an important part of the professional superstructure. Although not aimed at

HEADQUARTERS OF THE POLICE DEPARTMENT,
BOSTON, MASS.
SUPERINTENDENT'S OFFICE, 37 PEMBERTON SQUARE

Wanted on an Indictment Warrant,

For obtaining $6,000 by false pretences, with intent to cheat and defraud by means of the gold dust trick, a Russian Jew, known by the following names, Samuel Brotzski, Solomon Schwartzman, Solomon Tzigainer (means Gypsy), Samuel Schetman, Leitchman and Greenberg. He is from 45 to 50 years old, 5 feet 3 inches tall, 175 pounds weight, dark complexion, dark mustache mixed with gray, beard when worn will be mixed with gray, bluish-gray eyes, small nose, talks slowly and has a slow gait. Is a constant smoker of cigarettes that he makes himself, has small hands with tapering fingers, and full neck. Will be found amongst Jews, and is very fond of women.

If found, arrest, hold and notify me, and I will send for him. Send any information to

BENJAMIN P. ELDRIDGE,

Boston, Nov. 17, 1894.   Superintendent of Police.

Illus. 13. Wanted poster circulated by the Boston Police Department (1894).

Illus. 14. New York rogues' gallery photographs of female criminals (1886).

7

EDWARD DINKLEMAN,
ALIAS EDDIE MILLER—HUNTER—BOWMAN,
PICKPOCKET,
SHOP LIFTER, AND HOTEL THIEF.

8

WALTER SHERIDAN,
ALIAS RALSTON—KEENE,
BANK SNEAK, FORGER, AND
COUNTERFEITER.

9

WILLIAM COLEMAN,
ALIAS BILLY COLEMAN,
BURGLAR AND BANK SNEAK.

10

IKE VAIL,
ALIAS OLD IKE,
CONFIDENCE.

11

JOHN LARNEY,
ALIAS MOLLIE MATCHES,
BANK SNEAK AND BURGLAR

12

EDWARD RICE,
ALIAS BIG RICE,
CONFIDENCE AND HOTEL SNEAK.

Illus. 15. New York rogues' gallery photographs of male criminals (1886).

162

Illus. 16. Posed photograph of Detective Thomas Byrnes observing four policemen holding a criminal for the rogues' gallery photographer from *Professional Criminals of America* (1886).

COMPOSITE OF
6 BANK SNEAKS.

COMPOSITE OF
5 FORGERS.

COMPOSITE OF
4 BURGLARS.

COMPOSITE OF
5 CRIMINALS.

COMPOSITE OF
4 CRIMINALS.

COMPOSITE OF
9 CRIMINALS.

CO-COMPOSITE
OF ALL.

COMPOSITE OF
6 HOTEL THIEVES.

COMPOSITE OF
7 PICKPOCKETS.

CO-COMPOSITE OF
28 CRIMINALS.

The six outside portraits are original composite photographs.
The four central portraits are reproduced from Galton's work.

Illus. 17. Attempts to derive prototypical criminal visages by combining individual photographs from *Our Rival, The Rascal* (1897).

monetary profit as was the case with crime reporting and imagining, police and detective cultural work not only reflected but also helped constitute police and detective social practices.

The earliest of the memoirs—Edward Savage's *Police Records and Recollections* and George McWatters' *Knots Untied* of the 1870s—proffered humane, even troubled attempts to conceive the criminal. However, with the modern society's gears meshing more and more completely and police and detective institutions growing more certain of their functions in maintaining social order, the criminal frames in the police and detective writings change rapidly. Police histories, Allan Pinkerton's eighteen-volume crescendo, and the likes of *Our Rival, The Rascal* and *Professional Criminals of America* came to dominate with their boisterous, reified and unsympathetic conceptions of crime and the criminal. With this rigid criminal frame central in the police and detective works, the written products generated by police and detective professionals were by the end of the century predictable ideological defenses of both the social control institutions themselves and of the urban, industrial society to which the organizations were fundamental.

9.

Legitimate Illegitimacy:
The Criminal as Cultural Worker

In a study of the cultural portraiture of nineteenth-century American crime, it would be convenient if criminals corrected the images proffered by newspapers and fiction; it would be welcome if criminal authors, as organic spokesmen for the criminal classes, differed aggressively with police and detective memoirists. However, in the modern society that America had become by the final years of the nineteenth century, corrections and differences of opinion of these sorts are difficult to locate. Criminals of the period were men and women residing in the same world that enclosed law-abiding Americans. Their writings did not effectively challenge the writings of journalists, novelists and law enforcement officials but rather intersected with those writings in intriguing, telling ways.

In approaching the cultural work of the late nineteenth-century American criminals, it will be useful to recall this study's three basic categories of criminal conduct: personal violence crime, social disorder crime, and property crime. Criminals in each category temporarily became cultural workers. However, criminals turned writers from the first two categories are few in number, and only a handful contribute significantly to the nineteenth-century framing of the criminal. Property criminals turned writers, meanwhile, generated a surprisingly coherent and unified body of work. More so than other criminal writings, this body of work suggests the way the criminal's cultural practices were integrated in the dominant processes of the nineteenth century's final decades. The criminal turned cultural worker, it seems, was determined to stress the legitimacy of his life and activity.

Personal violence and social disorder crime are easily identified. The former includes rapes, child and wife beatings, and homicides. Sad and often bloody, these crimes are most frequently perpetrated by working class men and women. The perpetrators feel themselves fenced in by personal, social and economic barriers. Although crimes of this sort declined on a per capita basis in the years following the Civil War, they continued to harm substantial numbers of individuals and repeatedly fractured social decorum. Social disorder crime includes drunken carousing and disorderly conduct, the beating of ethnics and members of racial minorities, and the taunting of social misfits. It is most commonly perpetrated in the poorer neighborhoods of the modern city. On occasion, particularly in the final decades of the century, it took the form of rallies and protests concerning jobs and wages. Published writings by individuals who engaged in either personal violence or social disorder crime survive, but in neither category are the writings formally or substantively unified.

Only a few Gilded Age personal violence criminals published their reflections. Most had but a modicum of formal education, and although they might have conveyed their impressions orally, their lack of writing skills precluded the type of rendering so easy for the middle and upper classes. Then too, the publishing house with its stable of cultural workers who might have shaped their thoughts was for most personal violence criminals a truly foreign, barely recognizable enterprise. Lacking social connections and economic standing, the criminals could not "toss around ideas" with an editor.

In addition to several memoirs in which convicted personal violence criminals refuse to acknowledge their guilt,[1] there are other memoirs by personal violence criminals who accept the criminal mantle. In these short memoirs, the severe, wrenching dissociations that preceded the criminal acts continue afterwards and color the distressed commentaries. Jesse Pomeroy was only a confused fourteen-year-old. While growing up among poor Irish immigrants in the Boston area, he suffered from excruciating headaches and, according to subsequent testimony, had a proclivity for dismembering small animals. In 1874 Pomeroy killed and beheaded two of his working-class playmates in and around South Boston's stinking marshes. Expressing himself in a short pamphlet, Pomeroy is unable to focus on his heinous acts. He repeats time and again that he did not read cheap novels or make friends recite the Lord's Prayer with swear words interspersed.[2] He asserts pathetically, "I am not a cruel boy."[3]

Convicted murderess Bridget Durgan was similarly unable to make sense of what she had done. Born in County Sligo, Ireland, Durgan emigrated to the United States during the Civil War. Like many other single Irish women, she became a domestic servant for the established American elite, but first in New York City and later in New Jersey, her epilepsy made it difficult to retain a position. Only Dr. and Mrs. Coriell of New Brunswick seemed sympathetic to her plight, but the doctor's motivations were impure. Durgan sometimes awoke to find the doctor watching her. In one such nocturnal watch, he confided his wish that his wife should die, and shortly thereafter, Durgan responded to the suggestion by biting Mrs. Coriell, bashing her with a chair and stabbing her 60 times. "I made myself think . . . that the doctor liked me," Durgan says in a published jailhouse confession, "and I did really think that he wanted to get her out of the way, and this so preyed upon my mind that I thought I must kill her."[4]

The most sustained work by a Gilded Age personal violence criminal came from the pen of Charles Julius Guiteau. The son of a devout follower of John Humphrey Noyes, Guiteau grew up without a mother in antebellum Illinois. Throughout his boyhood and early adulthood, potential peers stepped away. At the University of Michigan Guiteau made few friends and with embarrassment enrolled in only a precollege program. In Noyes' Oneida Community, with its religious utopianism and sexual freedom, he could convince none of the men to promote his candidacy with the women, and in New York, Chicago and San Francisco he could never attract enough legal clients to prosper. Only the bill collectors called regularly, and Guiteau, himself a sometimes collection agent, relocated frequently in order to avoid their grasp.[5]

If there is anything surprising about Guiteau's life before he burst onto the nation's front pages with his 1881 murder of President Garfield, it was his activity as a cultural worker. Inspired by not only John Humphrey Noyes but also newspaperman Horace Greeley, Guiteau lectured on religious and business subjects in New York and in several cities in the Old Midwest. Reviews of his talks in the *Chicago Tribune* and elsewhere were negative, but at least Guiteau received the attention and company for which he so desperately longed. In addition, Guiteau managed during the 1870s to publish two short books. One was a discussion of Christ's second coming,[6] and the other was an idiosyncratic supplement to the Bible.[7] Neither attracted a substantial readership, but unlike other Gilded Age violent criminals, Guiteau could with justification consider himself an author.

It was in fact Guiteau's writing and publishing that gave him a tenuous link to James A. Garfield. In the months preceding the 1880 presidential election, Guiteau had privately printed his essay titled "Garfield Against Hancock" and distributed it to delegates at the Republican Party's New York convention. Few had time to study the work, but undaunted, Guiteau joined the Garfield campaign and on one occasion addressed a small rally of New York blacks. After the Garfield victory, the increasingly deranged Guiteau pressed members of the Garfield administration for a consulship if not to Austria then to France. One summer day he pressed again, this time on the trigger of a bulldog revolver, and the new president lay mortally wounded on the floor of the Baltimore and Potomac railroad depot. Aware that his act would cast a new light on his writings, Guiteau carried to the assassination a copy of his "Garfield Against Hancock" essay and also a newly edited version of *The Truth,* his Biblical companion.

After the smoke had cleared and the president had died, Guiteau remained a diligent cultural worker. The public was now hungry for his thoughts, and he met frequently with journalists in his jail cell. He urged them to describe carefully his dress and demeanor, he approached interviews with a list of subjects to be discussed, and he gave instructions regarding paragraphing and punctuation.[8] Furthermore, Guiteau was not about to allow only third parties to gain from his notoriety. He offered for sale the suit he had worn during the assassination and also marketed autographed photographs at one dollar each or twelve for nine dollars.[9] More importantly, Guiteau composed a lengthy autobiography, which appeared in both authorized and pirated editions.[10]

How did Guiteau perceive his crime? In matter-of-fact language he recalls the night of May 18, 1881, when thoughts of murder first occurred to him:

> I felt depressed and perplexed on account of the political situation, and I retired much earlier than usual. I felt wearied in mind and body, and I was in my bed about 9 o'clock, and the idea flashed through my brain that if the President was out of the way every thing would go better.[11]

Once established, the murderous idea, in Guiteau's words, "kept bearing and bearing and bearing down."[12] Newspaper reports suggested its necessity. Squabbles between Republican factions were opening the door for rebels and Democrats. Guiteau had not the slightest doubt of his duty. He felt he was acting with divine authority, and "this Divine pressure was upon me from the time when I fully resolved to remove him until I actually shot him."[13]

The key sensation in Guiteau's experience was pressure. Later he would rail about Half-Breeds and Stalwarts and argue he could not be convicted because he lacked technical legal malice: "I had none but the best of feelings, personally, toward the President."[14] Still, it was the pres-

THE ASSASSIN IN HIS CELL.

Illus. 18. Drawing of the assassin Guiteau staring through the bars of his cell from Guiteau's autobiography in *A Complete History of the Trial of Guiteau* (1882).

sure "bearing and bearing and bearing down." Guiteau was wracked by tension, pain and confusion. The world was squeezing angrily into his head. Explosion was the only way to relieve the pain.

Like personal violence criminals, most social disorder criminals of late nineteenth-century America lacked the social connections and formal education necessary for the production of fully shaped and coherent written works. Their impressions of a drunken night smashing windows are by and large lost. Their recollections of a rally to demand jobs or protest wage cuts do not survive in print. For the most part, only those social disorder criminals who had leadership positions in strikes and militant organizations, those who promoted the nonrecreational meaning of "party," have left their written reflections on crime, and even in these works, the authors' portrayals and discussions of crime seem naive and restricted.

Johann Most was more outspoken than other Gilded Age radicals. Born in 1846 in the Bavarian city of Augsburg, Most was mutilated in his youth by medical quacks who removed part of his jawbone to eliminate an infection. He took up bookbinding, and, in keeping with the trade's customary *Wanderschaft,* he traveled through the German-speaking duchies and principalities. Like many European migrant workers of the period, Most devoted his nights to reading in the natural sciences and social theory, and before long he became a leader of the International Workingmen's Association. Arrests, convictions and prison sentences followed. With Bismarck building an authoritarian German nation, Most moved to London to edit a revolutionary periodical named *Freiheit.* In 1882, after *Freiheit* articles commending Irish insurgency had prompted the destruction of the publication's offices, Most moved again—this time to the United States.[15]

Most found in America pockets of workers who had been radicalized by the extended depression of the 1870s and by several small revolutionary organizations. While still keeping an eye on European events, Most poured his energy into American speaking tours and radical publications. Along with several dozen other immigrant workers and intellectuals, he organized revolutionary parties. These parties split and recombined, but the International Working Peoples Association, Most's major party vehicle, was forceful enough to sap the strength of the more established but less revolutionary Socialist Labor Party. After only two years in America, Most had 8000 formally enrolled comrades.[16]

While engaged in party work, Most also continued to shape his critique of modern society. Influential in Most's thought were the writings of Karl Marx, and Most did his best to popularize Marx's theories. Most argued, simply, that the population of the capitalist West was divided into a proletariat of workers and a dominant bourgeoisie. The latter benefited from the exploitation and oppression of the former. Not only industry but also religion, journalism and literature, Most added, were active parts of the unjust social order. His prescription for change was inspired both by Marx's works and by those of Bakunin, Dave and particularly Kropotkin, leading nineteenth-century anarchists. Most felt radicals must organize workers, launch militant actions and smash the state. In its stead he hoped for a collectivist society, with workers' communes and agrarian committees united in a loosely structured federation.[17]

One focus in Most's writings was crime. There is a straightforwardness in his treatment of the subject: "All crime—except misconduct by the insane, which is the result of illness—is the result of the system of private property."[18] If workers should combine in order to obtain better wages, the propertied class decries it as conspiracy. If the worker is discharged or unable to find work and begins to beg, then the bourgeoisie calls it vagrancy. "Should the unemployed apply a little of the praised self-help, that is, should he steal on a small scale as the rich do daily with impunity on a large scale, the well-to-do will gather burning coals of moral indignation, and, with mean faces, turn him over to the state prisons so that he might be exploited more cheaply."[19] According to the 1883 declaration of principles of the International Working Peoples Association, the capitalist system "annually increases the percentage of the propertyless population, which becomes pauperized and is driven to crime, vagabondage, prostitution, suicide, starvation and general depravity."[20]

If Most had stopped there, with a simple radical criminology, his writings would deserve no further attention, but in addition to offering his social understanding of crime, Most called for crime of a particular sort. In *Revolutionary War Science,* a seventy-four page pamphlet published in 1885, he outlined a plan designed to disrupt the bourgeois social order.[21] Revolutionaries were to be criminals. Most told readers how to manufacture nitroglycerine and dynamite, a process he had learned while working undercover in a Jersey City explosives factory. He told them how to burglarize explosives works and to buy explosives on the black market. Once in hand, the explosives could be used to blast the dinner parties of the opulent into smithereens. If explosives failed or were unavailable, Most's *Revolutionary War Science* urged readers to rely instead on inflammable liquids, poisons and deadly chemicals, concoctions that the work told how to prepare.

Precise impact is difficult to gauge, but Most and his vision of revolutionary criminality had a role in three of the most infamous crimes of the period. Several of the Chicago anarchists accused of detonating the bomb that provoked the 1886 Haymarket Tragedy were Most's colleagues. Evidence linking these men to the bombing itself was flimsy, but prior to the incident, articles in *Alarm,* the English-language organ of the Chicago anarchist movement, had hailed the liberating potential of dynamite.[22] When Most first heard of the bombing, he assumed it was the work of his anarchist comrades.[23] Alexander Berkman, the Russian immigrant who in 1892 shot and stabbed but failed to kill Henry Frick, the general manager of the Carnegie Steel Company, was also affiliated with Most. After the crime, the two men had a falling out—Most repudiated Berkman's act and Berkman labeled Most "Wurst," that is, sausage.[24] Prior to the crime, however, Berkman had studied with Most in New York and, in keeping with Most's teachings, had understood his criminal act not as murder but rather *Attentat*—political assassination.[25] Even Leon Czolgosz, the shadowy immigrant who assassinated President McKinley at the 1901 Pan-American Exposition in Buffalo, had studied Most's pamphlets. Czolgosz had tried to secure a foothold in the anarchist movement, and Most himself edited the *Arbeiterzeitung,* a radical workers' newspaper, in Buffalo during the years shortly preceding the assassination.[26]

In conjunction with *Revolutionary War Science,* these events were more than enough to make Most the unrivaled bête noire of revolution on American shores. He was convicted and imprisoned after speaking at a New York rally in 1886 and again after a Chicago rally in 1891. He also went to jail in 1901 after republishing an earlier editorial that urged readers to "Murder the Murderers! Save humanity through blood and iron, poison and dynamite!"[27] Vigilantes beat Most's children on the streets. Prominent politicians called for his deportation. Standard histories of the late nineteenth century fail even to note Most,[28] but his own contemporaries, particularly the formal representatives of the social order, recognized the potential dangerousness of the revolutionary criminal and his theories.

How should Most and his theories of crime be evaluated? Emma Goldman, Most's one-time student and lover, set the tone for a modern appraisal. When Most died in 1906, in the midst of one last speaking tour, Goldman's obituary in *Mother Earth* was guarded indeed.[29] She praised his fire and commitment but diplomatically skirted his theories of revolutionary criminality. Most's basic perception of crime greatly reduces the variety and complexity of criminal conduct. His call for a range of criminal acts suffers from a revolutionary pubescence. An automatic inversion of legality and illegality betrays an ongoing susceptibility to the influence of dominant criminal conceptualizations. Convicted criminal and cultural worker, Most articulated neither a subtle understanding of crime nor a useful revolutionary criminal praxis.[30]

Guiteau and Most, respectively, are not typical personal violence and social disorder criminals, and their writings are not typical cultural work by criminals. Indeed, the "typical" is elusive. As a group, the personal violence criminals who managed to become cultural workers are too bewildered to provide analysis of crime in the modern society. Similarly, social disorder criminals did not easily engage in cultural work. The works from both categories do not establish enduring frames for the criminal. The works stand as intriguing exclamation points in American social and cultural history. They provide insight to the harshest moments and meanest attitudes of the period, but all told, a study of crime-related cultural work must look elsewhere for coherence and coordination.

The most shaped body of late nineteenth-century criminal writings comes from the period's property criminals. In the final decades of the century these criminals developed a recognizable superstructure. They nicknamed one another with such abandon that virtually none of them went only by baptismal names. Their specialized argot acknowledged the sweetness of money by calling it "sugar" and dividing it into such denominations as the "pheniff," "double pheniff" and "century."[31] The criminal mythology lionized particularly successful criminals and cast crimes such as the Lord Bond Robbery as bench marks.[32] Most importantly for purposes at hand, a half dozen sophisticated property criminals published memoirs. First issued by small, local publishers, these memoirs, in a few cases, were subsequently republished on a larger, more expensive scale. Sharing a form, a focus and an overall perspective, these memoirs may be thought of as a "literature."

The authors of the works were elite practitioners of property crime, men who had spent most of their adult years working as burglars and swindlers in the Boston to Philadelphia corridor. While perhaps graceful in their felonious practice, the authors proved awkward as cultural workers. Their reminiscences of planning crimes, life on the lam, and prison connect poorly to one another. Their addenda and supplements lack integration with their texts. Their literary voices clash and contradict, and each memoir at first seems a shouting match.

On the one hand, the authors seem to be speaking as repentant individuals, men who fell but have since seen the light. "Jim," the son of working-class Irish immigrants in New York, was impressed as a boy by the "swell" grafter with his "clean linen collar and shirt, a diamond in his tie, an air of leisure all about him."[33] He pursued this attractive image down the primrose path and a sad life of till tapping, moll buzzing, burglary and lengthy prison sentences followed. A fellow memoirist, counterfeiter and bank robber Langdon Moore one day stumbled onto the game of faro. Much later in life, after many crimes and twenty-five years in Maine and Massachusetts prisons, Moore was sure he had failed, "as all must do who lead a criminal life."[34] George Bidwell, a candy-maker from Michigan, began embezzling in order to avoid embarrassment before his wife of three months. He moved to New York, and one disastrous step followed another. "Success won in honest fight is sweet," Bidwell says, "but I know from my own experience that the success of crime brings no sweetness, no blessing with it, but leaves the mind a prey to a thousand haunting fears that make a shipwreck of peace."[35]

Surely this is the attitude most societies would like their criminals to acquire: repentance of misdeeds and determination to warn others away from similar mistakes. However, the criminal memoirists are not completely remorseful. Indeed, a distinct zestfulness rings in their published works. "Jim" proffers a chapter titled "When Graft Was Good," and Bidwell subtitles the first of his works "The Wonderful Life-Story of George Bidwell." After an enthusiastic account of his life on the lam in Ireland, Bidwell catches himself sounding insufficiently remorseful: "Readers who may discover any trace of exultation in my relation to the cool and skillful manner in which I eluded the detectives will bear in mind that the story is told from the standpoint of my then state of feeling."[36]

Can the contradictory voices be coordinated? H. Bruce Franklin, the scholar who has most extensively studied the writings of American criminals, thinks not. In one chapter of a work devoted to larger concerns, Franklin has argued that the writings of nineteenth-century criminals are laden with inconsistencies. He finds in criminal writings from early in the century a "purely confessional" voice, but he feels that by midcentury the confessional voice has merged with a "picaresque voice." During the remainder of the century the picaresque voice is dominant, but, according to Franklin, both voices continue to speak, often contradicting one another and confusing the reader.[37]

Franklin's observations are helpful in the study at hand. "Jim," Moore, Bidwell and the other memoirists do, after all, repent before the altar of legitimate society while simultaneously espousing an adventuresomeness. On the surface, the memoirs recall the portraits and portrayals of criminals in the early nineteenth-century crime-related pamphlets. They are confessional, and they are roguish. Seemingly contradictory, the memoirs may well stymie the scholar hoping to hear a steady criminal voice.

However, still another voice is present in these memoirs, one that Franklin fails to hear but one that eventually proves louder than either the voice of the confessant drawn sadly into the urban social swirl or the voice of the rogue rambunctiously on the illegitimate make. A major emergent social formation of the late nineteenth century engenders this voice. Unlikely as it may seem, special purpose occupationalism powerfully infuses the criminal memoirs. This infusion makes the memoirs truly modern and distinguishes them as cultural work of a particular historical juncture.

Throughout the works the authors manifest self-impressions grounded in a sense of their calling. For a man with a calling, the act of confessing can itself be boastful. Rather than fleeing their pasts, these men have the courage to confront their deeds. Their public remorse is nothing less momentous than "an awakening of the soul."[38] Seemingly picaresque adventures, meanwhile, become cohesive if placed in an occupational context. When George Bidwell sets out for Amsterdam in order to "pry out a good-sized nugget from the 'pocket' of one of those bulky—in body and estate—but justly cautious Hollanders,"[39] he has a specific occupational goal. When he becomes the first person to perpetrate a large-scale fraud on the Bank of England—"the Old Lady with impregnable vaults"[40]—he creates an occupational bench mark.

Admittedly, the criminal authors cannot completely remove insecurity from their voices; Moore, for example, offers to provide confirming references should anyone doubt him.[41] However, this fleeting self-doubt notwithstanding, the authors' claim is the assertion of elite professionalism. To use the language of bank robber George White, the authors are "high-class men, such as bank burglars, bank sneaks and big forgers"; certainly they should not be confused with "the small-fry thief."[42] They may lack formal training, a license, and a professional commitment to clients, but like members of other stabilizing occupational groups of the period, they are anxious to cast themselves in professional terms.[43] Time and again, the authors in fact refer to themselves as "professionals."[44] By way of justifying their claim to this social title, they ask us to believe they "never as a rule attempt any unfair means to induce each other to take part in crime."[45] They have character. They portray their lives as marked by consciously separated and sequentially ordered stages. As men who have climbed a social ladder, the authors understand themselves as careerists.[46]

The memoirists' portrayal of police, detectives, and law enforcement procedures is consistent with their professed professionalism. Through a range of anecdotes, the memoirists invite the reader to envision a friendly relationship between law enforcement officials and themselves. Langdon Moore wagers and drinks with policemen at Jim Colbert's Saloon, and even when he sets up three New Jersey detectives for a futile three-day stakeout, his motivations are less malicious than fraternal.[47] George Bidwell, meanwhile, recalls the time a group of counterfeiters wanted to give Boss Tweed's daughter a $500 silver punch bowl as a wedding gift. In order to avoid embarrassing the proud father and his daughter, the counterfeiters arranged to have the gift displayed in Tiffany's window and presented under the name of Superintendent of Police James Kelso. Catherine Tweed had her gift, the Boss knew who had truly given it, and Kelso was delighted the counterfeiters had made him appear a pillar of generosity.[48]

Given such cordial relations, it is hardly surprising that criminals and law enforcement officials reportedly work well together. Criminals allegedly paid police and detectives to turn the other way during the planning and perpetration of crimes. Police and detectives on the other hand contacted criminals with ideas for criminal ventures. George Bidwell recalls a New York City detective who came to him with news that a well-to-do German jeweler was to open a new shop. With the detective's cooperation, Bidwell rented a shop next door and easily stole the jeweler's stock even before the store opened for business. The detective received a standard percentage of the take. Had he physically participated in the heist itself, Bidwell notes matter-of-factly, he would have received a full share.[49]

According to the criminal memoirists, the working arrangements between law enforcement officials and criminals were most formalized in New York City. George White points out this had not always been the case:

> When I came to New York, the partnership of the police with professional criminals was of the go as you please sort. The fat, thin, great, small, long, and short hand of the copper was held out from all sides,—in Mulberry Street, in the police courts, on post. Everywhere protection was being paid for indiscriminately. If one copper got more from one crook than another, it was quite likely to create jealousy, and be certain that the crook got the worst end of the argument.[50]

Fortunately, Boss Tweed and other politicians helped straighten things out, and James Irving, the city's top detective, began serving as a coordinator. Eventually Irving's whole detective bureau, White asserts, became a "safety switch" for joint ventures involving criminals and law enforcement officials.[51]

The most fascinating part of the criminal authors' commentary on law enforcement concerns the Pinkerton National Detective Agency. As noted in the preceding chapter, the agency had by the final decades of the century become the nation's leading law enforcement organization. It marketed from a half-dozen branch offices a range of detective services to businesses and bankers. Criminal memoirists, one might expect, would rail against such an operation, but that is decidedly not the case. To a man, the criminal memoirists praise the Pinkertons as particularly honest, forceful and dependable. Like us, the memoirists imply, Pinkertons are the crème de la crème of their calling.

At times the memoirists' comments on the Pinkertons approach the obsequious. Even though the Pinkertons were responsible for his capture, Bidwell profusely thanks Allan Pinkerton's son William for visiting him in a Havana jail and for supplying cigars and wine.[52] Moore bursts with pride when Allan Pinkerton not only favorably compares Moore to Pinkerton Lieutenant George Bangs but also offers Moore the superintendent's position in the agency's New York office.[53] Professional criminals of late nineteenth-century urban America were prepared to measure themselves against the Pinkertons, but the measuring is marked more by shared goals and styles than by hostility or antagonism.[54]

The authors' elite professionalism also leads to empathic impressions of late nineteenth-century American businessmen. Pinkerton, as noted earlier, was at ease with the industrialists, bankers, and businessmen who purchased his detective services. Businessmen, he makes clear, are the natural colleagues of the elite professional detective.[55] The criminal authors were much less likely to be invited into the boardroom, but they too are fond of businessmen and business procedures. In hopes of dignifying criminal conduct as opposed to denigrating business practices, George Bidwell points out that both professional criminals and smart businessmen purchase goods without being certain they can pay for them.[56] Langdon Moore not only revels in his contacts with legitimate businessmen, Allan Pinkerton included, but also argues American prisons could be improved if "conducted on business principles" with the warden given authority comparable to "the head of a business house."[57]

The criminal authors' actual comments on crime also relate to their professionalism. One author vaguely suggests that social "circumstances" might lead one to a life of crime,[58] but he does not pursue his deterministic notion. Another seems prepared to take issue with "scientists" who argue criminals are mentally ill,[59] but he never makes an alternative environmentalist argument. Time and again the authors launch discussions of crime in general only to gravitate quickly to considerations of their own type of crime. They limit the range of their discussions, rarely considering personal violence or social disorder crime. They are, like most careerist professionals, consumed by what they themselves do.

According to the memoirs, the criminals' operations are quite sophisticated. George Bidwell's account of his swindle of the Bank of England is representative. After his investigation reveals the bank does not send bills of exchange to its acceptors for verification, Bidwell hatches his plan. He moves to London and during a span of six months frequently converts and reconverts his capital assets, each time passing legitimate bills of exchange through the bank. Then, as a respected and seemingly flush client, Bidwell one day presents a stack of expertly forged bills. The bank's clerks never bat an eye, and Bidwell absconds with £1,000,000.

The other criminal authors tell of similarly intricate operations. They communicate with lawyers, fences and criminal colleagues by telegraph and private messenger service. They assemble staffs of specialized "sneaks," "stalls" and "shoo-flies" who, dependable and brave, are always well groomed.[60] When the criminal authors enter into compromise agreements with banks and other legitimate businesses, they keep their ends of complicated bargains.

As part of their self-aggrandizing presentation, the authors attempt to correct any misimpressions the reader may have from journalistic, fictional or police sources. Police rogues' galleries in particular seem, from the criminals' perspective, misleading. Police obtain criminal photographs only through force, a point Bidwell seeks to prove by including a drawing of a criminal struggling desperately with a rogues' gallery photographer.[61] Furthermore, the numbered tintypes made available by police and prisons show visages which in the authors' opinions are too worn and sinister. Several of the authors provide alternative pictures of themselves as strong and attractive men.

The criminal author who most extensively employs photographs is Langdon Moore. After asserting that photographs might be used to identify Pinkerton agents as well as criminals,[62] Moore supplies pictures of his colleagues, his private residences and even his counterfeit bank bills. He also creates a photographic symbol for himself, namely, a small human figure wearing an overcoat and top hat. Moore inserts his dignified

AS I AM.
(Not copyrighted by the police.)

ORIGINAL IN ROGUES' GALLERY, BOSTON.
Obtained by fraud and falsehood, Feb. 21, 1880; since
copyrighted without my knowledge or consent, and
sent among the nations of the earth.

Illus. 19. Photographic composite of the author from *Langdon W. Moore: His Own Story of His Eventful Life* (1893).

little self into pictures of business streets, store fronts and bank interiors. The resulting composites convey an impression of bourgeois calm.

Overall, the criminal memoirists most likely overstated the collegiality of their relationships with police and businessmen and also the professionalism of their own operations, but this overstatement in itself is less intriguing than the strategies it suggests. Successful yet illegitimate, the memoirists supply images designed to garner respect. Lacking uniforms, badges and societal stamps of approval, they place themselves and their work in a positive light. Echoing the dominant prescriptions of a modern social order, they champion efficiency, organization and rational, photographic objectivity. As ironic as it may seem, the sophisticated property criminals want the reader to believe they are criminals who may be trusted.

The expressions of similar sentiments in the late nineteenth-century police and detective writing are not surprising. The authors, after all, represent and promote bulwarks of the modern society. However, when these sentiments are expressed by criminals, it is astounding. If even the criminal, the mythical social outsider, is grounded as felon and cultural worker in a social and cultural order, how firm and established that order must have been. If the criminal writings are strongly colored by dominant ideologies, how appropriate it is to think of the criminal's world as hegemonic.[63]

First visible in the early decades of the century, the institutions and ideologies of the hegemony were solidly in place by the final decades of the century. More and more Americans lived in cities, attended public schools, and served in the army. Some worked in factories. Others built professional careers. Dominant groups internalized and promoted a sanctification of private property, a belief in self-interested industriousness, and valorization of specialized organization and rational efficiency. While the lack of consensus necessitated a degree of coercion, the consent of subordinated social groups was even more important than coercion in preserving the social formation as a whole. Property criminals, like police and detectives, knew the hegemony as their fundamental social experience. It is little wonder their attempts to remember crime are shaped by the world they wanted to call home.

Epilogue

There are recognizable stages and an overall shift in alignment in crime-related cultural work produced in the United States during the nineteenth century. Early in the century a broadside and pamphlet literature similar to that which had been available in western Europe for almost three hundred years framed criminals as rogues and fiends. Then, during the antebellum period, with cities burgeoning and industrializing and emergent social groups struggling to define their relationships with one another, cultural work regarding crime briefly became more fluid. Cultural workers changed their specialties and even their occupations frequently, and crime reporting in the cheap press, popular crime fiction, and the very earliest police and detective memoirs provided criminal frames rich in aggressive critical meanings. By the final decades of the century specialization, genre, professionalism and bureaucratic institutionalism assumed hegemonic roles, and the reporting, imagining and remembering of crime lost its critical thrust. Even the memoirs of criminals revealed strong affiliations with the status quo and receptiveness to dominant values of efficiency, organization and scientific objectivity.

Our late twentieth-century society and crime-related cultural work of course derive more from the final than the middle decades of the nineteenth century. Social behavior and ideological presumptions that surfaced in midcentury achieved dominance by the end of the century and then consolidation in the twentieth century. Cultural work, a major aspect of and contributor to a new texture of life, has come in the twentieth century to include technologies that would surprise the cultural worker of the 1890s. However, that cultural worker, sprung from his or her own period into the present, would not be surprised to see professionalism intertwined with cultural work and highly specialized workers performing in well-organized branches of an immense culture industry. Nor would the time traveler find it surprising that the production, marketing and consumption of most cultural work are geared to genres and enfolded in consumer capitalism. All of these tendencies were well established by the final decades of the nineteenth century. Modern cultural work began then.

Indeed, our contemporary crime-related cultural works are themselves surprisingly similar to the works that existed in the 1890s. The reader need not seek the basic entertaining and informing modes of crime reporting in the bowels of a microfilm collection. These modes are for sale on the contemporary newsstand in the pages of the *New York Post* and *The New York Times*, to cite only two representative examples. Middle-class detective fiction with its charming puzzles has hardly expired but rather thrives, and while Old Sleuth and Old Cap. Collier may no longer be available in pulpy coverings, heroic crime-stopping descendants of Nick Carter provide thrills galore on movie and television screens. Police, detectives and criminals, less prone perhaps to memoir writing than their self-consciously professionalizing nineteenth-century ancestors, nevertheless express themselves in cultural products. Local police departments ape the Federal Bureau of Investigation, which itself earlier aped the Pinkerton National Detective Agency, and representatives of all three organizations tout their efficiency and organization while spouting streams of prototypical criminal profiles and brutally reified, often misleading crime statistics. Expert criminals, searching for approval, boast of their connections to other criminal colleagues, established businessmen and even presidents. The frames for crime that emerged in the nineteenth century—the patterns of selection, presentation, and emphasis—are in many ways our contemporary frames.

In addition, the criminal frames of today also resemble the dominant frames of one hundred years ago in the political meanings they convey. Occasionally, twentieth-century works, for example, the hard-boiled school of detective fiction, black prison writings of the 1960s and 1970s, and the television series "Hill Street Blues," suggest a highly charged, critical vision. In exceptional cases they explicitly link crime and politics, but much more commonly, crime-related cultural work of the twentieth century supports the status quo. It says forces and individuals are pursuing and capturing criminals. It insists crime can be recognized, tabulated and controlled. Only rarely does this cultural work suggest or facilitate a critical, political understanding of crime as a complex social phenomenon.

As consumers and potential cultural workers, we must find and place in our crime-related artifacts new frames and meanings. The process of framing the criminal is important and highly consequential. In the nineteenth century and today, the process normatively delineates the lines between social legitimacy and illegitimacy. Crime-related works contribute significantly to our values and very sense of reality. Without new frames and meanings, we are more likely to launch another century of oppression and alienation, of pain and melancholy. To do so would be criminal in a way our standard frames and ideologies do not suggest.

Notes

The Preface

1. Many historians have applied the concept of modernization to nineteenth-century America, but Richard D. Brown has been the most diligent and careful. For his summary of nineteenth-century modernization and bibliographic information regarding other secondary commentaries, see "Modernization: A Victorian Climax," *American Quarterly*, 27 (1975): 548–553. A longer study by Brown, which begins with the first colonial settlements in North America, is *Modernization: The Transformation of American Life, 1600–1865* (New York: Hill and Wang, 1976).

2. For a critique of works in American history employing the modernization model, see Thomas Bender, *Community and Social Change in America* (1978; reprint, Baltimore: Johns Hopkins University Press, 1982).

3. Herbert Gutman, *Work, Culture and Society in Industrializing America* (New York: Vintage Books, 1977).

4. Until the 1960s, mainstream criminologists were confident that crime and criminals were, respectively, recognizable social phenomena and actors. Criminology explored the "criminal subculture" to determine why persons committed deviant acts, and it proposed ways in which criminal justice institutions could train and reform criminals. Sheldon and Eleanor Glueck in their many published works illustrate the thrust of this approach. For insightful critiques of mainstream criminology, see Leon Radzinowicz, *In Search of Criminology* (Cambridge: Harvard University Press, 1962), and Ian Taylor, Paul Walton, and Jack Young, *The New Criminology: For a Social Theory of Deviance* (1973; reprint, New York: Harper & Row, 1974).

5. Even criminology has in recent years accepted and elaborated the notion of criminal labeling. See Howard S. Becker, *Outsiders: Studies in the Sociology of Deviance* (London: Free Press of Glencoe, 1963); Walter R. Gove, *The Labelling of Deviance: Evaluating a Perspective* (New York: Halsted Press, 1975); and Edwin M. Schur, *Labeling Deviant Behavior: Its Sociological Implications* (New York: Harper & Row, 1971).

6. Two fascinating works that incorporate this assumption are Kai T. Erikson, *The Wayward Puritans: A Study in the Sociology of Deviance* (New York: John Wiley & Sons, 1966), and Charles E. Rosenberg, *The Trial of the Assassin Guiteau: Psychiatry and the Law in the Gilded Age* (Chicago: University of Chicago Press, 1968). An excellent article reviewing American and European scholarly work utilizing this dialectical approach to crime is Robert A.

Nye, "Crime in Modern Societies: Some Research Strategies for Historians," *Journal of Social History,* 11 (1978): 491–508.

7. The theorist and historian Raymond Williams discusses changing meanings of the term "culture" in *Marxism and Literature* (Oxford: Oxford University Press, 1977), 11–20. For a summary of the term's meanings in the social sciences, see A. L. Kroeber and Clyde Kluckhohn, *Culture: A Critical Review of Concepts and Definitions* (1952; reprint, New York: Random House, 1963).

8. Robert Berkhofer underscores and comments upon this confusion in "Clio and the Culture Concept: Some Impressions of a Changing Relationship in American Historiography," in Louis Schneider and Charles Bonjean, eds., *The Idea of Culture in the Social Sciences* (Cambridge, England: University Press, 1973).

9. Louis Althusser approaches "practice" in much the way I approach "work," even dividing it into certain prototypical varieties. Louis Althusser, *For Marx,* trans. Ben Brewster (1965; reprint, London: Verso Editions, 1977), 166–70.

10. For an excellent discussion of this development in the United States, see Alan Trachtenberg, *The Incorporation of America: Culture and Society in the Gilded Age* (New York: Hill and Wang, 1982), 140–81.

11. For general discussions and applications by scholars self-consciously working on "popular culture," see Ray B. Browne, Sam Grogg, Jr., and Larry Landrum, eds., "Theories and Methodologies in Popular Culture," *Journal of Popular Culture,* 9 (1975): 351–508. For a comparable group of articles using and insisting on an alternative "mass culture" methodology, see Stanley Aronowitz, John Brenkman, and Frederic Jameson, eds., "Mass Culture," *Social Text,* 1 (1979): 94–181.

12. Williams, *Marxism and Literature,* 121–27.

13. Ibid., 196–205.

14. The most influential work employing the notion of a frame is Erving Goffman, *Frame Analysis: An Essay on the Organization of Experience* (New York: Harper & Row, 1974). Goffman stresses the frames of events and experiences, but more recent commentators have applied the concept of framing to texts and other cultural products. Recent examples are Todd Gitlin, *The Whole World is Watching: Mass Media and the Making and Unmaking of the New Left* (Berkeley and Los Angeles: University of California Press, 1980), and Gaye Tuchman, *Making News* (New York: The Free Press, 1978).

Chapter 1. Criminal Conduct in a Modernizing Society: A Social History of Nineteenth-Century American Crime

1. For a sketch of the arrangements of criminals in the Tombs, see George W. Walling, *Recollections of a New York Chief of Police: An Official Record of Thirty-*

Eight Years as Patrolman, Detective, Captain, Inspector and Chief of the New York Police (New York: Coxton, 1887), 398. For an additional sketch of the Tombs in this period, see James Dabney McCabe, *New York by Sunlight and Gaslight* (Philadelphia: Douglas Brothers, 1881), 409–16.

2. Popular histories of nineteenth-century criminals and crime have appeared throughout the twentieth century. Representative titles include Jules Archer, *Riot! A History of Mob Action in the United States* (New York: Hawthorne Books, 1974); Herbert Asbury, *The Barbary Coast—An Informal History of the San Francisco Underworld* (New York: Alfred A. Knopf, 1973); Allen Churchill, *A Pictorial History of American Crime, 1849–1929* (New York: Holt, Rinehart and Winston, 1964); Alfred H. Lewis, *Nation-Famous New York Murders* (Chicago: M. A. Donohue, 1914); James McConaughy, *From Cain to Capone: Racketeering through the Ages* (New York: Brentano's, 1931); and Jay R. Nash, *Bloodletters and Badmen: A Narrative Encyclopedia of American Criminals from the Pilgrims to the Present* (New York: M. Evans, 1973), *Hustlers and Con Men: An Anecdotal History of the Confidence Man and His Games* (New York: M. Evans, 1976), and *Murder, America: Homicide in the United States from the Revolution to the Present* (New York: Simon and Schuster, 1980).

3. David J. Bodenhamer, "Law and Disorder on the Early Frontier: Marion County, Indiana, 1823–1850," *Western History Quarterly,* 10 (1979): 323–56; Frank Browning and John Gerassi, *The American Way of Crime* (New York: G. P. Putnam's Sons, 1980); Theodore N. Ferdinand, "The Criminal Patterns of Boston Since 1849," *American Journal of Sociology,* 73 (1967): 84–99; Roger Lane, "Crime and Criminal Statistics in Nineteenth-Century Massachusetts," *Journal of Social History,* 2 (1968): 156–63; Lane, *Violent Death in the City: Suicide, Accident, and Murder in Nineteenth-Century Philadelphia* (Cambridge: Harvard University Press, 1979); Eric H. Monkkonen, *The Dangerous Class: Crime and Poverty in Columbus, Ohio, 1860–1885* (Cambridge: Harvard University Press, 1975); Monkkonen, "A Disorderly People: Urban Order in the Nineteenth and Twentieth Centuries," *Journal of American History,* 68 (1981): 539–59; Elwin H. Powell, "Crime as a Function of Anomie," *Journal of Criminal Law, Criminology and Police Science,* 57 (1966): 161–71. For a comparative perspective, see Howard Zehr, "The Modernization of Crime in Germany and France, 1830–1913," *Journal of Social History,* 8 (Summer, 1975): 117–41.

4. James A. Henretta, *The Evolution of American Society, 1700–1815* (Lexington, Massachusetts: D. C. Heath, 1973).

5. A full review of the secondary studies of early nineteenth-century change is beyond the scope of this work. For a review of the literature and a challenge to my simple reliance on modernization theory, see Thomas Bender, *Community and Social Change in America* (Baltimore: Johns Hopkins University Press, 1982), 86–108.

6. One scholar has characterized this breakdown of networks as "detribaliza-

tion." J. J. Tobias, *Crime and Industrial Society in the Nineteenth Century* (New York: Schocken Books, 1967), 249.

7. For the classic discussion of anomie, see Emile Durkheim, *The Division of Labor in Society,* trans. George Simpson (Glencoe, Illinois: Free Press, 1933), 368–73.

8. "Report of the Joint Special Committee Relative to Establishing a Preventive Police" (New York: William Denman, Printer, 1843), 188–89.

9. Ferdinand, "Criminal Patterns of Boston," 84–99.

10. Lane, "Crime and Criminal Statistics," 156–63.

11. For a comparative study of nineteenth-century crime in Massachusetts and South Carolina, see Stephen Hindus, *Prison and Plantation: Crime, Justice and Authority in Massachusetts and South Carolina, 1767–1878* (Chapel Hill: University of North Carolina Press, 1980).

12. For general reflections and for a study of the relation of homicide to the business cycle in the United States, see Andrew F. Henry and James F. Short, Jr., *Suicide and Homicide* (Glencoe, Illinois: The Free Press, 1954).

13. Quoted in Robert Sullivan, *The Disappearance of Dr. Parkman* (Boston: Little, Brown and Company, 1971), 183.

14. Emmanuel Tonay, "Psychiatric Study of Homicide," *American Journal of Psychiatry,* 125 (1969): 148.

15. Lane, *Violent Death in the City,* 59.

16. Ibid., 83.

17. David R. Johnson, *Policing the Urban Underworld: The Impact of Crime on the Development of the American Police, 1800–87* (Philadelphia: Temple University Press, 1979), 140. A fuller treatment of the development of nineteenth-century police departments appears in Chapter 7 of this work. Surely the development of citywide police departments in this period affected arrest totals, a figure some historians take as synonymous with crime totals.

18. For a suggestion of the complexities inherent in the police-citizenry relationship of the period, see David Reynold's sketch of affairs in antebellum Philadelphia, *George Lippard* (Boston: Twayne Publishers, 1982), 12.

19. Richard M. Brown, "Historical Patterns of Violence in America," in *The History of Violence in America: Historical and Comparative Perspectives,* eds. Hugh Graham and Ted Gurr (New York: Frederick A. Praeger, 1969), 54; Carl E. Prince, "The Great 'Riot Year': Jacksonian Democracy and Patterns of Violence in 1834," *Journal of the Early Republic* 5 (1985): 1–19.

20. Willard A. Heaps, *Riots, USA, 1765–1970* (New York: Seabury Press, 1966), 39–49.

21. Sam Bass Warner, Jr., *The Private City: Philadelphia in Three Periods of Its Growth* (Philadelphia: University of Pennsylvania Press, 1968), 151.

22. Heaps, *Riots, USA,* 52.

23. David R. Johnson, "Crime Patterns in Philadelphia, 1840–70," in *The Peoples of Philadelphia,* eds. Allen F. David and Mark H. Haller (Philadelphia: Temple University Press, 1973), 89–110.

24. Police and others often characterize this variety of property crime as "vice" and establish special departments and procedures to deal with it. While most property crimes involve theft of goods and services, vice involves selling illicit goods and services.

25. Powell, "Crime as a Function of Anomie," 161.

26. Douglas Hay *et al.*, *Albion's Fatal Tree: Crime and Society in Eighteenth-Century England* (New York: Pantheon Books, 1975); E. J. Hobsbawn, *Bandits* (New York: Pantheon Books, 1969); E. P. Thompson, *Whigs and Hunters: The Origin of the Black Act* (New York: Pantheon Books, 1975); Michael R. Weisser, *Crime and Punishment in Early Modern Europe* (Bristol, England: Harvester Press, 1979), 29–49.

27. Marshall B. Clinard, "The Process of Urbanization and Criminal Behavior," *American Journal of Sociology*, 48 (1942): 202–13; Frederick M. Thrasher, *The Gang* (Chicago: University of Chicago Press, 1936).

28. Paul Dolan, "The Rise of Crime in the Period 1830–1860," *Journal of the American Institute of Criminal Law and Criminology*, 30 (1939): 851; Browning and Gerassi, *American Way of Crime*, 134–39.

29. Browning and Gerassi, *American Way of Crime*, 137.

30. Edith Abbott, "The Civil War and the Crime Wave of 1865–70," *Social Science Review*, 1 (1927): 216–19.

31. Ibid., 219–22.

32. "The Reformation of Prison Reform," *North American Review*, 217 (1867): 580–81.

33. Abbott, "Civil War and the Crime Wave," 232.

34. Betty B. Rosenbaum, "The Relationship between War and Crime in the United States," *Journal of Criminal Law, Criminology and Police Science*, 30 (1939): 725–29, 738. Abbott also accepts this argument, citing post-Civil War commentators and drawing an analogy to the crime wave in England following the Crimean War. Abbott, "Civil War and the Crime Wave," 212, 232.

35. This development will be discussed at greater length in chapter 2.

36. Magali Sarfatti Larson, *The Rise of Professionalism: A Sociological Analysis* (Berkeley and Los Angeles: University of California Press, 1977).

37. R. Freeman Butts and Lawrence A. Cremin, *A History of Education in American Culture* (New York: Holt, Rinehart and Winston, 1953), 356–64, 415–21.

38. Daniel T. Rodgers, *The Work Ethic in Industrial America, 1850–1920* (Chicago: The University of Chicago Press, 1974), 153–81.

39. For an excellent local study of how the differentiation of nineteenth-century social zones led to a reduction of urban disorder and conflict, see John C. Schneider, *Detroit and the Problem of Order, 1830–80* (Lincoln: University of Nebraska Press, 1980).

40. Burton J. Bledstein, *The Culture of Professionalism: The Middle Class and the Development of Higher Education in America* (New York: W. W. Norton, 1976).

41. Recent historical works that employ the concept of hegemony in a rich and sophisticated manner are T. J. Jackson Lears, *No Place of Grace: Antimodernism and the Transformation of American Culture, 1880–1920* (New York: Pantheon Books, 1981), and Alan Trachtenburg, *The Incorporation of America: Culture and Society in the Gilded Age* (New York: Hill and Wang, 1982).

42. Ferdinand, "Criminal Patterns of Boston," 87.

43. Powell, "Crime as a Function of Anomie," 163–64.

44. Monkkonen, *The Dangerous Class*, 49–56.

45. Charlotte C. Rhines, "A City and Its Social Problems: Health and Crime in Baltimore, 1865–75" (Ph.D. diss., University of Maryland, 1975), 407–10.

46. Lane, *Violent Death in the City*, 71.

47. Powell, "Crime as a Function of Anomie," 163.

48. Lane, for example, notes the particularly large per capita incidence of homicide in late nineteenth-century Philadelphia's working-class black and Italian communities. *Violent Death in the City*, 103–4.

49. Joyce G. Williams, J. Eric Smithburn, and M. Jeanne Peterson, *Lizzie Borden: A Case Book of Family and Crime in the 1890's* (Bloomington, Indiana: T.I.S. Publications, 1980).

50. Graham J. Barker-Benfield, *The Horrors of the Half-Known Life: Male Attitudes toward Women and Sexuality in Nineteenth-Century America* (New York: Harper & Row, 1976); Michael Gordon, ed., *The American Family in Social-Historial Perspective* (New York: St. Martin's Press, 1973).

51. Monkkonen, "A Disorderly People," 551.

52. Ibid., 540–50.

53. Charles Tilly, "Collective Violence in European Perspective," in Graham and Gurr, *Violence in America*, 21.

54. Archer, *Riot!*, 85.

55. Robert V. Bruce, *1877: Year of Violence* (Indianapolis: Bobbs-Merrill, 1959), 57–58.

56. Archer, *Riot!*, 85.

57. Robert H. Wiebe, *The Search for Order, 1877–1920* (New York: Hill and Wang, 1967), 78–79.

58. For discussions of the relationship of urban gang activity and professional crime in the final decades of the twentieth century, see Jenna Weissman Joselit, *Our Gang: Jewish Crime and the New York Jewish Community* (Bloomington: Indiana University Press, 1983); John Landesco, "The Criminal Underworld of Chicago in the 1880s and 1890s," *Journal of Criminal Law and Criminology*, 25 (1934): 343–45; and Humbert S. Nelli, *The Business of Crime: Italians and Syndicate Crime in the United States* (New York: Oxford University Press, 1976).

59. The Ross kidnapping featured the first series of child ransom letters in American history. Churchill, *History of American Crime*, 20.

60. Quoted in Browning and Gerassi, *American Way of Crime*, 289.

61. For a discussion of the criminal conduct of Cooke, Gould, Morgan and Rockefeller, see Browning and Gerassi, *American Way of Crime*, 210–15 and

Ellen A. Knodt, "The American Criminal: The Quintessential Self-Made Man," *Journal of American Culture,* 2 (Spring, 1979): 30–35.

62. Matthew Josephson, *The Robber Barons: The Great American Capitalists, 1861–1901* (New York: Harcourt, Brace, 1934), 95–96, 141–48.

63. George Bidwell, *Bidwell's Travels: From Wall Street to London Prison* (Hartford, Connecticut: Bidwell Publishing, 1897), 41.

64. The authors of Gilded Age books on the urban scene were frequently struck by the development of fencing operations. For representative discussions, see Junius Henri Browne, *The Great Metropolis: A Mirror of New York* (Hartford: American Publishing, 1869), 481–83; Edward Crapsey, *The Nether Side of New York; or, the Vice, Crime and Poverty of the Great Metropolis* (New York: Sheldon, 1872), 83–91; and McCabe, *New York by Sunlight,* 432–39.

65. Richard H. Rovere, *Howe & Hummel: Their True and Scandalous History* (New York: Straus, 1947), 26–27.

66. Jürgen Thorwald, *The Century of the Detective,* trans. Richard and Clara Winston (New York: Harcourt, Brace & World, 1965), 96.

67. Walling, *Recollections,* 291.

Chapter 2. Rogues and Fiends: Criminal Frames in the Traditional Street Literature

1. Frank Luther Mott, *American Journalism: A History, 1690–1960,* 3rd ed. (1941; reprint, New York: Macmillan, 1962), 8.

2. Ibid., 9–30.

3. Ibid., 48–51.

4. Older scholarship dealing at least in part with this literature includes Frank Aydelotte, *Elizabethan Rogues and Vagabonds* (Oxford: Clarendon Press, 1913); Frank W. Chandler, *The Literature of Roguery* (1907; reprint, New York: Burt Franklin, 1958); Arthur Valentine Judges, ed., *The Elizabethan Underworld* (London: George Routledge and Sons, 1930); and E. J. Ribton-Turner, *A History of Vagrants and Vagrancy and Beggars and Begging* (London: Chapman and Hall, 1887).

5. David Kunzle, *The Early Comic Strip: Narrative Strips and Picture Stories in the European Broadsheet from c. 1450 to 1825* (Berkeley: University of California Press, 1973), 4, argues that the term "broadsheet" has acquired a pictorial connotation while the term "broadside" is reserved for sheets consisting primarily of text. I have not observed this distinction. Instead, I have used "broadsheet" to refer to both sheets with a preponderance of illustrations and those consisting primarily of text.

6. For a brief discussion of crime-related writings by Defoe and Fielding, see Alma E. Murch, *The Development of the Detective Novel* (London: Peter Owen, 1958), 23. For a comment on de Lacretelle, see Michel Foucault, *Discipline and Punish: The Birth of the Prison,* trans. Alan Sheridan (New York: Vintage, 1979), 68.

7. Twenty-seven surviving sermons have been studied by Ronald A. Bosco, "Lectures at the Pillory: The Early Execution Sermon," *American Quarterly* 30 (1978): 156–76. Although the practice of delivering a simple moral discourse or exhortation at the gallows was common in England, the Puritan practice of delivering and publishing more elaborate sermons was unique in English-speaking communities.

8. Daniel E. Williams, "Rogues, Rascals and Scoundrels: The Underworld Literature of Early America," *American Studies* 24 (1983): 8.

9. David H. Hall, "The World of Print and Collective Mentality in Seventeenth-Century New England," in *New Directions in American Intellectual History,* eds. John Higham and Paul K. Conklin (Baltimore: Johns Hopkins University Press, 1979), 176.

10. *Sinners directed to hear and fear, and do no more so wickedly. Being an impartial account of the inhumane and barbarous murder, committed by Jeremiah Meacham, on his wife and her sister, at Newport on Rhode Island, March 22, 1715* (Boston: printed by J. Allen, for N. Boone, at the Sign of the Bible in Cornhill, 1715) and *The sad effects of sin. A true relation of the murder committed by David Wallis, on his companion Benjamin Stolwood: on Saturday night, the first of August, 1713. With his carriage after condemnation; his confession and dying speech at the place of execution, &c.* (Boston: printed by J. Allen, for N. Boone, at the Sign of the Bible in Cornhill, 1713).

11. John Tebbel, *A History of Book Publishing in the United States* (New York: R. R. Bowker, 1972), 1:160.

12. Quoted in Mott, *American Journalism,* 55.

13. Williams, "Rogues, Rascals and Scoundrels," 13–14.

14. Ibid., 13–14.

15. Erwin C. Surrency, "Law Reports in the United States," *American Journal of Legal History* 25 (1981): 52–53.

16. *The Criminal Recorder or, An Awful Beacon to the Rising Generation of Both Sexes, Erected by the Arm of Justice to Persuade Them from the Dreadful Miseries of Guilt* (Philadelphia: Mathew Carey, 1812).

17. Ibid., v.

18. Ibid., 6.

19. Tebbel, *History of Book Publishing,* 160.

20. Ted Peterson, "British Crime Pamphleteers: Forgotten Journalists," *Journalism Quarterly* 22 (1945): 305–16.

21. Ted Peterson, "James Catnach: Master of Street Literature," *Journalism Quarterly* 27 (1950): 161.

22. Ibid., 162.

23. Ibid., 161.

24. Peterson, "British Crime Pamphleteers," 314.

25. The best source of crime-related street literature titles is Thomas M. McDade, comp., *The Annals of Murder: A Bibliography of Books and Pamphlets on American Murders from Colonial Times to 1900* (Norman, Oklahoma:

University of Oklahoma Press, 1961). Since McDade is concerned only with murders, his listing is not complete, but McDade, an FBI agent turned bibliographer, is accurate and thorough, listing 1,126 titles. For a comment on McDade's scholarship, from a book collector's perspective, see Patterson Smith, "Collecting True Crime Literature," *Bookman's Weekly* 69 (1982): 3435–58.

26. Thomas M. McDade, "Lurid Literature of the Last Century: The Publications of E. E. Barclay," *Pennsylvania Magazine of History and Biography*, 80 (1956): 455–56.

27. *The Only Copy of the Life, and the Testimony that Convicted Michl. Monroe, alias James Wellington, at Chester, Pennsylvania on the 20th of October, 1824* (Philadelphia: printed and for sale at 38 Chestnut St., 1824).

28. *Life and Confessions of Henry Wyatt, Who Was Executed at Auburn, for the Murder of James Gordon, A Fellow Convict* (Auburn, New York: Ivison, 1846), 56.

29. Ann Jones, *Women Who Kill* (New York: Fawcett Columbine, 1981), 111.

30. McDade, "Lurid Literature of the Last Century," 454.

31. Peterson, "James Catnach," 160.

32. Ribton-Turner, *History of Vagrants*, 471–72.

33. 14 Eliz., c. 5 (1572).

34. *The Autobiography of Charles Moore* (Baltimore: A. R. Orton, 1854).

35. William Stuart, *Sketches of the Life of William Stuart, The First and Most Celebrated Counterfeiter of Connecticut* (Bridgeport: printed by author, 1854).

36. Ibid., 63.

37. Ibid., 124.

38. *The Autobiography of Charles Moore*, 2.

39. *Sketches of the Life of William Stuart*, 220.

40. Roland Barthes, "From Work to Text," in *Textual Strategies: Perspectives in Post-Structuralist Criticism*, ed. Josue V. Harari (Ithaca: Cornell University Press, 1979), 76–78.

41. Peterson estimates Catnach's fortune at 5000 to 10,000 pounds, "James Catnach," 157.

42. Williams, "Rogues, Rascals and Scoundrels," 16–17.

43. Brian J. Burton, *Sweeney Todd the Barber* (Birmingham, England: C. Cambridge, 1962), 5.

44. *Trial and Execution of Thomas Barrett, Who First Committed a Rape on the Person of Mrs. Houghton, of Lunenburg, an Aged Lady of 70 Years, and then Foully Murdered Her to Conceal his Crime, on Sunday Evening, Feb. 18, 1844, and Who Was Hung at Worcester, January 3, 1845* (Boston: Skinner & Blanchard, 1845).

45. *Trial and Confession of Robt. McConaghy, the Inhuman Butcher of Mr. Brown's Family on Saturday, May 30th, 1840, in Huntington County* (Huntington County, Pennsylvania: 1840).

46. *The Confession of Adam Horn, alias Andrew Hellman, Embodying Particulars of*

His Life; Convicted on the 27th November 1843, in Baltimore County Court, of the Murder of His Wife (Baltimore: James Young, 1843).

47. *Trial of Dr. John K. Hardenbrook, Indicted for the Murder of Thos. Nott, By Administering Strychnine to Him in Sufficient Quantity to Produce Death, on the 5th of February, 1849 at Rochester, N. Y.* (Rochester: D. M. Dewey, 1849).

48. William G. McLoughlin, "Untangling the Tiverton Tragedy: The Social Meaning of the Terrible Haystack Murder of 1833," *Journal of American Culture* 7 (1984): 75.

49. McDade, *The Annals of Murder*, lists these 21 pamphlets, 13–19. Presumably there were others that were not located by McDade or that have not survived.

50. Crowds at the grave became so large that the family of the deceased decided to rebury her elsewhere. McLoughlin, "Untangling the Tiverton Tragedy," 83.

51. *Life, Trial, Execution and Dying Confession of John Erpenstein* (Newark: Daily Advertiser, 1852).

52. *Trial of Maurice Antonio, the Portuguese, for the Murder of Ignacio Teixeira Pinto, at Rochester, November 23, 1851* (Rochester: D. M. Dewey, 1852).

53. On women's lifestyles and roles in antebellum America, see Nancy F. Cott, *The Bonds of Womanhood: Woman's Sphere in New England, 1780–1835* (New Haven: Yale University Press, 1977), 63–100; Gerda Lerner, "The Lady and the Mill Girl: Changes in the Status of Women in the Age of Jackson, 1800–1840," in *A Heritage of Her Own: Toward a New Social History of American Women*, eds. Nancy F. Cott and Elizabeth H. Pleck (New York: Simon and Schuster, 1980), 182–96; Ann Oakley, *Woman's Work: The Housewife, Past and Present* (New York: Vintage Books, 1976), 1–59; and Mary P. Ryan, *Womanhood in America From Colonial Times to the Present* (New York: Franklin Watts, 1975), 137–92.

54. *Isabella Narvaez, the Female Fiend and Triple Murderess; or the Life, Confession and Execution of Isabella Narvaez, the Atrocious Murderess of Three Husbands, Who Was Hung at Shelbyville on Friday, September 30, 1853* (Baltimore: A. R. Orton, 1854).

55. Wyatt murdered James Gordon, a fellow inmate at the New York State Prison in Auburn, with a shears when Gordon told prison guards of Wyatt's earlier escapades. *Life and Confessions of Henry Wyatt*, 51.

56. Chandler, *Literature of Roguery*, 3–4.

57. Peterson, "James Catnach," 163.

58. McDade, "Lurid Literature of the Last Century," 460.

59. McDade, *The Annals of Murder*, 119–25, 271–73.

60. Ibid., 35–37.

61. William Denton, *Who Killed Mary Stannard?* (Boston: Colby & Rich, 1880); *Life, Trial and Execution of H. Ruloff* (Philadelphia: Barclay & Co., 1873); and E. H. Freeman, *The Only True and Authentic History of Edward H. Ruloff* (New York: Carl & Freeman, 1871).

62. *Autobiography of Jesse H. Pomeroy* (Boston: J. A. Cummings & Co., 1875).

63. McDade, *The Annals of Murder*, 205–7, 134–36.

64. Karen Halttunen has extensively studied Victorian culture's sustained condemnation of the painted woman and confidence man, the latter being at
least in part a variety of the traditional rogue. *Confidence Men and Painted
Women: A Study of Middle-class Culture in America, 1830–1870* (New Haven:
Yale University Press, 1982).

65. For a provocative commentary on the rags-to-riches literature and particu-
larly on the works of Horatio Alger, see William Coyle, "Introduction" in
Horatio Alger, *Adrift in New York and The World Before Him* (Indianapolis:
Odyssey Press, 1966), v-xvii.

Chapter 3. Politicized Crime Journalism:
The Midcentury Cheap Press

1. Kai Erikson, *Wayward Puritans: A Study in the Sociology of Deviance* (New
York: John Wiley & Sons, 1966), 1–30, 161–82.

2. Earlier historical studies of American journalism include William Grosvenor
Bleyer, *Main Currents in the History of American Journalism* (Boston:
Houghton-Mifflin, 1927); Alfred McClung Lee, *The Daily Newspaper in
America: The Evolution of a Social Instrument* (New York: Macmillan, 1937):
James Melvin Lee, *History of American Journalism* (1917; reprint, Garden
City, New York: Garden City Publishing, 1923); and George Henry Payne,
History of Journalism in the United States (New York: Appleton, 1920). All of
these works, in particular, Alfred McClung Lee's study employing sociologi-
cal perspectives, offer useful insights regarding the penny press. However,
two more recent works have been the most influential: Edwin Emery, *The
Press and America: An Interpretative History of Journalism* (Englewood Cliffs,
New Jersey: Prentice-Hall, 1962) and Frank Luther Mott, *American Journalism: A History, 1690–1960*, 3rd ed. (1941; reprint, New York: MacMillan,
1962). An even more recent work that argues that the *National Police Gazette*
(NPG) embodies certain core features of the American journalistic develop-
ments of the 1830s and 1840s is Dan Schiller, *Objectivity and the News: The
Public and The Rise of Commercial Journalism* (Philadelphia: University of
Pennsylvania Press, 1981).

3. James W. Carey, "The Problem of Journalism History," *Journalism History* 1
(1974): 3–4.

4. Emery, *The Press and America*, v.

5. Michael Schudson, *Discovering the News: A Social History of American Newspapers* (New York: Basic Books, 1978), 17, estimates that over one-half of all
newspapers published weekly or more frequently in Baltimore, Boston,
Charleston, New Orleans, New York, Philadelphia and Washington in 1820
had these words in their names.

6. For a discussion of *The Washington Globe* and politically affiliated newspapers in general, see John Tebbel, *The Compact History of the American Newspaper* (New York: Hawthorne Books, 1963), 89.

7. For a criticism of this tunnel vision, see David H. Weaver, "Frank Luther Mott and The Future of Journalism History," *Journalism History* 2 (1975), 44–47.

8. For an excellent discussion of the changes taking place among these social groups, see Douglas T. Miller, *Jacksonian Aristocracy: Class and Democracy in New York, 1830–1860* (New York: Oxford University Press, 1967), 26–55, 128–54.

9. Edwin Williams, ed., *New-York As It Is, In 1834* (New York: J. Disturnell, 1834), 175.

10. Historical studies of *The Sun*, like those of most individual newspapers, tend to be popular and lionizing. Works that address in part the nineteenth-century history of *The Sun* include Frank M. O'Brien, *The Story of The Sun* (New York: George H. Doran, 1918); Charles J. Rosebault, *When Dana Was The Sun: A Story of Personal Journalism* (New York: Robert M. McBride, 1931); and Candace Stone, *Dana and The Sun* (New York: Dodd, Mead, 1938).

11. Alexander Saxton, "Problems of Class and Race in the Origins of the Mass Circulation Press," *American Quarterly* 36 (1984): 215.

12. O'Brien, *The Story of the Sun*, 25.

13. *The Sun*, 3 September 1833, 1.

14. *The Sun*, 9 May 1834, 2.

15. Edward Crapsey, *The Nether Side of New York; or, The Vice, Crime and Poverty of the Great Metropolis* (New York: Sheldon, 1872), 83.

16. *The Herald*, 31 August 1835, 1.

17. Newspapers in London and in the United States had run police court columns earlier, but *The Sun* greatly expanded and improved this journalistic form. Mott, *American Journalism*, 222. Before Wisner assumed his New York Police Court duties, Day apparently rephrased reports from other newspapers for the column in *The Sun*. James Stanford Bradshaw, "George W. Wisner and the New York *Sun*," *Journalism History* 6 (1979), 117.

18. Saxton, "Problems of Class and Race," 232.

19. Bradshaw, "George W. Wisner," 121.

20. *The Sun*, 24 October 1833, 1.

21. Bradshaw, "George W. Wisner," 119.

22. *The Sun*, 12 December 1833, 2.

23. *The Sun*, 9 June 1836, 2.

24. *The Sun*, 11 February 1834, 2.

25. *The Sun*, 4 January 1835, 2.

26. O'Brien, *The Story of the Sun*, 54, 57.

27. *The Sun*, 30 June 1835, 2.

28. *The Sun*, 9 September 1835, 2.

29. Works tracing the nineteenth-century history of *The Herald* include Oliver Carlson, *The Man Who Made News: James Gordon Bennett* (New York: Duell, Sloan and Pearce, 1942); Albert Stevens Crockett, *When James Gordon Bennett Was Caliph of Bagdad* (New York: Funk & Wagnalls, 1926); and Richard O'Connor, *The Scandalous Mr. Bennett* (Garden City, New York: Doubleday, 1962).

30. When *The Herald* reappeared for the first time on August 31, 1835, Bennett sought to emphasize the newspaper's optimistic rebirth by designating the issue volume I, number I.

31. Mott, *American Journalism,* 234.

32. *The Herald,* 31 August 1835, 1.

33. Ibid., 2.

34. Ibid., 3.

35. *The Herald,* 1 September 1835, 2.

36. After the fire, the Police Court column appeared in only two issues, those of August 31 and September 1, 1835.

37. *The Herald,* 31 August 1835, 2.

38. The misogyny of *The Herald's* reporting deserves further attention. According to *The Herald,* Jewett's "great passion was to seduce young men, and particularly those who most resisted her charms. She seems to have declared war against the sex. 'Oh,' she would say, 'how I despise you all—you are a heartless, unprincipled set—you have ruined me—I'll ruin you—I delight in your ruin.' " *The Herald,* 12 April 1836, 1. Two days later, *The Herald* picked up on this theme by posing a series of questions. "Who is the murderer? It cannot be possible that Robinson was the person? How could a young man perpetrate so brutal an act? Is it not more like the work of a woman? Are [sic] not the whole train of circumstances within the ingenuity of a female, abandoned and desperate?" *The Herald,* 14 April 1836, 1.

39. Mott, *American Journalism,* 233.

40. *The Herald,* 12 April 1836, 4.

41. *The Herald,* 9 June 1836, 2.

42. *The Sun,* 9 June 1836, 2.

43. *The Herald,* 12 April 1836, 1.

44. *The Herald,* 10 June 1836, 1.

45. *The Herald,* 31 August 1836, 2.

46. *The Sun,* 9 November 1833, 2.

47. Perhaps more so than any other historian, Edward Pessen has laid to rest romantic notions that the 1830s and 1840s were decades of the common man in which class society broke down. Eschewing time-honored notions of Jacksonian Democracy, Pessen has convincingly argued that the period was marked by a "seeming deference to the common man by the uncommon men who actually ran things." Edward Pessen, *Jacksonian America: Society, Personality and Politics* (Howewood, Illinois: Dorsey Press, 1969), 351.

48. For traditional descriptions of the "moral war," see Emery, *The Press and America*, 222–23, and Mott, *American Journalism*, 235–38.

49. For studies addressing the involvement of Protestant revivalism in, respectively, labor movements, family life and political parties, see Paul Faler, "Cultural Aspects of the Industrial Revolution: Lynn, Massachusetts Shoemakers and Industrial Morality, 1826–1860," *Labor History* 15 (1974): 367–94; Bernard Wishy, *The Child and the Republic* (Philadelphia: University of Pennsylvania Press, 1968); and Paul Kleppner, *The Cross of Culture: A Social Analysis of Midwestern Politics* (New York: Free Press, 1970).

50. Quoted in Isaac C. Pray, *Memoirs of James Gordon Bennett and His Times* (1855; reprint, New York: Arno Press, 1970), 266.

51. Ibid., 236.

52. Mott, *American Journalism*, 237.

53. Schudson, *Discovering the News*, 55.

54. Pray, *Memoirs*, 265.

55. Peleg W. Chandler, *American Criminal Trials* (Boston: Charles C. Little and James Brown, 1841–44).

56. For biographical treatments of Camp and Wilkes, see Walter Davenport, "The Nickel Shocker," *Colliers*, 10 March 1928, 26, 28, 34, 40; Frank Luther Mott, *A History of American Magazines, 1850–1865* (Cambridge: Harvard University Press, 1938), 325–28; and Edward Van Every, *Sins of New York as "Exposed" by The Police Gazette* (New York: Frederick A. Stokes, 1930), 3–29. A detailed commentary on Wilkes' full life is Alexander Saxton, "George Wilkes: The Transformation of Radical Ideology," *American Quarterly* 33 (1981): 437–58.

57. George Wilkes, *The Mysteries of the Tombs, a Journal of Thirty Days Imprisonment in the New York City Prison* (New York: George Wilkes, 1844). For comments regarding the impact of Wilkes' book on municipal politics, see Davenport, "The Nickel Shocker," 26.

58. Wilkes, *Mysteries of the Tombs*, 55.

59. Davenport, "The Nickel Shocker," 5.

60. Schiller, *Objectivity and the News*, 27.

61. Alma E. Murch, *The Development of the Detective Novel* (London: Peter Owen, 1958), 21.

62. Mott, *A History of American Magazines*, 325; Schiller, *Objectivity and the News*, 98.

63. Murch, *Development of the Detective Novel*, 21.

64. Davenport, "The Nickel Shocker," 28.

65. Standard microfilm collections of the *NPG* do not include all issues. The first four issues, presumably issued individually, are available only in a special combined issue. This combined issue, *NPG* 1:1–4 (16 October 1845), 56, sets the weekly's original circulation at 8600. For circulation claims for 1850, see *NPG*, 5:9 (2 November 1850), 1.

66. *NPG*, 1:9 (8 November 1845), 89.

67. *NPG*, 5:9 (2 November 1850), 1.

68. Proud of the endorsements, the *NPG* reprinted them in 1:9 (8 November 1845), 96.

69. Ibid.

70. *NPG*, 1:1–4 (16 October 1845), 56.

71. The list of rich thieves appeared in the *NPG*, 1:9 (8 November 1845), 92. Reflecting an anti-English sentiment that permeated the NPG's early issues, the editors noted that all of the "rich thieves" were English. Albeit more sporadically, *The Sun* had earlier expressed similar anti-English attitudes. *The Sun*, 9 May 1834, 2.

72. *NPG*, 1:10 (15 November 1845), 104.

73. *NPG*, 2:47 (31 July 1847), 372.

74. *NPG*, 1:14 (13 December 1845), 132.

75. *NPG*, 1:1–4 (16 October 1845), 53.

76. *NPG*, 1:5 (11 October 1845), 58. In a subsequent issue, meanwhile, the *NPG*, perhaps inspired by readers' complaints, noted that complete, bound "Lives" were available at the *NPG*'s New York offices or through agents for 6 1/2¢ each. *NPG*, 1:6 (18 October 1845), 132–33.

77. Schiller, *Objectivity and the News*, 150–78.

78. Davenport, "The Nickel Shocker," 26.

79. Mott, *History of American Magazines*, 326.

80. Van Every, *Sins of New York*, 11–12.

81. *NPG*, 1:14 (13 December 1845), 130.

82. *NPG*, 2:40 (12 June 1847), 316.

83. *NPG*, 1:30 (4 April 1846), 260.

84. Titled "The Life of Richard P. Robinson, Comprising a full account of the history, career and horrible end of the lovely and profligate Helen Jewett," the serial began in *NPG*, 4:4 (30 September 1848).

85. George Wilkes, *The Lives of Helen Jewett and Richard Robinson* (New York: George Wilkes, 1867). For some editions of this work Wilkes used the pseudonym "H. R. Howard," a fact that has confused some scholars, e.g., David B. Davis, *Homicide in American Fiction, 1798–1860: A Study in Social Values* (Ithaca: Cornell University Press, 1957), 164.

Chapter 4. Information and Entertainment: Journalistic Frames for the Modern Society

1. For details on the Tribune Tower and World Building, see, respectively, Harry W. Baehr, Jr., *The New York Tribune Since the Civil War* (New York: Dodd, Mead, 1936), 126–28, and W. A. Swanberg, *Pulitzer* (New York: Charles Scribner's Sons, 1967), 162–64.

2. For a general treatment of prominent Gilded Age dailies and their editors,

see Edwin Emery, *The Press and America: An Interpretative History of Journalism* (Englewood Cliffs, New Jersey: Prentice-Hall, 1962), 386–413 and Frank Luther Mott, *American Journalism: A History, 1690–1960,* 3rd ed. (1941; reprint, New York: Macmillan, 1962), 446–58.

3. Albert Fein, "Centennial New York, 1876," in *New York: The Centennial Years, 1676–1976,* ed. Milton M. Klein (Port Washington, New York: Kennikat, 1976), 75.

4. Mott, *American Journalism,* 403.

5. For discussions of *The Sun* during the nineteenth century and of Charles A. Dana, see Frank M. O'Brien, *The Story of The Sun* (New York: George H. Doran, 1918); Charles J. Rosebault, *When Dana Was The Sun: A Story of Personal Journalism* (New York: Robert M. McBride, 1931); and Candace Stone, *Dana and The Sun* (New York: Dodd, Mead, 1938).

6. Junius Henri Browne, *The Great Metropolis: A Mirror of New York* (Hartford, Connecticut: American Publishing Company, 1869), 305.

7. For discussions of *The Herald* during the Gilded Age, see Oliver Carlson, *The Man who Made News: James Gordon Bennett* (New York: Duell, Sloan and Pearce, 1942); Albert Stevens Crockett, *When James Gordon Bennett Was Caliph of Bagdad* (New York: Funk & Wagnalls, 1926); and Richard O'Connor, *The Scandalous Mr. Bennett* (Garden City, New York: Doubleday, 1962).

8. According to one historian, "No other publisher, save William Randolph Hearst, equaled Bennett in irresponsible personal control of a journalistic enterprise." Emery, *The Press and America,* 507.

9. Mott, *American Journalism,* 403.

10. For discussions of *The New York Times* during the Gilded Age and of Henry Raymond, see Francis Brown, *Raymond of The Times* (New York: Norton, 1951), and Elmer Davis, *History of The New York Times 1851–1921* (New York: The New York Times, 1921).

11. *The New-York Times,* 18 September 1851, 2.

12. For discussions of *The Tribune* during the Gilded Age and of Horace Greeley, see Baehr, *The New York Tribune Since the Civil War,* and Glyndon G. Van Deusen, *Horace Greeley: Nineteenth Century Crusader* (Philadelphia: University of Pennsylvania Press, 1953).

13. Browne, *The Great Metropolis,* 307.

14. Mott, *American Journalism,* 423.

15. Emery, *The Press and America,* 316; Mott, *American Journalism,* 406; John Tebbel, *The Compact History of the American Newspaper* (New York: Hawthorne Books, 1963), 122.

16. Edward Winslow Martin [James Dabney McCabe], *The Secrets of the Great City: A Work Descriptive of the Virtues and the Vices, the Mysteries, Miseries and Crimes of New York City* (Philadelphia: Jones, Brothers & Co., 1868), 135, and Matthew Hale Smith, *Sunshine and Shadow in New York* (Hartford, Connecticut: J. B. Burr, 1869), 635.

17. Browne, *The Great Metropolis*, 296.

18. Figures for 1860 are in Browne, *The Great Metropolis*, 302; figures for 1872 are in Mott, *American Journalism*, 406.

19. Alan Trachtenberg, *The Incorporation of America: Culture and Society in the Gilded Age* (New York: Hill and Wang, 1982), 136.

20. Average annual advertising income for American newspapers during the early 1870s was $12–15 million. Mott, *American Journalism*, 397.

21. S. N. D. North, "History and Present Condition of the Newspaper and Periodical Press of the United States, with a Catalogue of the Publications of the Census Year," in *Tenth Census* (Washington D.C.: Department of the Interior, Bureau of the Census, 1884), VIII, 51.

22. *The Herald* had the largest. Excluding newsboys, it reached 500 in 1869. Smith, *Sunshine and Shadow*, 516.

23. Browne, *The Great Metropolis*, 296–98.

24. George G. Foster, *New York in Slices: by an Experienced Carver* (New York: W. F. Burgess, 1849), 103–7.

25. Harry Kelber and Carl Schlesinger, *Union Printers and Controlled Automation* (New York: The Free Press, 1967), 11.

26. Mott, *American Journalism*, 489.

27. In the opinion of the editors of *The Nation*, "A very slight attention to the actual conditions of a professional career will show how utterly unprofessional newspaper work must always be." Surely, the editors felt, journalists did not compare to doctors or lawyers. "Most generally they remain all their lives collecting news or writing brilliant accounts of murders or hangings." "The Future of the Newspaper," *The Nation*, 28 (1879), 432–33.

28. Harry W. Marks, *Small Change; or, Lights and Shades of New York* (New York: Standard Publishing, 1882), 7–9.

29. For data concerning the striking increase in evening newspapers during the post-Civil War years, see Alfred McClung Lee, *The Daily Newspapers in America: The Evolution of a Social Instrument* (1937; reprint, New York: Macmillan, 1947), 65.

30. Gunther Barth, *City People: The Rise of the Modern City Culture in Nineteenth-Century America* (New York: Oxford University Press, 1980), 80.

31. This contrasts significantly with the diversity of antebellum years. George G. Foster, himself a journalist of the 1840s and 1850s, praised the journalist for his ability to write for widely differing newspapers, for being "able to appreciate and assimilate himself with these peculiarities, and to write in turn for all the papers. . . ." Foster, *New York in Slices*, 55.

32. Meyer Berger, *The Story of The New York Times, 1851–1951* (New York: Simon and Schuster, 1951), 33–53.

33. William Grosvenor Bleyer, *Main Currents in the History of American Journalism* (Boston: Houghton Mifflin, 1927), 332.

34. Oliver Grambling, *AP: The Story of News* (New York: Farrar and Rinehart, 1940), 19–25.

35. *The Sun,* 12 December 1855, 2.

36. For an insightful discussion of the relationship between crime reporters and the police in contemporary England, see Steve Chibnall, *Law-and-Order News: An Analysis of Crime Reporting in the British Press* (London: Tavistock Publications, 1977), 146–54, 172–205.

37. *The Herald,* 5 July 1877, 10.

38. *The Herald,* 13 July 1874, 5.

39. *The Herald,* 14 July 1877, 8.

40. *The Herald,* 18 July 1877, 6.

41. *The New-York Times,* 18 July 1877, 4.

42. Emery, *The Press and America,* 315–34; Mott, *American Journalism,* 411–29.

43. For discussions of Joseph Pulitzer's early life and newspaper activities, see James W. Barrett, *The World, The Flesh, and Messrs. Pulitzer* (New York: Vanguard, 1931) and Swanberg, *Pulitzer.*

44. For discussions of Hearst's early life and newspaper activities, see Lindsay Chaney and Michael Cieply, *The Hearsts* (New York: Simon and Schuster, 1981); W. A. Swanberg, *Citizen Hearst* (New York: Scribner's, 1961); and John Tebbel, *The Life and Times of William Randolph Hearst* (New York: E. P. Dutton, 1952).

45. Emery, *The Press and America,* 369.

46. Ibid., 378–79.

47. In hopes of competing with *The World, The Herald* and *The New-York Times* lowered their daily prices from, respectively, 3¢ and 4¢ to, in both cases, 2¢. *The Tribune* lowered its price from 4¢ to 3¢. Bleyer, *Main Currents,* 330.

48. Ibid., 329.

49. Daily sales of the *New York Journal* topped 1.5 million on the day following the 1896 Presidential election. Hearst ran a front-page headline of "1,506,634" and an article about his newspaper's sales. Hearst concluded the article by stating, "So great is this feat that an attempt to boast of it would seem ridiculous and paltry." *New York Journal,* 5 November 1896.

50. Lincoln Steffens, "The Conduct of a Newspaper," *Scribner's Magazine,* 22 (1897), 447.

51. One year after Pulitzer took control, *The World's* advertising inches were four times that of *The New-York Times* and *The Tribune,* and in November, 1884 *The World* passed *The Herald.* Bleyer, *Main Currents,* 330.

52. Steffens, "Conduct of a Newspaper," 448.

53. Hearst went so far as to make *The Examiner* a typographical duplicate of *The World.* Ferdinand Lundberg, *Imperial Hearst: A Social Biography* (New York: Arno Press, 1970), 24.

54. Emery, *The Press and America,* 423.

55. Emery, *The Press and America,* 317, 355; Mott, *American Journalism,* 436–39.

56. Barth, *City People,* 84.

57. *The World,* 1 January 1884, 1.

58. For a biographical sketch of Matsell, see Augustine E. Costello, *Our Police Protectors: A History of the New York City Police* (1885; reprint, Montclair, New Jersey: Patterson Smith, 1972), 100–1. Regarding Richard K. Fox's editorship of the *Gazette*, see Walter Davenport, "The Dirt Disher," *Colliers*, 82 (March 24, 1928), 26, 30, 52, 53, and Edward Van Every, *Sins of New York as "Exposed" by the Police Gazette* (New York: Frederick A. Stokes, 1930), 145–71.

59. For discussion of *The World*'s headlines, see Bleyer, *Main Currents*, 328.

60. Mott, *American Journalism*, 543.

61. These headlines were supplemented by a dozen other comparable crime-related headlines in the same issue. The most amusing, "My Coats! My Boots," was followed by an account of the theft of a gentleman's horse show regalia. *New York Journal*, 10 November 1896, 3.

62. For examples, see *The World*, 2 July 1881, 1, and 26 January 1886, 1.

63. For an earlier study of "human interest journalism," see Helen MacGill Hughes, *News and The Human Interest Story* (Chicago: University of Chicago Press, 1940).

64. *The World*, 16 July 1885, 1.

65. *The World*, 30 July 1885, 1.

66. Lee, *Daily Newspaper*, 360–1; Ted Curtis Smythe, "The Reporter, 1800–1900," *Journalism History* 7 (Spring, 1980): 8.

67. Coverage of the Guldensuppe case began in the *New York Journal*, 28 June 1897, 1.

68. *New York Journal*, 4 July 1897, 1.

69. *New York Journal*, 8 July 1897, 1. The editorial then went on to suggest that Thorn was "one of those deliberate monsters that it is the duty of society to exterminate."

70. Richard Chase, *The American Novel and Its Tradition* (1957; reprint, Baltimore: Johns Hopkins University Press, 1980), 38.

71. Alleyne Ireland, *An Adventure with a Genius: Recollections of Joseph Pulitzer* (New York: E. P. Dutton, 1920), 113–15.

72. Bleyer, *Main Currents*, 332.

73. James Creelman, "Joseph Pulitzer—Master Journalist," *Pearson's Magazine*, 21 (March, 1909), 246.

74. Bleyer, *Main Currents*, 351.

75. For discussions of the origins of the phrase "yellow journalism," see Bleyer, *Main Currents*, 339, and Mott, *American Journalism*, 525–26.

76. Isaac C. Pray, *Memoirs of James Gordon Bennett and His Times* (New York: Stringer and Townsend, 1855), 205.

77. Mott, *American Journalism*, 540.

78. Ibid., 541.

79. Emery, *The Press and America*, 445.

80. Mott, *American Journalism*, 539.

81. For a provocative treatment of crime journalism in the tabloids of the 1920s,

see John R. Brazil, "Murder Trials, Murders and Twenties America," *American Quarterly* 33 (Summer, 1981): 166–68.

82. Barth, *City People* 94, 98; Emery, *The Press and America,* 379.

83. Pulitzer briefly terminated use of woodcuts in *The World* in the mid-1880s, but when circulation began slumping, he quickly ordered their resumed use. Emery, *The Press and America,* 378.

84. For discussions of Ochs and *The New York Times,* see Berger, *Story of The New York Times,* 87–128, and Davis, *History of The New York Times,* 175–242.

85. Berger, *Story of The New York Times,* 117.

86. For a discussion of the new slogan's meaning in historical context, see Davis, *History of The New York Times.* 197–200.

87. Michael Schudson, *Discovering the News: A Social History of American Newspapers* (New York: Basic Books, 1978), 89, is sensitive to the same division in American newspapers that this study explores. Schudson speaks of the "aesthetic function" of the journalism that Pulitzer and Hearst wrought, but I believe my use of "entertainment function" more accurately captures this journalism's character.

88. Raymond Williams, *Marxism and Literature* (London: Oxford University Press, 1977), 199.

Chapter 5. Pointed Political Meanings: Popular Antebellum Fiction

1. James D. Hart, *The Popular Book: A History of America's Literary Taste* (New York: Oxford University Press, 1950), 85–105; Frank L. Mott, *Golden Multitudes: A History of Best Sellers in the United States* (New York: Macmillan, 1947), 76–9; and Russel B. Nye, *Society and Culture in America, 1830–1860* (New York: Harper & Row, 1974), 75–77.

2. Frank L. Mott, *A History of American Magazines, 1741–1850* (New York: D. Appleton, 1930), 341–42.

3. Robert E. Spiller, et al., eds., *Literary History of the United States* (New York: Macmillan, 1974), 241.

4. British authors sold twice as many books as American authors in American markets in 1820, but by 1850 the ratio had been inverted.

5. Maria Monk, *Awful Disclosures of Maria Monk, as Exhibited in a Narrative of Her Suffering During a Residence of Five Years as a Novice, and Two Years as a Black Nun, in the Hotel Dieu Nunnery at Montreal,* republished many times, dripped with nativism and was an immense best seller during the 1830s and 1840s. Mott, *Golden Multitudes,* 245–46.

6. Best sellers in this domestic novel genre included E. D. E. N. Southworth's *The Curse of Clifton* (Philadelphia: Carey & Hart, 1852) and *The Hidden Hand* (Philadelphia: Peterson & Brothers, 1859), and Mary Jane Holmes' *Tempest and Sunshine* (New York: D. Appleton, 1854) and

Lena Rivers (New York: Miller, Orton, 1856). Mott, *Golden Multitudes,* 306–8; Nye, *Society and Culture,* 97–100.

7. Caroline Ticknor, *Hawthorne and His Publisher* (Boston: Houghton-Mifflin, 1913), 141.

8. Frank L. Mott defines a best seller as a work whose sales equal or exceed one percent of the population for the decade in which the work was published. Admitting the arbitrariness of this approach, the scholar might nevertheless find useful and be intrigued by the extensive lists of nineteenth-century American best-sellers that Mott has compiled. Mott, *Golden Multitudes,* 304–312.

9. However, certain important minor works by writers of books in the American canon did concern crime in the urban surround. Herman Melville, for example, probed crime and social life in New York in *Pierre; or, The Ambiguities* and evoked the urban horror of London in *Redburn.*

10. Standard biographies of Poe include Hervey Allen, *Israfel: The Life and Times of Edgar Allan Poe* (New York: Farrar & Rinehart, 1934); William Bittner, *Poe: A Biography* (Boston: Little, Brown, 1962); and Arthur Hopson Quinn, *Edgar Allan Poe: A Critical Biography* (1941; reprint, New York: Cooper Square Publishers, 1969). For a shorter treatment of Poe's life, see Julian Symons, *The Tell-Tale Heart: The Life and Works of Edgar Allan Poe* (New York: Harper & Row, 1978). Symons fiercely insists on maintaining a critical division between Poe's life and work.

11. William T. Bandy, *The Influence and Reputation of Edgar Allan Poe in Europe* (Baltimore: C. T. Cimino, 1962); Helen Muchnic, *The Unhappy Consciousness: Gogol, Poe, Baudelaire* (Baltimore: Barton-Gillet, 1967); and G. R. Thompson, *Poe's Fiction: Romantic Irony in the Gothic Tales* (Madison: University of Wisconsin Press, 1973).

12. For a discussion of Poe's complicated relationship with Mrs. Clemm and Virginia, see Symons, *The Tell-Tale Heart,* 32, 54.

13. Bittner, *Poe,* 162; Mott, *A History of American Magazines,* 341–42; and Symons, *The Tell-Tale Heart,* 73.

14. For a discussion of Poe's relationship with Burton, see Bittner, *Poe,* 444–50.

15. Edgar Allan Poe, *The Complete Works of Edgar Allan Poe,* ed. James A. Harrison (New York: John D. Morris, 1902), 4:134. The Harrison edition of Poe's works is the most useful and accessible. All quotations from Poe's works are footnoted to this edition.

16. Allen, *Israfel,* 384.

17. For an extended account of Poe's tiring work for the Broadway Journal, see Quinn, *Edgar Allan Poe,* 451–95.

18. Ibid., 615–16.

19. For reproduced newspaper notices of Poe's death, see Quinn, *Edgar Allan Poe,* 644–46.

20. Thomas Bender, *Community and Social Change in America* (1978; reprint, Baltimore: The Johns Hopkins University Press, 1982), 93–94.

21. Poe knew well that successful stories might appear in foreign journals. Howard Haycraft, *Murder for Pleasure: The Life and Times of the Detective Story* (New York: D. Appleton-Century, 1941), 14, and Stephan Peithman, ed., *The Annotated Tales of Edgar Allan Poe* (Garden City, New York: Doubleday, 1981), 196, note that Poe's "The Murders in the Rue Morgue" was pirated by Parisian periodicals. Poe's "The Purloined Letter" had just barely appeared in a Christmas gift anthology when a shortened unauthorized version of the same story appeared in *Chambers' Edinburgh Journal,* a cheap penny-weekly. Haycraft, *Murder for Pleasure,* 18–20.

22. The three stories first appeared, respectively, in the April, 1841 issue of *Graham's Magazine;* in the November and December, 1842, and February, 1843, issues of the *Ladies' Companion;* and in *The Gift* (Philadelphia: Carey and Hart, 1844).

23. Haycraft, *Murder for Pleasure,* 21; Symons, *The Tell-Tale Heart,* 224.

24. Haycraft, *Murder for Pleasure,* 7; Peithman, *Annotated Tales,* 195.

25. Early codifications of detective fiction rules include Ronald A. Knox, *The Best Detective Stories of 1928* (London: Faber, 1929), introduction, and S. S. Van Dine [Willard Huntington Wright] "Twenty Rules for Writing Detective Stories," *American Magazine,* September, 1928: 129–31. For a modern codification of detective fiction rules, see John C. Cawelti, *Adventure, Mystery and Romance: Formula Stories as Art and Popular Culture* (Chicago: University of Chicago Press, 1976), 132.

26. Poe, *The Complete Works,* 4:151.

27. Poe, *The Complete Works,* 6:28.

28. Poe, *The Complete Works,* 5:3.

29. For a discussion from a modern perspective of the mimetic contract, see Jonathan Culler, *Structuralist Poetics: Structuralism, Linguistics and the Study of Literature,* (Ithaca: Cornell University Press, 1975), 192–94.

30. Haycraft, *Murder for Pleasure,* 7.

31. Bittner, *Poe,* 154.

32. The major exception to this simple plot is "The Mystery of Marie Rogêt," which lacks the investigative forays. In the tale Dupin bases his deductions solely on newspaper reports. While an intriguing critique of antebellum newspaper reporting, this mode of detection is less engaging than the detection including physical investigation.

33. Poe, *The Complete Works,* 4:192.

34. Poe, *The Complete Works,* 5:8.

35. Ibid., 5:7.

36. Poe, *The Complete Works,* 6:30.

37. Poe, *The Complete Works,* 4:150.

38. Ibid., 4:152.

39. Ibid., 4:152–56.

40. Ibid., 4:152.

41. Ibid., 4:179.

42. Poe, *The Complete Works,* 6:29.

43. The most noted example of this juxtaposition is Doyle's Sherlock Holmes and Scotland Yard.

44. Investigations of the Mary Rogers murder in fact complicated Poe's writing and publishing of the story. After Poe had already published two installments of the story, New York police discovered new clues in the case, and Poe had to rewrite and delay publishing the final installment.

45. Poe, *The Complete Works*, 5:66.

46. Poe, *The Complete Works*, 6:152. The lines might be translated, "A design so deadly, even if not worthy of Atreus, is worthy of Thyestes."

47. Nineteenth-century critics would be surprised by the development, but the editor of at least one important contemporary research guide ranks Poe among the eight most significant American authors of the nineteenth century. See James Woodress, ed., *Eight American Authors* (New York: W. W. Norton, 1971).

48. Mott, *Golden Multitudes*, 306–8.

49. "Recent French Novelists," *The American Review*, 3 (1846):244.

50. N. Atkinson, *Eugène Sue et le roman-feuilleton* (Paris: A. Lesot, 1929); Jean Bory, *Eugène Sue; le roi du roman populaire* (Paris: Hatchette, 1962); Lucian W. Minor, *The Militant Hackwriter; French Popular Literature, 1800–1848* (Bowling Green, Ohio: The Popular Press, 1975), 102–51.

51. One of the first and most widely circulated translations was Eugène Sue, *The Mysteries of Paris*, trans. Charles H. Town (New York: Harper & Brothers, 1843).

52. An early American translation was Eugène Sue, *The Wandering Jew*, trans. H. W. Herbert (New York: J. Winchester, 1845).

53. Quoted in Lee Baxandall and Stefan Morawski, eds., *Karl Marx and Frederick Engels on Literature and Art* (New York: International General, 1974), 119.

54. Raymond Williams, *Marxism and Literature* (London: Oxford University Press, 1977), 201.

55. David S. Reynolds, *George Lippard* (Boston: Twayne Publishers, 1982), 12, suggests that the work of Lippard "gave impetus" to the body of works, but although, as subsequent discussion will concede, Lippard was no doubt influential, Sue was even more so.

56. The most comprehensive study of Ingraham is Robert W. Weathersby's *J. H. Ingraham* (Boston: Twayne Publishers, 1980).

57. Mott, *Golden Multitudes*, 94.

58. Joseph Holt Ingraham, *The Miseries of New York; or, The Burglar and Counsellor* (Boston: Yankee Office, 1844).

59. A popular yet still comprehensive study of Judson is Jay Monaghen's *The Great Rascal: The Life and Adventures of Ned Buntline* (Boston: Little, Brown, 1952).

60. Ibid., 87–88.

61. Ned Buntline, *The Mysteries and Miseries of New York; A Story of Real Life* (New York: E. Z. C. Judson, 1848).

62. New York: Berford and Company, 1848.

63. Monaghen, *The Great Rascal*, 141.

64. Ibid., 147.

65. *The B'hoys of New York. A Sequel to the Mysteries and Miseries of New York* (New York: Dick & Fitzgerald, 1849); *The G'hals of New York. A Novel* (New York: Dewitt and Davenport, 1850); *The Mysteries and Miseries of New Orleans* (New York: Akarman and Ormsby, 1851); *Three Years After: A Sequel to the Mysteries and Miseries of New York* (New York: W. F. Burgess, 1849).

66. The canon should always be approached as both a guide and a hindrance to the study of American literature. For warnings on the dangers of the canon, see Brent Harold and the Marxist Educational Collective, "The Marxist Survey of American Fiction," *Radical Teacher*, March 1980:43–50.

67. Buntline, *Mysteries and Miseries*, 5.

68. Ibid., 7.

69. Ibid.

70. Ibid., 5.

71. An early and widely distributed edition of the work is Joseph Holt Ingraham, *The Prince of the House of David* (New York: Pudney & Russell, 1855).

72. Quoted without citation in Leslie Fiedler, "The Male Novel," *Partisan Review*, 37 (1970):75.

73. David S. Reynold's previously cited *George Lippard* is the most comprehensive study of the writer and his works.

74. Quoted without citation in Alexander Cowie, *The Rise of the American Novel* (New York: American Book Company, 1951), 319.

75. While working as an intern for the Attorney General, Lippard came to think of the office as "the Confessional of our Protestant communities." George Lippard, *The Quaker City; or, the Monks of Monk Hall* (1845; reprint, Philadelphia: Leary, Stuart, 1876), preface to the edition.

76. Lippard did not complete and publish the novel until 1843. George Lippard, *Ladye Annabel* (Philadelphia: George Lippard, 1843).

77. The full work appeared as George Lippard, *Herbert Tracy; or, the Legend of the Black Rangers* (Philadelphia: R. G. Berford, 1844).

78. George Lippard, *The Quaker City; or, the Monks of Monk Hall* (Philadelphia: George Lippard, 1845). Since this edition is rare, subsequent footnotes are to the more accessible and previously cited Leary, Stuart edition of 1876.

79. Reynolds, *George Lippard*, 12.

80. Lippard, *The Quaker City*, 1.

81. Reynolds, *George Lippard*, preface.

82. Lippard, *The Quaker City*, 2.

83. For stimulating essays on Philadelphia social turmoil in the nineteenth century, see Allen F. Davis and Mark H. Haller, eds., *The Peoples of Philadelphia* (Philadelphia: Temple University Press, 1973).

84. In 1843 Philadelphian Singleton Mercer was acquitted after killing Mahlon

Herberton, who had cultivated an affair with Mercer's sister and allegedly raped her at gunpoint.

85. Quoted in Reynolds, *George Lippard*, 12.

86. Lippard, *The Quaker City*, 220, 238, 252, 258.

87. An aggressively and self-consciously "male" stance was not rare among actual cultural commentators of the nineteenth century. For a suggestive discussion, see Alan Trachtenberg, *The Incorporation of America: Culture and Society in the Gilded Age* (New York: Hill & Wang, 1982), 163.

88. Lippard, *The Quaker City*, 21.

89. Ibid., 155.

90. Ibid., 8.

91. Ibid., 140, 148.

92. Ibid., 4.

93. Ibid., 146.

94. Ibid., 404.

95. The second subtitle of *The Quaker City* is "A Romance of Philadelphia Life, Mystery and Crime."

96. Lippard, *The Quaker City*, 20.

97. Fiedler, "The Male Novel," 88–89.

98. Lippard, *The Quaker City*, 1.

99. Ibid., 2.

100. J. V. Ridgely, "George Lippard's The Quaker City: The World of the American Porno-Gothic," *Studies in Literary Imagination*, 7 (Spring 1974): 81–83.

101. Cowie, *The Rise of the American Novel*, 320.

102. Lippard, *The Quaker City*, 160.

103. Ibid., 253.

104. Fiedler, "The Male Novel," 78–79.

105. The serial was later published in one volume, namely, George Lippard, *The Killers* (Philadelphia: Hankinson and Bartholomew, 1850).

106. A popular bound edition of the serial was George Lippard, *The Empire City; or, New York by Night and Day* (New York: Stringer and Townsend, 1850).

107. Quoted in Reynolds, *George Lippard*, 19.

Chapter 6. Escapist Reinforcement: The Detective and Crime Thriller Genres

1. David S. Reynolds, *George Lippard* (Boston: Twayne Publishers, 1982), 23.

2. Henry Nash Smith, *Popular Culture and Industrialism, 1865–1900* (New York: New York University Press, 1967), v–vi.

3. During the antebellum years New York and Philadelphia had vied with one another for the leading position in fiction publishing, but after the Civil War New York periodicals and publishing houses won control of the Ohio Valley. William Charvat, *Literary Publishing in America, 1770–1850* (Philadelphia: University of Pennsylvania Press, 1959), 23–37.

4. Russel B. Nye, *Society and Culture in America, 1830–1860* (New York: Harper & Row, 1974), 368–69.

5. Mary Noel, *Villains Galore . . . The Heyday of the Popular Story Weekly* (New York: Macmillan, 1954), 138.

6. Nye, *Society and Culture,* 369.

7. Ibid., 75; Charvat, *Literary Publishing,* 38–60.

8. Mary Noel, "Dime Novels," *American Heritage,* 7 (February, 1956):55.

9. Edmund Pearson, *Dime Novels; or, Following an Old Trail in Popular Literature* (Boston: Little, Brown, 1929), 49.

10. John Tebbel, *A History of Book Publishing in the United States* (New York: R. R. Bowker, 1975), 2:511–20.

11. Writers customarily received less than $100 from a novelette publisher for all rights to a work, but a writer's income could multiply quickly as he composed dozens or even hundreds of similar works. In 1868 Beadle and Adams delighted the writers' community by paying Mayne Reid $700 for *The White Squaw;* it was the largest amount paid for a single work during the Gilded Age. Pearson, *Dime Novels,* 46–47.

12. For the full text of the opinion, see Albert Johannsen, *The House of Beadle and Adams* (Norman: University of Oklahoma Press, 1950), 43–44.

13. Morton J. Horwitz has provocatively discussed the role of the courts in restructuring the commercial economy in *The Transformation of American Law, 1780–1860* (Cambridge: Harvard University Press, 1977).

14. For provocative comments on the period's sentimental romance and other mass cultural artifacts appealing primarily to women, see Ann Douglas, *The Feminization of American Culture* (New York: Avon Books, 1977). An excellent article on the rags-to-riches novel is Richard Weiss, "Horatio Alger, Jr., and the Response to Industrialism," in Frederic C. Jahn, ed., *The Age of Industrialism in America: Essays in Social Structure and Cultural Values* (New York: Free Press, 1968). John C. Cawelti, in *Adventure Mystery, and Romance: Formula Stories as Art and Popular Culture* (Chicago: University of Chicago Press, 1976), incorrectly suggests that he is breaking new ground by focusing on mass fiction genres; nevertheless, his work impressively attempts to raise genre studies to the level of theory.

15. Two generations of scholarship on the western are represented by Henry Nash Smith, *Virgin Land: The American West as Symbol and Myth* (1950; reissued with a new preface by the author, Cambridge: Harvard University Press, 1970), 51–120, and Daryl Jones, *The Dime Novel Western* (Bowling Green, Ohio: Popular Press, 1978).

16. Smith, *Virgin Land,* 90–91.

17. James' comments are from "The Question of Opportunities," *Literature* 2 (1898):357. For comments on this essay, see Alan Trachtenberg, *The Incorporation of America: Culture and Society in the Gilded Age* (New York: Hill and Wang, 1982), 195.

18. One of the earliest works of detective fiction was "A Detective's Story," *The Continental Magazine* 4 (1863): 474–77. In the story an unnamed author

recounts a fictional detective's investigation and termination of a New York counterfeiting operation.

19. François Fosca, *Histoire et technique du roman policier* (Paris: Nouvelle revue critique, 1937); Alma E. Murch, *The Development of the Detective Novel* (London: Peter Owen, 1958), 244; John M. Reilly, ed., *Twentieth-Century Crime and Mystery Writers* (London: Macmillan, 1980), 1540–41; S. S. Van Dine [Willard Huntington Wright], *The World's Great Detective Stories* (New York: Scribners, 1927), 14.

20. Robert Ashley, "Wilkie Collins and the Detective Story," *Nineteenth-Century Fiction,* 6 (June, 1951): 47–60, and Ian Ousby, *Bloodhounds of Heaven: The Detective in English Fiction from Godwin to Doyle* (Cambridge: Harvard University Press, 1976), 11–36.

21. Mike Pavett, "Introduction: Before the Fiction," in *Crime Writers,* ed. H. R. F. Keating (London: British Broadcasting Company, 1978), 16.

22. When Doyle published his "A Study in Scarlet" in 1886, the story received little notice in England. However, it did catch the eye of American editors at *Lippincott's Magazine.* They commissioned Doyle's subsequent "Sign of Four" and thereby helped accelerate his writing career.

23. "To sum up, detection is a game that must be played according to Doyle." Jacques Barzun and Wendell Hertig Taylor, *A Catalogue of Crime* (New York: Harper & Row, 1971), 5.

24. Nuel P. Davis, *The Life of Wilkie Collins* (Urbana: University of Illinois Press, 1956), 258–59. Even Charles Dickens, Collins' brother-in-law, recognized the generic nature of Collins' work. According to some, Dickens' *Mystery of Edwin Drood,* unfinished at the time of his death, was an attempt to invade Collins' literary domain. Howard Haycraft, *Murder for Pleasure: The Life and Times of the Detective Novel* (London: Chatto and Winders, 1953), 179.

25. "Crime in Fiction," *Blackwood's Edinburgh Magazine,* 148 (August, 1890): 172–89.

26. Murch, *The Development of the Detective Novel,* 80.

27. Quoted in Murch, *The Development of the Detective Novel,* 83.

28. For a sketch of Emerson's popularity with nineteenth-century American college students, see Burton J. Bledstein, *The Culture of Professionalism: The Middle Class and the Development of Higher Education in America* (1976; reprint, New York: Norton Paperback, 1978).

29. Ralph Waldo Emerson to Miss Ann Green, June 30, 1968, in Ralph L. Rusk, ed., *The Letters of Ralph Waldo Emerson* (New York: Columbia University Press, 1939), 6:22–23. Emerson goes on in the letter to appraise several poems Green had sent him, to distinguish between writing and creative power, and to urge Green to read Milton and Shakespeare.

30. Anna Katharine Green, *The Defence of the Bride, and Other Poems* (New York: Putnam's Sons, 1882); *Risifi's Daughter: A Drama* (New York: Putnam's Sons, 1887).

31. For a full bibliography of Green's works, see Merle Johnson, ed., "America's First Editions: Anna Katharine Green, 1846–1935," *Publishers' Weekly,* 127 (1935):1617–18. For a sketch of Green during her final years, see Kathleen Woodward, "Anna Katharine Green," *Bookman,* 70 (October, 1929):168–70.

32. For representative Gilded Age reviews of *The Leavenworth Case,* see "Editor's Literary Record," *Harper's New Monthly Magazine,* 57 (1879): 467, and "Recent Novels," *The Nation,* 29 (1879): 214. The latter review wishes the novel did not have so many young ladies appearing in "wrappers" before strange men but admits this may be "too much to ask of American writers."

33. The first of the ten imprints was *The Leavenworth Case: A Laywer's Story* (New York: Putnam, 1878). For a listing of other nineteenth-century imprints, see *The National Union Catalogue, Pre–1956 Imprints* (Chicago: American Library Association, 1977) 501:442–43. Frank L. Mott, *Golden Multitudes: A History of Best Sellers in the United States* (New York: Harper & Row, 1947), 310, lists the work as one of sixteen American best-sellers in the 1870s.

34. Van Dine, *The World's Great Detective Stories,* 7.

35. Green, *The Leavenworth Case,* 12.

36. Ibid., 7.

37. Ernst Kaemmel, "Literature under the Table: The Detective Novel and the Social Mission," in *The Poetics of Murder: Detective Fiction and Literary Theory,* ed. Glenn W. Most and William W. Stowe (New York: Harcourt, Brace, 1983), 57. Citing the *Encyclopedia Britannica* (1946), the East German scholar Kaemmel notes that 1300 different detective novels were published in England and the United States between 1841 and 1920.

38. Ibid., 56.

39. Noel, *Villains Galore,* 122–24, and Pearson, *Dime Novels,* 191–95.

40. Old Sleuth, *Old Sleuth, Badger & Co.* (New York: George Munro, 1891), 7.

41. Johannsen, *The House of Beadle and Adams,* 4.

42. Ironclad, *Old Cap. Collier & Co.; or, "Piping" the Stewart Vault Mystery* (New York: Norman L. Munro, 1883).

43. Ibid., 7.

44. W.I. James, *Old Cap. Collier; or, "Piping" the New Haven Mystery* (New York: Norman L. Munro, 1883), 80.

45. 2 *New York Supp.* 313 (1888) and 8 *New York Supp.* 414 (1890).

46. Johannsen, *The House of Beadle and Adams,* 67.

47. The exploits of the Alvarez twins are featured in Old Sleuth, *The Twin Athletes; or, Always on Top* (New York: Parlor Car Publishing, 1898). Other boy detectives appear in Old Sleuth, *Daring Tom Cary; or, a Farm Boy's Adventures in New York* (New York: George Munro's Sons, 1901), and in Old Sleuth, *Jack Gameway; or, A Western Boy in New York* (New York: George Munro, 1885).

48. Old Sleuth, *The Lady Detective* (New York: George Munro, 1885), and *Lady Kate, the Dashing Detective* (New York: George Munro, 1886).

49. Old Cap. Collier in particular seemed an inspiration for ethnic detectives. His assistants included Patrick Dillon, "the great Irish detective," and the indomitable Harry Doyle.

50. The term "intertextuality" customarily denotes the way one literary text is linked to other texts through citations and allusions, assimilation of features, and a charged usage of literary codes and conventions. Jonathan Culler, *Structuralist Poetics: Structuralism, Linguistics and the Study of Literature* (Ithaca: Cornell University Press, 1975), 139–40.

51. Arthur Orrmont, *Master Detective: Allan Pinkerton* (New York: Julian Messner, 1965), 177.

52. See, for example, A. Frank Pinkerton, *Dyke Darrel, The Railroad Detective; or, The Crime of the Midnight Express* (Chicago: Fred C. Laird, 1886) and *Jim Cummings; or, the Great Adams Express Robbery* (Chicago: Laird & Lee, 1887), and Ernest Stark, *Ed Sommer, The Pinkerton Detective* (New York: J. S. Oglivie, 1886).

53. Old Sleuth, *Old Puritan, The Old-Time Yankee* (New York: George Munro, 1891).

54. Old Sleuth, *Daring Tom Cary*, 13.

55. Old Sleuth, *Jack Gameway*.

56. Old Sleuth, *The Lady Detective*.

57. Old Sleuth, *Old Puritan*.

58. Secondary studies that address the confidence man convention include Karen Halttunen, *Confidence Men and Painted Women: A Study of Middle-class Culture in America, 1830–1870* (New Haven: Yale University Press, 1982); William E. Lenz, *Fast Talk and Flush Times: The Confidence Man as a Literary Convention* (Columbia: University of Missouri Press, 1984); and Warwick Wadlington, *The Confidence Game in American Literature* (Princeton: Princeton University Press, 1975).

59. Old Sleuth, *Old Sleuth, Badger & Co.*, 14; *Old Sleuth, the Detective; or, the Bay Ridge Mystery* (New York: George Munro, 1885), 21.

60. Old Sleuth, *Lady Kate*, 38.

61. Old Sleuth, *Old Sleuth, Badger & Co.*, 25.

62. Merle Curti, "Dime Novels and the American Tradition," *Yale Review*, 26 (1971):761.

63. Old Sleuth, *Daring Tom Cary*, 13.

64. Old Sleuth, *Jack Gameway*, 4.

65. Frank Luther Mott lists Clemens' *Tom Sawyer* and *Huckleberry Finn* as best sellers, respectively, of the 1870s and 1880s. *Golden Multitudes*, 310. Both works are rich in crime-related themes, but neither is set in the modern urban setting. Written with James Dudley Warner, *The Gilded Age* is a better indication of Clemens' sensitivity to crime in the urban setting. Clemens' later *Pudd'nhead Wilson* and *Tom Sawyer, Detective*, meanwhile, actively engage the detective fiction genre discussed in this chapter. His *A Connecticut Yankee in King Arthur's Court* proffers a chilling portrayal of modernization's impact on social life and relationship to crime.

66. For a discussion of these naturalists and their works, see Larzer Ziff, *The American 1890s: Life and Times of a Lost Generation* (Lincoln: University of Nebraska Press, 1966), and, in particular, Ziff's consideration of Stephen Crane, ibid., 185–205.

67. Anna Katharine Green, *The Doctor, His Wife and The Clock* (New York: G. P. Putnam's Sons, 1895).

68. Anna Katharine Green, *The Circular Study* (New York: McClure, Phillips, 1900), 21.

69. Anna Katharine Green, *The Mystery of the Hasty Arrow* (New York: Dodd, Mead, 1917), 28.

70. Miss Butterworth appears in *That Affair Next Door* (New York: Putnam's Sons, 1897), *Lost Man's Lane* (New York: Putnam's Sons, 1898), and *The Circular Study*, noted earlier. Strange appears in *The Golden Slipper and Other Problems for Violet Strange* (New York: Putnam's Sons, 1898), and Van Arsdale appears in *The Woman in the Alcove* (Indianapolis: Bobbs-Merrill, 1906).

71. Green, *The Circular Study*, 96.

72. For a brief analysis of the feminist potential of the female detective and passing references to Green's work, see Barbara Lawrence, "Female Detectives: The Feminist—Anti-Feminist Debate," *Clues,* 3 (1982): 38–48.

73. Frank Luther Mott, *A History of American Magazines, 1885–1905* (Cambridge: Harvard University Press, 1957), 118–19.

74. Russell M. Coryell, "The Birth of Nick Carter," *The Bookman,* 69 (1929): 495–502.

75. Ibid., 499.

76. Smith, *Virgin Land,* 119–20.

77. "Crickety junebugs" tumbles from the lips of Obadia Crabtree, a rube from Brown's Hollow, New Jersey, featured in *The Gold Brick Swindlers; or, Nick Carter's Exposure* (New York: Street and Smith, 1895). Other expletives in Crabtree's vernacular include "Bustin' snakeweed" and "Tearin' squash-vines."

78. For interesting reflections on mass fiction genres of the 1920s, see John R. Brazil, "Murder Trials, Murders and Twenties America," *American Quarterly,* 33 (1981): 168–74. For a suggestion that Mario Puzo's *The Godfather* is a prototype for late twentieth-century crime fiction, see Cawelti, *Adventure, Mystery and Romance,* 65–79.

Chapter 7. From Memoir to Ideology: Gilded Age Police Writings

1. Lincoln Steffens, *The Autobiography of Lincoln Steffens* (1931; reprint, New York: Harcourt, Brace and World), 1:224–26.

2. James F. Richardson, *Urban Police in the United States* (Port Washington, New York: Kennikat, 1974), 1–34, provides the standard analysis of the origins of American police departments. For a Marxist critique of the

Richardson analysis, one that emphasizes instead the development of industrial capitalism and the class struggle, see Sidney Harring, "The Development of the Police Institution in the United States," *Crime and Social Justice*, 5 (1976): 54–59.

3. The American experiment with private urban police forces continued through the antebellum years. In Detroit, for example, private police patrolled the downtown throughout the 1850s. John C. Schneider, *Detroit and the Problem of Order, 1830–1880* (Lincoln: University of Nebraska Press, 1980), 65–75.

4. Each of the major studies of nineteenth-century police recounts American fascination with the London police model. Wilbur R. Miller's *Cops and Bobbies: Police Authority in New York and London, 1830–1870* (Chicago: University of Chicago Press, 1977) pays particular attention to the development.

5. David R. Johnson's *Policing the Urban Underworld: The Impact of Crime on the Development of American Police, 1800–1887* (Philadelphia: Temple University Press, 1979) traces the ways in which nineteenth-century policemen dealt with criminals not as symbols but as real people with a structured underworld.

6. During the 1860s state legislatures and governors took control of the police departments of Baltimore, Cleveland, Detroit, Kansas City, New Orleans and St. Louis. Theodore N. Ferdinand, "Introduction to the Reprint Edition," in Augustine E. Costello, *Our Police Protectors: A History of the New York Police* (Montclair, New Jersey: Patterson Smith, 1972), xiii.

7. Allan Silver, "The Demand for Order in Civil Society: A Review of Some Themes in the History of Urban Crime, Police and Riot," in David J. Bordua, ed., *The Police: Six Sociological Essays* (New York: John Wiley & Sons, 1967), 12–13.

8. The best studies of individual police departments are Kenneth Alfers, *Law and Order in the Capital City: A History of the Washington Police, 1800–86* (Washington, D. C.: George Washington University Press, 1976); Roger Lane, *Policing the City, Boston 1822–85* (Cambridge: Harvard University Press, 1967); and James F. Richardson, *The New York Police—Colonial Times to 1901* (New York: Oxford University Press, 1970). Robert M. Fogleson, *Big-City Police* (Cambridge: Harvard University Press, 1977), and Thomas A. Reppetto, *The Blue Parade* (New York: Free Press, 1978), address the relationships between nineteenth-century police and machines. Additional important studies include Eric H. Monkkonen, *Police in Urban America, 1860–1920* (Cambridge: Cambridge University Press, 1981), and Samuel Walker, *A Critical History of Police Reform* (Lexington, Massachusetts: Lexington Books, 1977). For a review of the secondary police history literature, see Samuel Walker, "The Urban Police in Urban America: A Review of the Literature," *Journal of Police Science and Administration*, 4 (1976): 252–60.

9. W. W. Walbridge, reporter, *Official Proceedings of the National Police Convention* (St. Louis: Ennis, 1871), 101.

10. Metropolitan police forces doubled or even tripled in size during the Gilded Age. Harring, "The Development of the Police Institution," 55.

11. While memoirs juxtapose the self and events, autobiographies more fully examine just the self. For definitive discussions of the differences between memoirs and autobiographies, see Roy Pascal, *Design and Truth in Autobiography* (Cambridge: Harvard University Press, 1960), and James Olney, *Metaphors of Self: The Meaning of Autobiography* (Princeton: Princeton University Press, 1972).

12. Edward H. Savage, *Police Records and Recollections; or, Boston by Daylight and Gaslight for Two Hundred and Forty Years* (Boston: John P. Dale, 1873). An earlier and smaller edition of this work was privately published by Savage in 1865. George W. Walling, *Recollections of a New York Chief of Police; An Official Record of Thirty-Eight Years as Patrolman, Detective, Captain and Chief of the New York Police* (New York: Caxton, 1887).

13. Savage, *Police Records and Recollections*, 215.

14. Walling, *Recollections*, 322.

15. For biographical information regarding Savage, see Lane, *Policing the City*, 157–59, 175–78, 201. For comments on Walling, see Reppetto, *The Blue Parade*, 43, 47–57.

16. Edward H. Savage, *Boston Events* (Boston: Tolman & White, 1884).

17. Savage, *Police Records and Recollections*, 6.

18. Walling, *Recollections*, 4.

19. Savage, *Police Records and Recollections*, 340.

20. Walling, *Recollections*, 194.

21. Savage, *Police Records and Recollections*, 147.

22. Ibid., 172.

23. Walling, *Recollections*, 331.

24. Ibid., 597.

25. Ibid., 596.

26. Ibid., 576.

27. Barbara Raffel Price, *Police Professionalism: Rhetoric and Action* (Lexington, Massachusetts: Lexington Books, 1977), 8 and Walker, *A Critical History of Police Reform*, 34.

28. Walker, *A Critical History of Police Reform*, 35.

29. *Our Police Protectors—A History of the New York Police* (1885; reprint, Montclair, New Jersey: Patterson Smith, 1972); *History of the Fire and Police Departments of Minneapolis* (Minneapolis: Relief Association, 1890); *Commercial History of Syracuse and History of the Police Department* (Syracuse, New York: Commercial, 1887); *History of the Police Department of Jersey City* (Jersey City: Police Relief Association, 1891); *History of the Fire and Police Departments of Paterson, New Jersey* (Paterson: Relief Association, 1877); *History of the Police Department of New Haven From the Period of the Watch in Colonial*

Times to the Present Time (New Haven: Relief Association, 1892); and *Our Firemen—A History of the New York Fire Department, Volunteer and Paid* (New York: A. E. Costello, 1887).

30. *Recollections of a New York Chief of Police and The Historic Supplement of the Denver Police* (Denver: specially issued, 1890).

31. Howard O. Sprogle, *The Philadelphia Police, Past and Present* (Philadelphia: specially issued, 1887), iii.

32. J. Birney Tuttle, ed., *An Illustrated Sketch of the Guardians of the Peace and Prosperity of New Haven* (New Haven: Evans, Gardner, 1889), 37.

33. Costello, *Our Police Protectors,* 163, and John J. Flinn, *History of the Chicago Police from the Settlement of the Community to the Present Time* (Chicago: Police Book Fund, 1887), 278.

34. Flinn, *History of the Chicago Police,* 166.

35. Costello, *Commercial History of Syracuse,* 100.

36. Sprogle, *The Philadelphia Police,* 330.

37. For representative police history accounts of rogues' galleries see Costello, *Our Police Protectors,* 403; Flinn, *History of the Chicago Police,* 455; and Sprogle, *The Philadelphia Police,* 274.

38. Works in this largely unstudied "lights and shadows" literature include Junius Henri Browne, *The Great Metropolis; A Mirror of New York Life* (Hartford: American Publishing, 1869); Edward Crapsey, *The Nether Side of New York; or, The Vice, Crime and Poverty of the Great Metropolis* (New York: Sheldon, 1872); Benjamin E. Lloyd, *Lights and Shadows in San Francisco* (San Francisco: A. L. Bancroft, 1876); James D. McCabe, *New York by Sunlight and Gaslight* (Philadelphia: Douglas Brothers, 1881); *The Secrets of the Great City: A Work Descriptive of the Virtues and the Vices, The Mysteries, Miseries and Crime of New York City* (Philadelphia: Jones, 1868); and Matthew Hale Smith, *Sunshine and Shadow in New York* (Hartford: J.B. Burr, 1869). The subtitle of Savage's work, "Boston by Daylight and Gaslight for Two Hundred and Forty Years," suggests the work's cultural comradeship with this literature.

Chapter 8. Looking through Private Eyes: Late Nineteenth-Century Detective Writings

1. James D. Horan and Howard Swiggert, *The Pinkerton Story* (Melbourne: William Heinemann, 1952), 289.

2. Roger Lane, *Policing the City, Boston 1822–85* (Cambridge: Harvard University Press, 1967), 146–56; and James F. Richardson, *Urban Police in the United States* (Port Washington, New York: Kennikat, 1974), 207–13.

3. Edward Crapsey, *The Nether Side of New York; or, The Vice, Crime and Poverty of New York* (New York: Sheldon, 1872), 61. This volume is a collection of pieces from *The Galaxy,* a popular periodical of the 1860s and 1870s.

4. Matthew Hale Smith, *Sunshine and Shadow in New York* (Hartford: J. B. Burr, 1869), 162.

5. For a detailed discussion of Chapman's career, see Lane, *Policing the City,* 146–47.

6. For a discussion of assorted Broadway detective offices and their fee schedules, see Crapsey, *The Nether Side of New York,* 55.

7. Smith, *Sunshine and Shadow,* 146–47.

8. Thomas A. Reppetto, *The Blue Parade* (New York: Free Press, 1978), 256–63.

9. Ibid.

10. Horan and Swiggert, *The Pinkerton Story,* 188, 206.

11. The association set up the National Bureau of Criminal Identification located in Chicago. In 1924 photographs and records from the Bureau were transferred to the Identification Division of the Federal Bureau of Investigation. Horan and Swiggert, *The Pinkerton Story,* 208.

12. Sigmund A. Lavine, *Allan Pinkerton—America's First Private Eye* (New York: Dodd, Mead, 1963), 140.

13. Ida M. Tarbell, "Identification of Criminals: The Scientific Method in Use in France," *McClure's Magazine,* 2 (1894), 355–69; and Jürgen Thorwald, *The Century of the Detective,* trans. Richard and Clara Winston (New York: Harcourt, Brace & World, 1965), 6–30, 94.

14. Norma B. Cuthbert, *Lincoln and the Baltimore Plot* (San Marino, California: Huntington Library, 1949).

15. Eugène François Vidocq, *Memoires de Vidocq, chef de police sûreté, jusqu'en 1827, aujourd'hui proprietaire et fabricant du papiers à Saint Mandé* (Paris: Tenon, 1828).

16. Michel Foucault, *Discipline and Punish: The Birth of the Prison,* trans. Alan Sheridan (New York: Vintage Books, 1979), 283.

17. George S. McWatters, *Knots Untied; or, Ways and By-ways in the Hidden Lives of American Detectives* (Hartford: J. B. Burr and Hyde, 1871), xix.

18. George P. Burnham, *Three Years With Counterfeiters, Smugglers and Boodle Carriers* (Boston: Lee and Shepard, 1872), iv.

19. David J. Cook, *Hands Up; or, Twenty Years of Detective Life in the Mountains and on the Plains* (1882; reprint, Norman, Oklahoma: University of Oklahoma Press, 1958), 14. Everett L. Degolyer notes in an introduction to this volume that Cook's adventures were rendered by either journalist Thomas Dawson or by Cook's cousin John W. Cook. However, neither is listed as author.

20. McWatters, *Knots Untied,* 26.

21. Ibid., 649, 665.

22. Ibid., 194, 665.

23. Ibid., 193.

24. Ibid., 644.

25. Ibid., 645.

NOTES

26. While the secondary literature concerning Allan Pinkerton is relatively large, it consists mostly of popular works that rehash the same episodes in Pinkerton's life. Representative works include Horan and Swiggert, *The Pinkerton Story;* Lavine, *Allan Pinkerton;* Arthur Orrmont, *Master Detective: Allan Pinkerton* (New York: Julian Messner, 1965); and Richard Wilmer Rowan, *The Pinkertons—A Detective Dynasty* (Boston: Little, Brown, and Company, 1931). A more critical recent study is Frank Morn, *"The Eye that Never Sleeps": A History of the Pinkerton National Detective Agency* (Bloomington: Indiana University Press, 1982). For a comment on Pinkerton's involvement with the Underground Railroad, see Henrietta Buckmaster, *Let My People Go: The Story of the Underground Railroad and Growth of the Abolition Movement* (Boston: Beacon Press, 1941), 259.
27. Orrmont, *Master Detective,* 177.
28. Lavine, *Allan Pinkerton,* 186.
29. Rowan, *The Pinkertons,* 299.
30. Lavine, *Allan Pinkerton,* 185.
31. Orrmont, *Master Detective,* 179.
32. One can see clearly the work of different ghost writers by juxtaposing standard scenes from assorted Pinkerton memoirs. Compare, for example, the concluding trial scenes in *The Expressman and the Detective* (1874; reprint, New York: G. W. Dillingham, 1900) and *The Model Town and Detectives* (1876; reprint, New York: G. W. Dillingham, 1900) with the concluding trial scene in the later *Mississippi Outlaws and the Detectives* (1878; reprint, G. W. Dillingham, 1900).
33. Burton J. Bledstein, *The Culture of Professionalism: The Middle Class and the Development of Higher Education in America* (New York: W. W. Norton, 1976), 31.
34. Ibid., 112.
35. Pinkerton recounts with pride his decision to hire a woman operative: "I finally became convinced that it would be a good idea to employ her. True, it was the first experiment of the sort that had ever been tried, but we live in a progressive age, and in a progressive country." Pinkerton, *The Expressman and the Detective* (Chicago: W. B. Keen, 1874), 95.
36. Charles A. Siringo, *Two Evil Isms: Pinkertonism and Anarchism* (Chicago: Charles A. Siringo, 1915).
37. Allan Pinkerton, *The Molly Maguires and the Detectives* (1877; reprint, New York: G. W. Dillingham, 1900), 25.
38. Allan Pinkerton, *The Rail-Road Forger and the Detectives* (1881; reprint, New York: G. W. Dillingham, 1900), xii.
39. Allan Pinkerton to George Bangs, March 30, 1877, Pinkerton Manuscripts, Library of Congress.
40. Pinkerton, *Molly Maguires,* 146.
41. Allan Pinkerton, *Strikers, Communists, Tramps and Detectives* (1877; reprint, New York: G. W. Dillingham, 1900), 215.
42. Ibid., 86.

43. Ibid.
44. Allan Pinkerton, *A Double Life and the Detectives* (1884; reprint, New York: G. W. Dillingham, 1900), 225–26.
45. In writing of MacDonald, Pinkerton says, "The life of this man affords a strangely sad study to the philosophic mind." Ibid., v.
46. Allan Pinkerton, *Thirty Years a Detective* (1884; reprint, New York: G. W. Dillingham, 1900), 17.
47. Allan Pinkerton, *The Model Town and the Detectives* (1876; reprint, New York: G. W. Dillingham, 1900), 208.
48. George S. McWatters, *Detectives of Europe and America or Life in the Secret Service* (Chicago: Laird and Lee, 1892). The Pinkerton Detective Series consisted of crime-related memoirs and novels; it was published sporadically between 1886 and 1895 in inexpensive editions. The secondary literature on Allan Pinkerton and his agency mentions neither the series nor its most prolific writer, A. Frank Pinkerton. One concludes that the marketers of the series selected an appropriate marketing name but lacked formal affiliations with the Pinkerton family and interests.
49. Theodore N. Ferdinand, "Introduction to the Reprint Edition," in Augustine E. Costello, *Our Police Protectors: A History of the New York Police* (1885; reprint, Montclair, New Jersey: Patterson Smith, 1972), xi–xii.
50. Jonathon Gilmer Speed, "New York's Police Chieftans," *Harper's Weekly*, 36 (1892), 404–5.
51. Lincoln Steffens, *The Autobiography of Lincoln Steffens* (1931; reprint, New York: Harcourt, Brace & World, 1958), 1:201. Byrnes not only borrowed from fiction when speaking with reporters but also collaborated with the novelist Julian Hawthorne in a half-dozen fictionalized accounts of his work, perhaps the best of which is *The Great Bank Robbery, From the Diary of Inspector Byrnes* (New York: Cassell & Company, 1887).
52. Benjamin P. Eldridge and William B. Watts, *Our Rival, The Rascal* (Boston: Pemberton, 1896), viii.
53. Byrnes' types are bank burglars, bank sneaks, forgers, hotel and boarding house thieves, sneak and house thieves, store and safe burglars, shoplifters and pickpockets, confidence and banco men, receivers of stolen goods, sawdust men, and horse thieves. *Professional Criminals of America* (New York: Cassell, 1886).
54. Eldridge and Watts, *Our Rival*, 338.
55. Ibid., 377.

Chapter 9. Legitimate Illegitimacy: The Criminal as Cultural Worker

1. Fascinating examples of self-impression in tension with social judgment, these works include Thomas J. Cluverius, *Cluverius—My Life, Trial and Conviction* (Richmond: Andrews, Baptist & Clemmitt, 1887), and Sarah M.

Victor, *The Life Story of Sarah M. Victor* (Cleveland: Williams Publishing, 1887).

2. Jesse H. Pomeroy, *Autobiography of Jesse H. Pomeroy* (Boston: J. A. Cummings, 1875).

3. Ibid., 26. Much later in life, as a man who had spent over 40 years in prison, Pomeroy was known as "Grandpa" and endorsed clean-living, character, cheerfulness and obedience. Pomeroy's later prison writings are collected in *Selections from the Writings of Jesse Harding Pomeroy* (private printing, 1920).

4. *The Life and Confession of Bridget Dergan {sic} Who Murdered Mrs. Ellen Coriell, The Lovely Wife of Dr. Coriell* (Philadelphia: Barclay, 1867), 40.

5. Guiteau's assassination of Garfield provoked a great outpouring of medical, religious and legal commentaries. The work that most successfully synthesizes and addresses this literature is Charles E. Rosenberg, *The Trial of the Assassin Guiteau: Psychiatry and Law in the Gilded Age* (Chicago: University of Chicago Press, 1968).

6. Charles J. Guiteau, *A Lecture on Christ's Second Coming A.D. 70* (Albany: Weed, Parsons, 1877).

7. Charles J. Guiteau, *The Truth: A Companion to the Bible* (Chicago: Donnelly, Gassette, Loyd, 1879).

8. H. C. and C. J. Hayes, *A Complete History of the Trial of Guiteau, Assassin of President Garfield* (Philadelphia: Hubbard Brothers, 1882), 405–6.

9. Guiteau's brother John cited these acts as proof of insanity. John W. Guiteau, *Letters and Facts, Not Heretofore Published Touching on the Mental Condition of Charles J. Guiteau Since 1865* (submitted to the President of the United States, 1882), 28.

10. The autobiography is preserved in Hayes, *A Complete History of the Trial of Guiteau, Assassin of President Garfield,* cited above.

11. Ibid., 428.

12. Ibid.

13. Ibid., 436.

14. Ibid., 449.

15. Rudolf Rocker, *Johann Most: Das Leben Eines Rebellen* (Berlin: Fritz Kater, 1924), and Frederic Trautman, *The Voice of Terror: A Biography of Johann Most* (Westport, Connecticut: Greenwood Press, 1980).

16. Max Nomad, *Apostles of Revolution* (Boston: Little, Brown, 1939), 281.

17. Most's American writings were inexpensively printed and often republished. They include *Die Anarchie* (New York: J. Müller, 1888); *Die Eigenthumsbestie* (New York: J. Müller, 1887); *Die freie Gesellschaft* (New York: Samisch & Goldman, 1884); *Die Gottespest* (New York: J. Müller, 1887); *Die Hoelle von Blackwells Island* (New York: J. Müller, 1887); *Memoiren, Erlebtes, Erforschtes und Erdachtes, von John Most* (New York: Selbstverlag des Verfassers, 1903–5); *Der Narrenthurm* (New York: J. Müller, 1888); *Die Nihilisten* (Chicago: Commune-feier, 1882); *Stammt der Mensch vom Affen ab?* (New York: J. Müller, 1887); *Der Stimmkasten* (New York: J. Müller, 1888); *Unsere Stellung*

in der Arbeiterbewegung (New York: J. Müller, 1890); and *Zwischen Galgen und Zuchthaus* (New York: J. Müller, 1887).

18. Most, *Die Anarchie*, n.p. The quotations from this work and from Most's other works in German are my own translations.

19. Most, *Die Eigenthumsbestie*, 3.

20. *To the Workingman of America* (Chicago: International Working Peoples Association, 1883), 2.

21. The full German title of Most's pamphlet is *Revolutionäre Kriegswissenschaft: Ein Handbuchlein zur Anleitung betreffend Gebrauches und Herstellung von Nitro-Glycerin, Dynamit, Shiessbaumwolle, Knallsquecksilber, Bomben, Brandsätzen, Giften u.s.w., u.s.w.* (New York: Internationaler Zeitungs-Verein, 1885).

22. Nomad, *Apostles of Revolution*, 289, and Trautman, *Voice of Terror*, 114.

23. Henry David, *The History of the Haymarket Affair*, 2nd ed. (New York: Russell & Russell, 1958), 521–22.

24. Alexander Berkman, *Prison Memoirs of an Anarchist* (New York: Mother Earth Publishing, 1912), 136.

25. Ibid., 33–35.

26. Trautman, *Voice of Terror*, 251.

27. Quoted in Nomad, *Apostles of Revolution*, 298.

28. Ray Ginger, *Age of Excess: The United States from 1877 to 1914*, 2nd ed. (New York: Macmillan, 1975); Alan Trachtenberg, *The Incorporation of America: Culture and Society in the Gilded Age* (New York: Hill and Wang, 1982); and Robert Wiebe, *The Search for Order: 1877–1920* (New York: Hill and Wang, 1967).

29. Emma Goldman, "John Most," *Mother Earth*, 1:2 (April, 1906): 17–20.

30. Georg Lukács, "Legality and Illegality," in *History and Class Consciousness*, trans. Rodney Livingstone (Cambridge: Massachusetts Institute of Technology Press, 1968), 256–71, is a provocative critique of overly simple revolutionary criminologies. The revolutionary, in Lukács' opinion, should not assume that criminal conduct per se is desirable but rather should commit criminal acts and engage in other social conduct only after a reasoned consideration of the action's impact on the social order and the public's impressions of the action's meaning. Lukács, himself a radical, says, "The risks of breaking the law should not be regarded any differently than the risk of missing a train connection on an important journey," 263.

31. The argot was in fact so specialized that several criminal memoirs include glossaries. The terms at hand come from J. Harrie Banka, *State Prison Life: By One Who Has Been There* (Cincinnati: C. F. Vent, 1871), 492–93. For general discussions of criminal argots, see David W. Maurer, *Language of the Underworld* (Lexington: University Press of Kentucky, 1981).

32. George Bidwell, *Bidwell's Travels: From Wall Street to London Prison* (Hartford: Bidwell Publishing, 1897), 41.

33. Hutchins Hapgood, *The Autobiography of a Thief* (1903; reprint, New York: Johnson Reprint Corporation, 1970), 27–28.

34. Langdon W. Moore, *Langdon W. Moore: His Own Story of His Eventful Life* (Boston: Langdon W. Moore, 1893), x.

35. Bidwell, *Bidwell's Travels,* 91.

36. George Bidwell, *Forging His Own Chains: The Wonderful Life-Story of George Bidwell* (Hartford: The Bidwell Publishing Company, 1891), 257.

37. H. Bruce Franklin, *The Victim as Criminal and Artist: Literature from the American Prison* (New York: Oxford University Press, 1978), 127–33.

38. Hapgood, *Autobiography,* 343.

39. Bidwell, *Forging His Own Chains,* 198.

40. Bidwell, *Bidwell's Travels,* 193.

41. Moore, *His Own Story,* 331.

42. George M. White, *From Boniface to Bank Burglar* (Bellows Falls, Vermont: Truax Printing, 1905), 309.

43. For a light-hearted discussion of the attempt by nineteenth-century under-takers to convert their trade into a profession, see Burton J. Bledstein, *The Culture of Professionalism: The Middle Class and the Development of Higher Education in America* (New York: W. W. Norton, 1976), 34.

44. For examples of criminal authors speaking of themselves as "professionals," see Bidwell, *Forging His Own Chains,* 601; Hapgood, *Autobiography,* 39–40; and White, *Boniface to Bank Burglar,* 309.

45. Bidwell, *Forging His Own Chains,* 601.

46. Bledstein, *The Culture of Professionalism,* 129–202, expertly develops the notions of character and career central in late nineteenth-century professional self-perceptions.

47. Moore, *His Own Story,* 645.

48. Bidwell, *Bidwell's Travels,* 44–45.

49. Bidwell, *Forging His Own Chains,* 580.

50. White, *Boniface to Burglar,* 305.

51. Ibid.

52. Bidwell, *Bidwell's Travels,* 372.

53. Moore, *His Own Story,* 324–25.

54. It is interesting to compare the professional, urban criminals' collective opinion of the Pinkertons with that held by a rural criminal of the same period. Jim Cummins, who rode with the James and Younger gangs in the South and Midwest, suggests the Pinkertons and other detectives for that matter were "blooded horses" lacking a pedigree. Jim Cummins, *Jim Cummins' Book* (Denver: Reed, 1903), x–xi.

55. Allan Pinkerton, *Thirty Years a Detective* (1884; reprint, New York: G. W. Dillingham, 1900), 16.

56. Bidwell, *Forging His Own Chains,* 73.

57. Moore, *His Own Story,* 636–67.

58. Bidwell, *Forging His Own Chains,* 257.

59. Moore, *His Own Story,* 645.

60. According to "Jim," "The world thinks that a thief is a dirty, disreputable

looking object, next door to a tramp in appearance, but this idea is far from being true. Every grafter of any standing in the profession is very careful about his clothes. He is always neat, clean, and as fashionable as his income will permit." Hapgood, *Autobiography,* 39–40.

61. Bidwell, *Forging His Own Chains,* 288.
62. Moore, *His Own Story,* 279.
63. For initial discussions regarding the capitalist hegemony, see Antonio Gramsci, *Selections from the Prison Notebooks,* trans. and ed. Quintin Hoare and Geoffrey Nowell Smith (New York: International Publishers, 1971). For an attempt to pull together and expand on Gramsci's thoughts regarding hegemony, see Raymond Williams, *Marxism and Literature* (Oxford: Oxford University Press, 1977), 108–14.

Selected Bibliography

The organization of the titles below corresponds roughly to the organization of the body of this work. The first section of the selected bibliography corresponds to the introductory chapter and includes articles, books and dissertations concerned with the history of crime. Most of the titles focus on nineteenth-century American crime, but several titles focus on other periods and settings and provide a comparative perspective. The second section corresponds to Part I of this work and concerns crime reporting. It includes primary newspapers, articles, books and pamphlets as well as secondary articles and books concerning or touching upon nineteenth-century American journalism. The third section corresponds to Part II of this work and concerns crime imagining. It includes primary works of crime fiction as well as secondary articles and books concerning nineteenth-century fiction. The fourth section corresponds to Part III of this work and concerns crime remembering. It includes primary works by policemen, detectives and criminals as well as secondary articles and books regarding the same social groups or individuals within the groups. In reality, of course, certain titles in the selected bibliography are relevant to more than one part of the whole work, but an individual title appears only in the section of the selected bibliography for which it is most appropriate.

I. History of Crime

A. Articles

Abbott, Edith. "The Civil War and the Crime Wave of 1865–70." *Social Science Review* 1 (1927): 212–34.

Bodenhamer, David J. "Law and Disorder on the Early Frontier: Marion County, Indiana, 1823–1850." *Western History Quarterly* 10 (1979): 323–56.

Brazil, John R. "Murder Trials, Murder, and Twenties America." *American Quarterly* 33 (1981): 163–84.

Calahan, Margaret. "Trends in Incarceration in the United States Since 1880." *Crime and Delinquency* 25 (1979): 9–41.

Clinnard, Marshall B. "The Process of Urbanization and Criminal Behavior." *American Journal of Sociology* 48 (1942): 202–13.

Dolan, Paul. "The Rise of Crime in the Period 1830–1860." *Journal of the American Institute of Criminal Law and Criminology* 30 (1939): 857–64.

Ferdinand, Theodore N. "The Criminal Patterns of Boston Since 1849." *American Journal of Sociology* 73 (1967): 84–99.

Garfinkel, Harold. "Conditions of Successful Degradation Ceremonies." *The American Journal of Sociology* 61 (1955): 420–24.

Grumstead, David. "Rioting in the Jacksonian Setting." *American Historical Review* 77 (1972): 361–97.

Harring, Sidney L. "Class Conflict and the Suppression of Tramps in Buffalo, 1892–1894." *Law and Society Review* 11 (1977): 873–911.

Hobbs, A. H. "Criminality in Philadelphia." *American Sociological Review* 8 (1943): 198–202.

Holmes, Kay Ann. "Reflections by Gaslight: Prostitution in Another Age." *Issues in Criminology* 7 (1972): 83–101.

Knodt, Ellen Andrews. "The American Criminal: The Quintessential Self-Made Man?" *Journal of American Culture* 2 (1979): 30–41.

Landesco, John. "The Criminal Underworld of Chicago in the 1880s and 1890s." *Journal of Criminal Law and Criminology* 25 (1934): 343–45.

Lane, Roger. "Crime and Criminal Statistics in Nineteenth-Century Massachusetts." *Journal of Social History* 2 (1968): 156–63.

———. "Crime and the Industrial Revolution: British and American Views." *Journal of Social History* 7 (1973): 287–303.

McLoughlin, William G. "Untangling the Tiverton Tragedy: The Social Meaning of the Terrible Haystack Murder of 1833." *Journal of American Culture* 7 (1984): 75–84.

Monkkonen, Eric H. "A Disorderly People? Urban Order in the Nineteenth and Twentieth Centuries." *Journal of American History* 68 (1981): 539–59.

Nye, Robert A. "Crime in Modern Societies: Some Research Strategies for Historians." *Journal of Social History* 11 (1978): 491–508.

O'Brien, Patricia. "Crime and Punishment as a Historical Problem." *Journal of Social History* 11 (1978): 508–20.

Phelps, Harold A. "Frequency of Crime and Punishment." *Journal of the*

American Institute of Criminal Law and Criminology 19 (1928): 165–80.

Powell, Elwin H. "Crime as a Function of Anomie." *Journal of Criminal Law, Criminology and Police Science* 57 (1966): 161–71.

Prince, Carl E. "The Great 'Riot Year': Jacksonian Democracy and Patterns of Violence in 1834." *Journal of the Early Republic* 5 (1985): 1–19.

Rosenbaum, Betty B. "The Relationship Between War and Crime in the United States." *Journal of Criminal Law, Criminology and Police Science* 30 (1939): 722–40.

Tanay, Emanuel. "Psychiatric Study of Homicide." *American Journal of Psychiatry* 125 (1969): 146–52.

Zehr, Howard. "The Modernization of Crime in Germany and France, 1830–1913." *Journal of Social History* 8 (1975): 117–41.

B. Books

Archer, Jules. *Riot! A History of Mob Action in the United States.* New York: Hawthorne Books, 1974.

Asbury, Herbert. *The Barbary Coast—An Informal History of the San Francisco Underworld.* New York: Alfred A. Knopf, 1933.

Aydelotte, Frank. *Elizabethan Rogues and Vagabonds.* Oxford: Clarendon Press, 1913.

Becker, Howard S. *Outsiders: Studies in the Sociology of Deviance.* London: Free Press of Glencoe, 1963.

Bell, Daniel. *The End of Ideology.* New York: The Free Press, 1960.

Boyer, Paul. *Urban Masses and Moral Order in America, 1820–1920.* Cambridge: Harvard University Press, 1978.

Browning, Frank, and Gerassi, John. *The American Way of Crime.* New York: G. P. Putnam's Sons, 1980.

Bruce, Robert V. *1877: Year of Violence.* Indianapolis: Bobbs-Merrill Company, 1959.

Churchill, Allen. *A Pictorial History of American Crime, 1849–1929.* New York: Holt, Rinehart and Winston, 1964.

David, Henry. *The History of the Haymarket Affair.* New York: Russell & Russell, 1958.

Erikson, Kai T. *The Wayward Puritans: A Study in the Sociology of Deviance.* New York: John Wiley & Sons, 1966.

Fink, Arthur E. *Causes of Crime: Biological Theories in the United States, 1800–1915.* Philadelphia: University of Pennsylvania Press, 1938.

Friedman, Lawrence M., and Percival, Robert V. *The Roots of Justice: Crime and Punishment in Alameda County, California, 1870–1910.* Chapel Hill: University of North Carolina Press, 1981.

Graham, Hugh, and Gurr, Ted, eds. *History of Violence in America: Historical and Comparative Perspectives.* New York: Frederick A. Praeger, 1969.

Hay, Douglas, et al. *Albion's Fatal Tree: Crime and Society in Eighteenth-Century England.* New York: Pantheon Books, 1975.

Heaps, Willard A. *Riots, U. S. A., 1765–1970.* New York: Seabury Press, 1966.

Henry, Andrew F., and Short, James R. *Suicide and Homicide.* Glencoe, New York: The Free Press, 1954.

Hibbert, Christopher. *The Roots of Evil: A Social History of Crime and Punishment.* Boston: Little, Brown and Company, 1963.

Hindus, Stephen. *Prison and Plantation: Crime, Justice and Authority in Massachusetts and South Carolina, 1767–1878.* Chapel Hill: University of North Carolina Press, 1980.

Hobsbawn, E. J. *Bandits.* New York: Pantheon Books, 1969.

Jones, Ann. *Women Who Kill.* New York: Fawcett Columbine, 1981.

Joselit, Jenna Weissman. *Our Gang: Jewish Crime and the New York Jewish Community.* Bloomington: Indiana University Press, 1983.

Josephson, Matthew. *The Robber Barons: The Great American Capitalists, 1861–1901.* New York: Harcourt, Brace & Co., 1934.

Judges, Arthur Valentine, ed. *The Elizabethan Underworld.* London: George Routledge & Sons, 1930.

Lane, Roger. *Violent Death in the City: Suicide, Accident and Murder in Nineteenth-Century Philadelphia.* Cambridge: Harvard University Press, 1979.

Lewis, Alfred H. *Nation-Famous New York Murders.* Chicago: M. A. Donohue, 1914.

McConaughy, James. *From Cain to Capone: Racketeering Through the Ages.* New York: Brentano's, 1931.

Mohr, James C. *Abortion in America: The Origins and Evolution of National Policy, 1800–1900.* New York: Oxford University Press, 1978.

Monkkonen, Eric H. *The Dangerous Class—Crime and Poverty in Columbus, Ohio, 1860–1885.* Cambridge: Harvard University Press, 1975.

Moquin, Wayne, ed. *The American Way of Crime. A Documentary History.* New York: Praeger Publishers, 1976.

Nash, Jay R. *Bloodletters and Badmen: A Narrative Encyclopedia of American Criminals from the Pilgrims to the Present.* New York: M. Evans, 1973.

————. *Hustlers and Con Men: An Anecdotal History of the Confidence Man and His Games*. New York: M. Evans, 1976.

————. *Murder, America: Homicide in the United States from the Revolution to the Present*. New York: Simon and Schuster, 1980.

Nelli, Humbert S. *The Business of Crime: Italians and Syndicate Crime in the United States*. New York: Oxford University Press, 1976.

Palmer, Stuart. *The Violent Society*. New Haven: College and University Press, 1972.

Radzinowicz, Leon. *Ideology and Crime*. New York: Columbia University Press, 1966.

————. *In Search of Criminology*. Cambridge: Harvard University Press, 1962.

Ribton-Turner, C. J. *A History of Vagrants and Vagrancy and Beggars and Begging*. London: Chapman and Hall, 1887.

Rosenberg, Charles E. *The Trial of the Assassin Guiteau: Psychiatry and Law in the Gilded Age*. Chicago: University of Chicago Press, 1968.

Rothman, David J. *Conscience and Convenience: The Asylum and Its Alternatives in Progressive America*. Boston: Little, Brown and Company, 1980.

————. *The Discovery of the Asylum: Social Order and Disorder in the New Republic*. Boston: Little, Brown and Company, 1971.

Rovere, Richard H. *Howe & Hummel: Their True and Scandalous History*. New York: Straus, 1947.

Schneider, John C. *Detroit and the Problem of Order, 1830–1880*. Lincoln: University of Nebraska Press, 1980.

Sullivan, Robert. *The Disappearance of Dr. Parkman*. Boston: Little, Brown and Company, 1971.

Taylor, Ian, et al. *The New Criminology: For a Theory of Social Deviance*. New York: Harper Colophon Books, 1973.

Thompson, E. P. *Whigs and Hunters: The Origin of the Black Acts*. New York: Pantheon Books, 1975.

Tobias, J. J. *Crime and Industrial Society in the Nineteenth Century*. New York: Schocken Books, 1967.

Walker, Samuel. *Popular Justice—A History of American Criminal Justice*. New York: Oxford University Press, 1980.

Warner, Sam Bass. *Crime and Criminal Statistics in Boston*. Cambridge: Harvard University Press, 1934.

Weisser, Michael R. *Crime and Punishment in Early Modern Europe*. Bristol: Harvester Press, 1979.

Williams, Joyce C.; Smithburn, J. Eric; and Peterson, M. Jeanne. *Lizzie Borden: A Case Book of Family and Crime in the 1890s*. Bloomington, Indiana: T. I. S. Publications, 1980.

C. Dissertations

Caye, James F. "Crime and Violence in the Heterogeneous Urban Community, Pittsburgh, 1870–89" (Ph.D. diss., University of Pittsburgh, 1977).

Fabian, Ann V. "Rascals and Gambling: The Meaning of American Gambling, 1820–1890" (Ph.D. diss., Yale University, 1982).

Freedman, Estelle Brenda. "Their Sisters' Keepers: The Origins of Female Corrections in America" (Ph.D. diss., Columbia University, 1976).

Green, Harvey. "Structures of Stone, Language and Feeling: The Cultural Response to the Criminal in New York, 1925–35" (Ph.D. diss., Rutgers University, 1976).

Guillot, Ellen E. "Social Factors in Crime; As Explained by American Writers of the Civil War and Post Civil War Period" (Ph.D. diss., University of Pennsylvania, 1943).

Houston, Susan E. "The Impetus to Reform: Urban Crime, Poverty and Ignorance in Ontario, 1850–75" (Ph.D. diss., University of Toronto, 1974).

Kuntz, William F. "Criminal Sentencing in Three Nineteenth-Century Cities: A Social History of Punishment in New York, Boston and Philadelphia" (Ph.D. diss., Harvard University, 1979).

Langsam, Miriam Z. "The Nineteenth Century Wisconsin Criminal: Ideologies and Institutions" (Ph.D. diss., University of Wisconsin, 1967).

McGowen, Randall. "Rethinking Crime: Changing Attitudes Towards Law-Breakers in Eighteenth- and Nineteenth-Century England" (Ph.D. diss., University of Illinois, 1979).

Naylor, Timothy J. "Criminals, Crime and Punishment in Philadelphia, 1866–1916" (Ph.D. diss., University of Chicago, 1979).

Salkin, Barry L. "Crime in Pennsylvania, 1786–1859. A Legal and Sociological Study" (Ph.D. diss., Harvard University, 1975).

II. Reporting Crime

A. Primary Works

1. Newspapers

The Herald, 1835–1900.
National Police Gazette, 1845–1900.
New York Journal, 1895–1900
The New York Times, 1851–1900.
The Sun, 1833–1900.

The Tribune, 1841–1900.
The World, 1883–1900.

2. Articles

"The Future of the Newspaper." *The Nation,* 28 (1879): 432–3.

North, S. N. D. "History and Present Condition of the Newspaper and Periodical Press of the United States." In *Tenth Census.* Washington, D.C.: Department of the Interior, 1884.

Shanks, W. F. G. "How We Get Our News." *Harper's New Monthly Magazine,* 34 (1867): 511–22.

Steffens, Lincoln. "The Conduct of a Newspaper." *Scribner's Magazine,* 22 (1897): 447–52.

3. Books and Pamphlets

Chandler, Peleg W. *American Criminal Trials.* Vol. 1. Boston: Charles C. Little and James, 1841.

————. *American Criminal Trials.* Vol. 2. Boston: Timothy H. Carter and Company, 1844.

The Confession of Adam Horn, alias Andrew Hellman, Embodying the Particulars of His Life. Baltimore: James Young, 1843.

Confessions, Trials, and Biographical Sketches of the Most Cold Blooded Murderers Who Have Been Executed in This Country From Its First Settlement Down to the Present Time. Boston: George N. Thompson and E. Littlefield, 1840.

The Criminal Recorder; or, An Awful Beacon to the Rising Generation of Both Sexes, Erected by the Arm of Justice to Persuade Them from the Dreadful Miseries of Guilt. Philadelphia: Mathew Carey, 1812.

Denton, William. *Who Killed Mary Stannard?* Boston: Colby & Rich, 1880.

Fenner, Ball. *Raising the Veil; or, Scenes in the Courts.* Boston: James French & Company, 1856.

Foster, George G. *New York in Slices: by an Experienced Carver.* New York: W. F. Burgess, 1849.

Freeman, E. H. *The Only True and Authentic History of Edward H. Ruloff.* Binghamton, New York: Carl and Freeman, 1871.

The Goss-Udderzook Tragedy: Being a History of a Strange Case of Deception and Murder. Baltimore: Baltimore Gazette, 1873.

The Life and Confessions of Bridget Dergan, Who Murdered Mrs. Ellen Coriell, The Lovely Wife of Dr. Coriell, of New Market, New Jersey. Philadelphia: Barclay & Company, 1867.

Life, Trial, Confession and Conviction of John Hanlon for the Murder of Little Mary Mohrman. Philadelphia: Barclay & Company, 1870.

Life, Trial and Execution of Edward H. Ruloff. Philadelphia: Barclay and Company, 1873.

Life, Trial, Execution and Dying Confession of John Erpenstein. Newark, New Jersey: Daily Advertiser, 1852.

Marks, Harry W. *Small Change; or, Lights and Shades of New York.* New York: The Standard Publishing Company, 1882.

Moore, Charles. *The Autobiography of Charles Moore.* Baltimore: A. R. Orton, 1854.

Narvaez, Isabella. *Isabella Narvaez, the Female Fiend and Triple Murderess.* Baltimore: A. R. Orton, 1854.

Renault, J. Edwards. *The Car-Hook Tragedy—The Life, Trial, Conviction and Execution of William Foster for the Murder of Avery D. Putnam.* Philadelphia: Barclay & Company, 1873.

Report of the Case of Ephraim Gilman, Indicted for the Murder of Mrs. Harriet B. Swan. Portland, Maine: Stephen Berry, 1863.

Stuart, William. *Sketches of the Life of William Stuart, The First and Most Celebrated Counterfeiter of Connecticut.* Bridgeport, Connecticut: printed by the author, 1854.

Trial and Confession of Robt. McConaghy, the Inhuman Butcher of Mr. Brown's Family on Saturday, May 30, 1840, in Huntington County. Huntington County, Pennsylvania, 1840.

Trial and Execution of Thomas Barrett. Boston: Skinner & Blanchard, 1845.

Trial of Maurice Antonio, The Portuguese, for the Murder of Ignacio Teixeira Pinto, at Rochester, November 23, 1851. Rochester: D. M. Dewey, 1852.

Wilkes, George. *Life and Adventures of the Accomplished Forger and Swindler, Colonel Monroe Edwards.* New York: H. Long & Brother, 1848.

———. *The Lives of Helen Jewett and Richard Robinson.* New York: George Wilkes, 1867.

———. *The Mysteries and Miseries of the Tombs, A Journal of Thirty Days Imprisonment in the New York City Prison for Libel.* New York: George Wilkes, 1844.

Wyatt, Henry. *Life and Confession of Henry Wyatt, Who Was Executed at Auburn, For the Murder of James Gordon, A Fellow Convict.* Auburn, New York: Ivison and Company, 1846.

B. Secondary Works

1. Articles

Attunes, George E. "The Presentation of Criminal Events in Houston's Daily Newspapers." *Journalism Quarterly* 54 (1977): 756–60.

Bosco, Ronald A. "Lectures at the Pillory: The Early American Execution Sermon." *American Quarterly* 30 (1978): 156–76.

Bradshaw, James Standorf. "George W. Wisner and the New York *Sun.*" *Journalism History* 6 (1979): 112–21.

Carey, James W. "The Problem of Journalism History." *Journalism History* 1 (1974): 3–4.

Chibnall, Steve. "The Crime Reporter: A Study in the Production of Commercial Knowledge." *Sociology* 9 (1975): 49–65.

Cochran, Thomas. "Media as Business: A Brief History." *Journal of Communication* 25 (1975): 155–65.

Davenport, Walter. "The Dirt Disher." *Colliers* (March 24, 1928): 26, 30, 52–53.

———. "The Nickel Shocker." *Colliers* (March 10, 1928): 26, 28, 38, 48.

Fulcher, James. "Murder Reports: Formulaic Narrative and Cultural Context." *Journal of Popular Culture* 18 (1985): 31–42.

McDade, Thomas M. "Lurid Literature of the Last Century: The Publications of E. E. Barclay." *Pennsylvania Magazine of History and Biography* 80 (1956): 452–64.

Peterson, Ted. "James Catnach: Master of Street Literature." *Journalism Quarterly* 27 (1959): 157–63.

———. "British Crime Pamphleteers: Forgotten Journalists." *Journalism Quarterly* 22 (1945): 305–16.

Saxton, Alexander. "George Wilkes: The Transformation of a Radical Ideology." *American Quarterly* 33 (1981): 437–58.

———. "Problems of Class and Race in the Origins of the Mass Circulation Press." *American Quarterly* 36 (1984): 211–34.

Smythe, Ted Curtis. "The Reporter, 1880–1900: Working Conditions and Their Influence on the News." *Journalism History* 7 (1980): 1–10.

Surrency, Erwin C. "Law Reports in the United States." *American Journal of Legal History* 25 (1982): 48–66.

Weaver, David H. "Frank Luther Mott and the Future of Journalism History." *Journalism History* 2 (1975): 44–47.

Weiss, Harry B. "A Brief History of American Jest Books." *Bulletin of the New York Public Library* 47 (1943): 273–89.

Williams, Daniel E. "Rogues, Rascals and Scoundrels: The Underworld Literature of Early America." *American Studies* 24 (1983): 5–18.

2. Books

Baehr, Harry W. *The New York Tribune Since the Civil War.* New York: Dodd, Mead & Company, 1936.

Barrett, James W. *The World, the Flesh, and Messrs. Pulitzer.* New York: Vanguard, 1931.

Barth, Gunther. *City People: The Rise of Modern City Culture in Nineteenth-Century America.* New York: Oxford University Press, 1980.

Berger, Meyer. *The Story of the New York Times, 1851–1951.* New York: Simon and Schuster, 1951.

Bleyer, William Grosvenor. *Main Currents in the History of American Journalism.* Boston: Houghton Mifflin Company, 1927.

Brown, Francis. *Raymond of the Times.* New York: Norton, 1951.

Carlson, Oliver. *The Man Who Made News: James Gordon Bennett.* New York: Duell, Sloan and Pearce, 1942.

Chandler, Frank W. *The Literature of Roguery.* 2 vols. Boston: Houghton Mifflin Company, 1907. Reprint. New York: Burt Franklin, 1958.

Chaney, Lindsay, and Cieply, Michael. *The Hearsts.* New York: Simon and Schuster, 1981.

Chibnall, Steve. *Law-and-Order News: An Analysis of Crime Reporting in the British Press.* London: Tavistock Publications, 1977.

Cohen, Herbert J. *125 Years of Famous Front Pages from the New York Times, 1851–1976.* New York: Arno Press, 1976.

Davis, Elmer. *History of the New York Times.* New York: The New York Times, 1921.

Emery, Edwin. *The Press and America: An Interpretative History of Journalism.* New York: Prentice-Hall, 1954. Reprint. Englewood Cliffs, New Jersey: Prentice-Hall, 1962.

Gitlen, Todd. *The Whole World is Watching: Mass Media and the Making and Unmaking of the New Left.* Berkeley and Los Angeles: University of California Press, 1980.

Goffman, Erving. *Frame Analysis: An Essay on the Organization of Experience.* New York: Harper & Row, 1974.

Grambling, Oliver. *AP: The Story of News.* New York: Farrar and Rinehart, 1940.

Hughes, Helen MacGill. *News and the Human Interest Story.* Chicago: University of Chicago Press, 1940.

Ireland, Alleyne. *An Adventure with a Genius: Recollections of Joseph Pulitzer.* New York: E. P. Dutton, 1920.

Kelber, Harry, and Schlesinger, Carl. *Union Printing and Controlled Automation.* New York: The Free Press, 1967.

Kobre, Sidney. *Development of American Journalism.* Dubuque, Iowa: William C. Brown Company, 1969.

Kunzle, David. *The Early Comic Strip: Narrative Strips and Picture Stories in the European Broadsheet from c. 1450 to 1825.* Berkeley and Los Angeles: University of California Press, 1973.

Lee, Alfred McClung. *The Daily Newspaper in America: the Evolution of a Social Instrument.* New York: Macmillan Company, 1937.

Lee, James Melvin. *History of American Journalism.* Boston: Houghton Mifflin Company, 1917.

Lundberg, Ferdinand. *Imperial Hearst: A Social Biography.* New York: Arno Press, 1970.

McDade, Thomas M., comp. *The Annals of Murder: A Bibliography of Books and Pamphlets on American Murders from Colonial Times to 1900.* Norman: University of Oklahoma Press, 1961.

Mott, Frank Luther. *American Journalism: A History, 1690–1960.* 3rd ed. New York: Macmillan Publishing Company, 1962.

————. *A History of American Magazines, 1741–1850.* New York: D. Appleton, 1930.

————. *A History of American Magazines, 1850–1865.* Cambridge: Harvard University Press, 1938.

O'Brien, Frank M. *The Story of The Sun.* New York: George H. Doran, 1918.

O'Connor, Richard. *The Scandalous Mr. Bennett.* New York: Doubleday, 1962.

Payne, George Henry. *History of Journalism in the United States.* New York: Appleton, 1920.

Rosebault, Charles J. *When Dana Was The Sun: A Story of Personal Journalism.* New York: Robert M. McBride, 1931.

Rutland, Robert A. *The Newsmongers: Journalism and the Life of the Nation, 1690–1972.* New York: Dial Press, 1973.

Schiller, Dan. *Objectivity and the News: The Public and the Rise of Commercial Journalism.* Philadelphia: University of Pennsylvania Press, 1981.

Schudson, Michael. *Discovering the News: A Social History of American Newspapers.* New York: Basic Books, 1978.

Steffens, Lincoln. *The Autobiography of Lincoln Steffens.* Vol. 1, *A Boy on Horseback/Seeing New York First.* New York: Harcourt, Brace & World, 1931; Harvest Books, 1958.

Stone, Candace. *Dana and The Sun.* New York: Dodd, Mead & Company, 1938.

Swanberg, W. A. *Citizen Hearst.* New York: Scribner's, 1961.

———. *Pulitzer.* New York: Scribner's, 1967.

Tebbel, John. *The Compact History of the American Newspaper.* New York: Hawthorne Books, 1963.

———. *The Life and Times of William Randolph Hearst.* New York: E. P. Dutton, 1952.

Tuchman, Gaye. *Making News.* New York: The Free Press, 1978.

Van Deusen, Glyndon G. *Horace Greeley: Nineteenth-Century Crusader.* Philadelphia: University of Pennsylvania Press, 1953.

Van Every, Edward. *Sins of New York as "Exposed" by the Police Gazette.* New York: Frederick A. Stokes Company, 1930.

Ziff, Larzer. *The American 1890s: Life and Times of a Lost Generation.* New York: Viking Press, 1966. Reprint. Lincoln: University of Nebraska Press, 1979.

III. Imagining Crime

A. Primary Works

Carter, Nick. *The Gold Brick Swindlers; or, Nick Carter's Exposure.* New York: Street & Smith, 1895.

———. *Patsy's Live Wire and the Way It Worked with a Stranger.* New York: Street & Smith, 1896.

"A Detective's Story." *The Continental Magazine,* 4 (1863): 474–77.

Farrars, Francis. *Jim Cummings; or, the Crime of the Frisco Express.* Chicago: R. R. Publishing Company, 1887.

Green, Anna Katharine. *The Circular Study.* New York: McClure, Phillips, 1900.

———. *The Defence of the Bride and Other Poems.* New York: Putnam's Sons, 1882.

———. *The Doctor, His Wife and the Clock.* New York: G. P. Putnam's Sons, 1895.

———. *The Golden Slipper and Other Problems for Violet Strange.* New York: Putnam's Sons, 1915.

———. *The Leavenworth Case.* New York: G. P. Putnam's Sons, 1879.

———. *Lost Man's Lane.* New York: Putnam's Sons, 1898.

———. *The Mystery of the Hasty Arrow.* New York: Dodd, Mead & Company, 1917.

———. *Risifi's Daughter: A Drama.* New York: G. P. Putnam's Sons, 1887.

————. *That Affair Next Door*. New York: Putnam's Sons, 1897.

————. *The Woman in the Alcove*. Indianapolis: Bobbs-Merrill, 1906.

Ingraham, Joseph Holt. *The Miseries of New York; or, the Burglar and Counsellor*. Boston: Yankee Office, 1844.

Ironclad. *Old Cap. Collier & Co.; or, "Piping" the Stewart Vault Mystery*. New York: Norman L. Munro, 1883.

James, W. I. *Old Cap. Collier; or, "Piping" the New Haven Mystery*. New York: Norman L. Munro, 1883.

Jerome, Gilbert. *Old Roulette; or, Red and Black*. New York: Norman L. Munro, 1884.

Judson, Edward Z. *The B'hoys of New York*. New York: Dick & Fitzgerald, 1849.

————. *The G'hals of New York*. New York: Dewitt and Davenport, 1850.

————. *The Mysteries and Miseries of New Orleans*. New York: Akarman and Ormsby, 1851.

————. *The Mysteries and Miseries of New York; A Story of Real Life*. New York: E. Z. C. Judson, 1848.

————. *Three Years After: A Sequel to the Mysteries and Miseries of New York*. New York: W. F. Burgess, 1849.

Lippard, George. *The Empire City; or, New York by Night and Day*. New York: Stringer and Townsend, 1850.

————. *Herbert Tracy; or, the Legend of the Black Rangers*. Philadelphia: R. G. Berford, 1844.

————. *The Killers*. Philadelphia: Hankinson & Bartholomew, 1850.

————. *Ladye Annabel*. Philadelphia: George Lippard, 1843.

————. *The Quaker City; or, the Monks of Monk Hall*. Philadelphia: published by the author, 1844. Reprint. Philadelphia: Leary, Stuart & Company, 1876.

Old Sleuth. *Daring Tom Cary; or, A Farm Boy's Adventures in New York*. New York: George Munro's Sons, 1901.

————. *Jack Gameway; or, A Western Boy in New York*. New York: George Munro, 1885.

————. *The Lady Detective*. New York: George Munro, 1885.

————. *Lady Kate, The Dashing Detective*. New York: George Munro, 1886.

————. *Old Puritan, The Old-Time Yankee Detective*. New York: George Munro, 1887.

————. *Old Sleuth, Badger & Co.* New York: George Munro, 1891.

————. *Old Sleuth, the Detective; or, the Bay Ridge Mystery*. New York: George Munro, 1885.

————. *The Twin Athletes; or, Always on Top*. New York: Parlor Car Publishing Company, 1898.

Pinkerton, A. Frank. *Jim Cummings or the Great Adams Express Robbery*. Chicago: Laird & Lee, 1887.

————. *A Race for Life*. Chicago: Laird & Lee, 1886.

————. *Saved at the Scaffold or Nic Brown, the Chicago Detective*. Chicago: Laird & Lee, 1888.

————. *Dyke Darrel, The Railroad Detective; or, The Crime of the Midnight Express*. Chicago: Fred C. Laird, 1886.

Pinkerton, Myron. *The Stolen Will or the Rokewood Tragedy*. Chicago: Laird & Lee, 1887.

Poe, Edgar Allan. *The Complete Works of Edgar Allan Poe*. Edited by James A. Harrison. New York: John D. Morris, 1902.

Simpson, Charles. *Life in the Far West; or, A Detective's Thrilling Adventures Among the Indians and Outlaws of Montana*. Chicago: Rhodes and McClure Publishing Company, 1896.

Stark, Ernest. *Ed Sommer, The Pinkerton Detective*. New York: J. S. Oglivie, 1886.

Sue, Eugène. *The Mysteries of Paris*. Translated by Charles H. Town. New York: Harper & Brothers, 1843.

————. *The Wandering Jew*. Translated by J. W. Herbert. New York: J. Winchester, 1845.

B. Secondary Works

1. Articles

Ashley, Robert. "Wilkie Collins and the Detective Story." *Nineteenth-Century Fiction* 6 (1951): 47–60.

Aydelotte, W. O. "The Detective Story as a Historical Source." *Yale Review* 39 (1949): 76–95.

Coryell, Russell M. "The Birth of Nick Carter." *The Bookman* 69 (1929): 495–502.

Curti, Merle. "Dime Novels and the American Tradition." *Yale Review* 26 (1937): 761–78.

Fiedler, Leslie. "The Male Novel." *Partisan Review* 37 (1970): 74–89.

French, Warren. "A Hundred Years of a Religious Bestseller. *Western Humanities Review* 10 (1955): 45–54.

————. "A Sketch of the Life of Joseph Holt Ingraham." *The Journal of Mississippi History* 11 (1949): 155–71.

————. "The Twice-Told Travels of Joseph Holt Ingraham." *American Notes and Queries* 1 (1962): 51–52.

James, Henry. "The Question of Opportunities." *Literature* 2 (1898): 356–58.

Lawrence, Barbara. "Female Detectives—The Feminist–Anti-Feminist Debate." *Clues* 3 (1982): 38–48.

Noel, Mary. "Dime Novels." *American Heritage* 7 (1956): 50–55, 112–113.

Ridgely, J. V. "George Lippard's The Quaker City: The World of the American Porno-Gothic." *Studies in Literary Imagination* 7 (1974): 77–94.

Rohlfs, Charles. "American First Editions: Mrs. Anna K. Green, 1846–1935." *Publishers' Weekly* 127 (1935): 1617–18.

Seitz, Don C. "A Prince of Best Sellers." *Publishers' Weekly* 119 (1931): 940.

Wimsatt, William K. "Poe and the Mystery of Mary Rogers." *Publication of the Modern Language Association* 56 (1941): 230–48.

Woodward, Kathleen. "Anna Katharine Green." *Bookman* 70 (1929): 168–70.

2. Books

Allen, Hervey. *Israfel: The Life and Times of Edgar Allan Poe.* New York: Farrar & Rinehart, 1934.

Atkinson, N. *Eugène Sue et le roman-feuilleton.* Paris: A. Lesot, 1929.

Bandy, William T. *The Influence and Reputation of Edgar Allan Poe in Europe.* Baltimore: C. T. Cimino, 1962.

Barnes, Melvyn. *Best Detective Fiction—A Guide from Godwin to the Present.* London: Clive Bangley, 1975.

Barzun, Jacques, and Taylor, Wendell Hertig. *A Catalogue of Crime.* New York: Harper & Row, 1971.

Bittner, William. *Poe: A Biography.* Boston: Little, Brown and Company, 1962.

Bory, Jean. *Eugène Sue; le roi du roman populaire.* Paris: Hatchette, 1962.

Buranelli, Vincent. *Edgar Allan Poe.* New York: Twayne Publishers, 1961.

Cawelti, John C. *Adventure, Mystery and Romance: Formula Stories as Art and Popular Culture.* Chicago: University of Chicago Press, 1976.

Charvat, William. *Literary Publishing in America, 1790–1850.* Philadelphia: University of Pennsylvania Press, 1959.

Chase, Richard. *The American Novel and Its Tradition.* New York: Doubleday & Company, 1957. Reprint. Baltimore: Johns Hopkins University Press, 1980.

Cobb, Irwin S. *A Plea for Old Cap. Collier.* New York: George H. Doran Company, 1921.

Cowie, Alexander. *The Rise of the American Novel.* New York: American Book Company, 1948.

Culler, Jonathan. *Structuralist Poetics: Structuralism, Linguistics, and the Study of Literature.* Ithaca: Cornell University Press, 1975.

Davis, David Brion. *Homicide in American Fiction, 1798–1860.* Ithaca: Cornell University Press, 1957.

Davis, Nuel P. *The Life of Wilkie Collins.* Urbana: University of Illinois Press, 1956.

Douglas, Ann. *The Feminization of American Culture.* New York: Avon Books, 1977.

Exman, Eugene. *The Brothers Harper: A Unique Publishing Partnership and Its Impact Upon the Cultural Life of America from 1817 to 1853.* New York: Harper & Row, 1965.

Fiedler, Leslie. *Love and Death in the American Novel.* New York: Stein & Day, 1966.

Fosca, François. *Histoire et technique du roman policier.* Paris: Nouvelle revue critique, 1937.

Hart, James D. *The Popular Book: A History of America's Literary Taste.* New York: Oxford University Press, 1950.

Haycraft, Howard. *Murder for Pleasure: The Life and Times of the Detective Story.* New York: D. Appleton-Century, 1941.

Hubbell, Jay B. *The South in American Literature, 1607–1900.* Durham, North Carolina: Duke University Press, 1954.

Johannsen, Albert. *The House of Beadle and Adams.* Norman: University of Oklahoma Press, 1950.

Jones, Daryl. *The Dime Novel Western.* Bowling Green, Ohio: The Popular Press, 1978.

Keating, H. R. F., ed. *Crime Writers.* London: British Broadcasting Corporation, 1978.

Ketterer, David. *The Rationale of Deception in Poe.* Baton Rouge: Louisiana State University Press, 1979.

Minor, Lucian W. *The Militant Hackwriter: French Popular Literature, 1800–1848.* Bowling Green, Ohio: The Popular Press, 1975.

Monaghen, Jay. *The Great Rascal: The Life and Adventures of Ned Buntline.* Boston: Little, Brown and Company, 1952.

Most, Glenn W., and Stowe, William W., eds. *The Poetics of Murder: Detective Fiction and Literary Theory.* New York: Harcourt, Brace, 1983.

Mott, Frank Luther. *Golden Multitudes: The Story of Best Sellers in the United States*. New York: Macmillan, 1947.

Muchnic, Helen. *The Unhappy Consciousness: Gogol, Poe, Baudelaire*. Baltimore: Barton-Gillet, 1967.

Murch, Alma E. *The Development of the Detective Novel*. London: Peter Owen, 1958.

Noel, Mary. *Villains Galore . . . The Heyday of the Popular Story Weekly*. New York: Macmillan, 1954.

Nye, Russel B. *Society and Culture in America, 1830–1860*. New York: Harper & Row, 1974.

———. *The Unembarrassed Muse: The Popular Arts in America*. New York: Dial Press, 1970.

Ounsby, Ian. *Bloodhounds of Heaven: The Detective in English Fiction from Godwin to Doyle*. Cambridge: Harvard University Press, 1976.

Pearson, Edmund. *Dime Novels; or, Following an Old Trail in Popular Literature*. Boston: Little, Brown and Company, 1929.

Quinn, Arthur Hopson. *Edgar Allan Poe: A Critical Biography*. New York: Cooper Square Publishers, 1969.

Reynolds, David S. *George Lippard*. Boston: Twayne Publishers, 1982.

Reynolds, Quentin. *The Fiction Factory or From Pulp Row to Quality Street*. New York: Random House, 1955.

Routley, Erik. *The Puritan Pleasures of the Detective Story*. London: Victor Gollancz, 1972.

Smith, Henry Nash. *Virgin Land: The American West as Symbol and Myth*. Cambridge: Harvard University Press, 1950. Reprint. Cambridge: Harvard University Press, 1970.

———, ed. *Popular Culture and Industrialism, 1865–1900*. New York: New York University Press, 1967.

Symons, Julian. *The Tell-Tale Heart: The Life and Works of Edgar Allan Poe*. New York: Harper & Row, 1978.

Tebbel, John. *A History of Book Publishing in the United States*. New York: R. R. Bowker, 1972.

Ticknor, Caroline. *Hawthorne and His Publisher*. Boston: Houghton Mifflin Company, 1913.

Thompson, G. R. *Poe's Fiction: Romantic Irony in the Gothic Tales*. Madison: University of Wisconsin Press, 1973.

Trachtenberg, Alan. *The Incorporation of America: Culture and Society in the Gilded Age*. New York: Hill and Wang, 1982.

Walsh, John. *Poe the Detective: The Curious Circumstances Behind "The Mystery of Marie Rogêt."* New Brunswick, New Jersey: Rutgers University Press, 1968.

Weathersby, Robert W. *Joseph Holt Ingraham.* Boston: Twayne Publishers, 1980.

Williams, Raymond. *Marxism and Literature.* London: Oxford University Press, 1977.

IV. *Remembering Crime*

A. Primary Works

Banka, J. Harrie. *State Prison Life: By One Who Has Been There.* Cincinnati: C. F. Vent, 1871.

Berkman, Alexander. *Prison Memoirs of an Anarchist.* New York: Mother Earth Publications, 1912.

Bidwell, Austin. *From Wall Street to Newgate Via the Primrose Way.* Hartford, Connecticut: Bidwell Publishing Company, 1895.

Bidwell, George. *Bidwell's Travels: From Wall Street to London Prison.* Hartford, Connecticut: Bidwell Publishing Company, 1897.

————. *Forging His Own Chains: The Wonderful Life-Story of George Bidwell.* Hartford, Connecticut: Bidwell Publishing Company, 1891.

Burnham, George P. *Three Years With Counterfeiters, Smugglers and Boodle Carriers.* Boston: Lee & Shepard, 1872.

Byrnes, Thomas B. *Professional Criminals of America.* New York: Cassell & Company, 1886.

Cluverius, Thomas J. *Cluverius—My Life, Trial and Conviction.* Richmond, Virginia: Andrews, Baptist & Clemmitt, 1887.

Cook, D. J. *Hands Up; or, Twenty Years of Detective Life in the Mountains and on the Plains.* Denver: W. F. Robinson Printing Company, 1897. Reprint. Norman: University of Oklahoma Press, 1958.

Costello, Augustine E. *Commercial History of Syracuse and History of the Police Department.* Syracuse: Commercial Book Publishing Company, 1892.

————. *History of the Fire and Police Departments of Minneapolis.* Minneapolis: Relief Association, 1890.

————. *History of the Fire and Police Departments of Paterson, New Jersey.* Paterson, New Jersey: Relief Association, 1877.

————. *History of the Police Department of Jersey City.* Jersey City: Police Relief Association, 1891.

————. *History of the Police Department of New Haven From the Period of the Watch in Colonial Times to the Present Time.* New Haven: Relief Association, 1892.

————. *Our Police Protectors—A History of the New York Police.* New York: A. E. Costello. 1885. Reprint. Montclair, New Jersey: Patterson Smith, 1972.

Cummins, Jim. *Jim Cummins' Book.* Denver: Reed Publishing Company, 1903.

Eaglin, Thomas. *The Walls of Limbo: A Convict's Story of Prison Life.* Philadelphia: National Printing Company, 1895.

Eldridge, Benjamin, and Watts, William B. *Our Rival, The Rascal.* Boston: Pemberton Publishing Company, 1896.

Flinn, John J. *History of the Chicago Police from the Settlement of the Community to the Present Time.* Chicago: Police Book Fund, 1887.

Guiteau, Charles J. "Autobiography." In *A Complete History of the Trial of Guiteau. Assassin of President Garfield.* Edited by H. G. and C. J. Hayes. Philadelphia: Hubbard Brothers, 1882.

————. *A Lecture on Christ's Second Coming, A.D. 70.* Albany: Weed, Parsons, 1877.

————. *The Truth: A Companion to the Bible.* Chicago: Donnelley, Gassette & Loyd, 1879.

Hapgood, Hutchins. *The Autobiography of a Thief.* New York: Fox, Duffield & Company, 1903.

McWatters, George S. *Knots Untied; or, Ways and By-Ways in the Hidden Life of American Detectives.* Hartford, Connecticut: J. B. Burr and Hyde, 1871.

————. *Detectives of Europe and America; or, Life in the Secret Service.* Chicago: Laird & Lee, 1892.

Matsell, George Washington. *Vocabulum; or, the Rogue's Lexicon.* New York: G. W. Matsell & Company, 1859.

Moore, Charles Chilton. *Behind the Bars; 31498.* Lexington, Kentucky: Blue Grass Printing Company, 1899.

Moore, Langdon W. *Langdon W. Moore. His Own Story of His Eventful Life.* Boston: Langdon W. Moore, 1893.

Most, Johann. *Die Anarchie.* New York: J. Müller, 1887.

————. *Die Eigenthumsbestie.* New York: J. Müller, 1887.

————. *Die freie Gesellschaft.* New York: J. Müller, 1887.

————. *Memoiren, Erlebtes, Erforschtes und Erdachtes von John Most.* New York: Selbstverlag des Verfassers, 1903.

————. *Die Narrenthurm.* New York: J. Müller, 1888.

————. *Die Nihilisten.* Chicago: Commune-feier, 1882.

————. *Revolutionäre Kriegswissenschaft: Ein Handbuchlein zur Anleitung betreffend Gebrauches und Herstellung von Nitro-Glycerin, Dynamit,*

*Shiessbaumwolle, Knallsquecksilber, Bomben, Brandsätzen, Giften u.s.
w., u.s.w.* New York: Internationaler Zeitungs-Verein, 1885.

———. *Stammt der Mensch von Affen ab?* New York: J. Müller, 1887.

———. *Der Stimmkasten.* New York: J. Müller, 1888.

———. *Unsere Stellung in der Arbeiterbewegung.* New York: J. Müller,
1890.

———. *To the Workingmen of America.* Chicago: International Working
Peoples Association, 1883.

———. *Zwischen Gallen und Zuchthaus.* New York: J. Müller, 1887.

Payne, Seth Williams. *Behind the Bars: A Book by Seth William Payne.* New
York: Vincent & Company, 1873.

Pinkerton, Allan. *Allan Pinkerton's Great Detective Series.* 18 vols. New
York: G. W. Dillingham Company, 1900.

Pomeroy, Jesse H. *Autobiography of Jesse H. Pomeroy.* Boston: J. A.
Cummings, 1875.

———. *Selections from the Writings of Jesse Harding Pomeroy.* Boston: private
printing, 1920.

*Recollections of a New York Chief of Police and The Historic Supplement of the
Denver Police.* Denver: specially issued, 1890.

Report of the Joint Special Committee Relative to Establishing a Preventive Police.
New York: William Denman, 1842.

Savage, Edward H. *Boston Events.* Boston: Tolman & White, 1884.

———. *Police Records and Recollections; or, Boston by Daylight and Gaslight
for Two Hundred and Forty Years.* Boston: John P. Dale & Company, 1873.

Sprogle, Howard O. *The Philadelphia Police, Past and Present.* Philadelphia: specially issued, 1887.

Tuttle, J. Birney, ed. *An Illustrated Sketch of the Guardians of the Peace and
Prosperity of New Haven.* New Haven: Evans, Gardner & Company,
1889.

Victor, Sarah M. *The Life Story of Sarah M. Victor.* Cleveland: Williams
Publishing Company, 1887.

Vidocq, Eugène François. Memoires de Vidocq, chef de police sûreté,
jusqu'en 1827, aujourd'hui proprietaire et fabricant du papiers à
Saint Mandé. Paris: Tenon, 1828.

Walbridge, W. W., reporter. *Official Proceedings of the National Police
Convention.* St. Louis: Ennis, 1871.

Walling, George W. *Recollections of a New York Chief of Police.* New York:
Caxton Book Concern, 1887.

White, George M. *From Boniface to Bank Burglar.* Bellows Falls: Truax
Printing Company, 1905.

B. Secondary Works

1. Articles

Goldman, Emma. "John Most." *Mother Earth* 1 (1906): 17–20.

Harring, Sidney. "The Development of the Police Institution in the United States." *Crime and Social Justice* 5 (1976): 54–59.

Smith, Patterson. "Collecting True Crime Literature." *Bookman's Weekly* 69 (1982): 3435–58.

Walker, Samuel. "The Urban Police in Urban America: A Review of the Literature." *Journal of Police Science and Administration* 4 (1976): 252–60.

2. Books

Alfers, Kenneth. *Law and Order in the Capital City: A History of the Washington Police, 1800–86*. Washington, D.C.: George Washington University Press, 1976.

Bledstein, Burton J. *The Culture of Professionalism: The Middle Class and the Development of Higher Education in America*. New York: W. W. Norton, 1976.

Block, Eugene B. *Famous Detectives—True Stories of Great Crime Detection*. Garden City, New York: Doubleday & Company, 1967.

Bordua, David J., ed. *The Police: Six Sociological Essays*. New York: John Wiley & Sons, 1967.

Cuthbert, Norma B. *Lincoln and the Baltimore Plot*. San Marino, California: Huntington Library, 1949.

Fogelson, Robert M. *Big-City Police*. Cambridge: Harvard University Press, 1977.

Foucault, Michel. *Discipline and Punish—The Birth of the Prison*. Translated by Alan Sheridan. New York: Pantheon Books, 1978.

Franklin, H. Bruce. *The Victim as Criminal and Artist: Literature from the American Prison*. New York: Oxford University Press, 1978.

Friedman, Morris. *The Pinkerton Labor Spy*. New York: Wilshire Book Company, 1907.

Henderson, Bruce, and Summerlin, Sam. *The Super Sleuths*. New York: Macmillan Publishing Company, 1976.

Horan, James D., and Swiggert, Howard. *The Pinkerton Story*. Melbourne: William Heinemann, 1952.

Johnson, David R. *Policing the Urban Underworld: The Impact of Crime on the Development of the American Police, 1800–1887*. Philadelphia: Temple University Press, 1979.

Lane, Roger. *Policing the City, Boston 1822–85*. Cambridge: Harvard University Press, 1967.

Larson, Magali Sarfatti. *The Rise of Professionalism: A Sociological Analysis*. Berkeley and Los Angeles: University of California Press, 1977.

Lavine, Sigmund A. *Allan Pinkerton—America's First Private Eye*. New York: Dodd, Mead & Company, 1963.

Maurer, David W. *Language of the Underworld*. Lexington: University of Kentucky Press, 1981.

Miller, Wilbur R. *Cops and Bobbies: Police Authority in New York and London, 1830–1870*. Chicago: University of Chicago Press, 1977.

Monkkonen, Eric H. *Police in Urban-America, 1860–1920*. Cambridge: Harvard University Press, 1981.

Morn, Frank. *"The Eye That Never Sleeps": A History of the Pinkerton National Detective Agency*. Bloomington: Indiana University Press, 1982.

Olney, James. *Metaphors of Self: The Meaning of Autobiography*. Princeton: Princeton University Press, 1972.

Orrmont, Arthur. *Master Detective: Allan Pinkerton*. New York: Julian Messner, 1965.

Pascal, Roy. *Design and Truth in Autobiography*. Cambridge: Harvard University Press, 1960.

Price, Barbara Raffel. *Police Professionalism: Rhetoric and Action*. Lexington, Massachusetts: Lexington Books, 1977.

Reppetto, Thomas A. *The Blue Parade*. New York: The Free Press, 1978.

Richardson, James F. *The New York Police: Colonial Times to 1901*. New York: Oxford University Press, 1970.

———. *Urban Police in the United States*. Port Washington, New York: Kennikat Press, 1974.

Rocker, Rudolf. *Johann Most: Das Leben Eines Rebellen*. Berlin: Fritz Kater, 1924.

Rowan, Richard Wilmer. *The Pinkertons—A Detective Dynasty*. Boston: Little, Brown and Company, 1931.

Sayre, Robert F. *The Examined Self: Benjamin Franklin, Henry Adams, Henry James*. Princeton: Princeton University Press, 1964.

Shallo, J. P. *Private Police—With Special Reference to Pennsylvania*. Philadelphia: American Academy of Political and Social Science, 1933.

Siringo, Charles A. *Two Evil Isms: Pinkertonism and Anarchism*. Chicago: Charles A. Siringo, 1915.

Thorwald, Jürgen. *The Century of the Detective*. New York: Harcourt, Brace & World, 1964. Reprint. New York: Harcourt, Brace & World, 1965.

Trautman, Frederic. *The Voice of Terror: A Biography of Johann Most.* Westport, Connecticut: Greenwood Press, 1980.

Walker, Samuel. *A Critical History of Police Reform.* Lexington, Massachusetts: Lexington Books, 1977.

Index